Job #: 89398

Author name: Smith

Title of book: Disruptive Religion The Force or Faith

ISBN number: 0415914051

DISRUPTIVE RELIGION

THE FORCE OF FAITH
IN SOCIAL-MOVEMENT
ACTIVISM

DISRUPTIVE RELIGION

THE FORCE OF FAITH IN SOCIAL-MOVEMENT ACTIVISM

EDITED BY

CHRISTIAN SMITH

ROUTLEDGE
NEW YORK • LONDON

Published in 1996 by
Routledge
29 West 35th Street
New York, NY 10001

Published in Great Britain by
Routledge
11 New Fetter Lane
EC4P 4EE

Aldon Morris' "The Black Church in the Civil Rights Movement: the SCLC as the Decentralized,
Radical Arm of the Black Church" reprinted with the permission of The Free Press, a Division of
Simon & Schuster from *The Origins of the Civil Rights Movement: Black Communities
Organizing for Change*, by Aldon D. Morris. Copyright © 1984 by The Free Press.

June Nash's "Religious Rituals of Resistance and Class Consciousness in Bolivian Tin-Mining
Communities" reprinted with the permission of The University of California Press, from *Power
and Popular Protest: Latin American Social Movements*, edited by Susan Eckstein. Copyright ©
1989 by the Regents of the University of California.

M.M. Salehi's "Radical Islamic Insurgency in the Iranian Revolution of 1978–1979" reprinted
with permission of Greenwood Publishing Group, Inc., Westport, CT, from *Insurgency Through
Culture and Religion*, Praeger Publishing. Copyright © 1988.

Library of Congress Cataloging-in-Publication Data

Disruptive religion: the force of faith in social movement activism / edited by Christian Smith
        p. cm.
    Includes bibliographical references
    ISBN 0-415-91404-3 — ISBN 0-415-91405-1
    1. Social movements — Religious aspects. 2. Religion and social problems   I. Smith,
Christian (Christian Stephen).
    BL65.S64D57   1996
    291.1'71—dc20   95-40059
                                                                        CIP

FOR ERIN,
my brave little fighter,
whose very life is for me everyday
a sacrament of grace and mercy

CONTENTS

ACKNOWLEDGEMENTS

I owe a debt of gratitude to a number of people who helped me pull this book together. Thanks first to Bill Gamson and N.J. Demerath for encouraging me at the earliest stage to pursue this project. Pam Oliver and Hank Johnston also encouraged me to follow-through with my idea for this book. Doug McAdam, Robert Wuthnow, John McCarthy, David Meyer, and Mark Chaves all made very valuable suggestions early on about the conceptual shape of this volume, as well as helpful recommendations about potential contributors. I am grateful to four anonymous reviewers for their constructive, critical evaluations of my original proposal for this book. Thanks, of course, to all of the chapter contributors for their cooperation and timeliness. I was greatly assisted by the typing skills of Vickie Wilson and Nina Liou, and by the editing ability of Chris Bartley. I am indebted to Mark Mazuzan for allowing me to use his graphic for the book's cover. Grady Spires graciously assisted me in my Latin translations. And David Meyer, Stan Gaede, Stephen Hart, and Dave Sikkink all read and gave me smart feedback on earlier drafts of my Introduction. Thanks to Curt Faught for help with the index. Marlie Wasserman, my well-known and liked editor at Routledge, has been supportive of this project from the start, and a real pleasure to work with. Thank you all. Finally, the one who deserves far and away the most thanks for helping me accomplish all of my work is the love of my life, Emily.

ABOUT THE CONTRIBUTORS

James Aho is professor of sociology at Idaho State University.

Jeffrey Blackburn is a graduate student at Southern Illinois University, Carbondale.

Tristan Anne Borer is assistant professor of political science at Connecticut College.

Aldon Morris is professor of sociology at Northwestern University.

June Nash is professor of anthropology at the City College of New York.

Sharon Erickson Nepstad is a graduate student at the University of Colorado, Boulder.

Maryjane Osa is assistant professor of political science at the University of South Carolina, Colombia.

Ron Pagnucco is assistant professor of sociology at Mount Saint Mary's College.

Mark Regnerus is a graduate student at the University of North Carolina, Chapel Hill.

M.M. Salehi received his PhD in sociology from Michigan State University, and is completing a second PhD in Industrial Relations at Wayne State University.

David Sikkink is a graduate student at the University of North Carolina, Chapel Hill.

Christian Smith is assistant professor of sociology at the University of North Carolina, Chapel Hill.

Rhys H. Williams is associate professor of sociology at Southern Illinois University, Carbondale.

Correcting a Curious Neglect, or Bringing Religion Back In

Christian Smith

Disruptive religion? For many, the phrase is an oxymoron. Integrating religion? Sure. Consoling religion? Okay. Legitimating religion? Right. But disruptive religion? Since when is religion in the business of social disorder, collective confrontation, or political protest? When was the last time anyone saw a nun rioting, or heard of a Sunday school teacher plotting to subvert a government, or knew of a rabbi arrested for civil disobedience? Religion is too busy conducting funerals, expounding theology, collecting tithes, burning incense, and offering opening prayers at local Kiwanis luncheons to be mobilizing protests, boycotts, and insurrections. Right?

Partly right. Religion typically *is* in the business of supplying meaningful worldviews and moral systems that help to integrate and harmonize societies; of providing comforting theodicies to those distressed and suffering; of rendering ideologies that legitimate the oftentimes unjust status quo. There certainly are plenty of military chaplains who sanctify the work of war, theologies that proffer health-and-wealth and pie-in-the-sky bye-and-bye, pastors who preach patient submission to injustice and indignity, and parishioners whose faith rouses them to little more than regular church attendance and charity.

But there is another face to the sacred-social phenomena we call religion. For the worldviews, moral systems, theodicies, and organizations of religion can serve not only to legitimate and preserve, but also to challenge and overturn social, political, and economic systems. Religion *can* help to keep everything in its place. But it can *also* turn the world upside-down.

This book is about the disruptive, defiant, unruly face of religion. It is particularly concerned with religion's capacity to mobilize, promote, and abet *social movements*—organized efforts of challenger groups to promote or resist social change through disruptive means.

This volume was begotten as a response to a glaring incongruity that is evident to those who study both social movements and religion. Namely, on the one hand, it is clear that religion has often played, and today still plays, an absolutely central role in a number of important social and political movements. Indeed, in a host of cases, religion has served as the primary source of many of the necessary ingredients of social-movement emergence and success. From the black civil rights movement to Poland's Solidarity movement, from the Nicaraguan revolution of 1979 to the South African anti-apartheid movement, from Ghandi's movement for Indian independence to the U.S. Central America peace movement of the 1980s, people and organizations of faith have contributed indispensable resources to the mobilization of disruptive political activism. Yet, on the other hand, religion's important contribution to social movements remains conspicuously under-explored—arguably virtually ignored—in the academic literature on social movements. Students of disruptive politics have simply paid very little sustained, focused attention to the often-present religious dynamics in their field of study. And students of religion have done an inadequate job of building bridges from their field of study to that of social movements. Of course, scholars in both areas rarely *deny* the important role religion often plays in social-movement activism. But neither do they give that role the studied attention it deserves.[1] So, there remains a gaping void where there should stand a rich, illuminating body of publications. This book is intended to help redress this neglect and to begin filling that void.

WHY THE NEGLECT?

It would seem prudent, before pressing on with our analysis, to first consider reasons why religion has been neglected in the literature on social movements. If we are to redress this neglect, we will need to be aware of, and responsive to, its possible causes.

The first likely reason why the role of religion in disruptive politics has been neglected is the long domination of the social sciences by secularization theory. From its earliest years, many formative thinkers in the social sciences, such as August Compte and Karl Marx—influenced by nineteenth-century faith in evolutionary historical progress—predicted and, in some cases, championed the decline and eventual disappearance of religion. The view that modernization erodes the social importance of religion became for decades the conventional wisdom in the social sciences. By the 1960s, when many of today's most influential social-movement scholars were in college and graduate school, secularization theory had reached its zenith in the popular works of Peter Berger (1967), David Martin (1969), and Bryan Wilson (1966). At that time, it was largely taken for granted in the social sciences that religion was in decline and, therefore, increasingly becoming a marginal factor shaping the social world. It is no wonder why, in this intellectual climate, few aspiring social-movement scholars looked to religion to explain the political problems that engaged them.

Second, and reinforcing this tendency, was the theoretical domination of American sociology from the 1940s to the early 1970s by structural-functionalism. This school of thought viewed religion as serving society's macro-functional need for cultural consensus and social integration—what Talcott Parsons called "latent pattern maintenance." To the extent that religion survived the forces of secularization, it did so because it provided the shared values and norms necessary to promote social harmony and equilibrium (see Nottingham 1954; Parsons 1951: 163—67). At the micro level, structural-functionalism saw religion as providing meaning, belonging, and identity for individuals. But, since modern society was viewed as effecting progressive differentiation between the religious and secular spheres, religion was also thought to be undergoing increasing compartmentalization and privatization (Parsons 1963). Although many structural-functionalists, including Parsons, recognized religion's potential as a force for social change, this recognition was often eclipsed by the larger theoretical framework's emphasis on religion as a source of consensus, integration, and equilibrium. Importantly for our purposes, this emphasis has retained to this day considerable influence in sociology—especially among those not studying religion—despite the fact that structural-functionalism has been out of fashion since the early 1970s.[2] Therefore it is not surprising that social-movement scholars—to the extent that they have operated with a background impression of religion as a source of consensus and integration—have generally not utilized religion to help illuminate the problems of conflict and confrontation they study.

The third likely reason for the neglect of religion in social-movement literature derives from the fragmented nature of contemporary academic inquiry. Regrettably, in general, scholars from one field of study rarely converse extensively with those from other fields. Too often, different fields of inquiry operate on separate but parallel tracks, with few idea-diffusing ties linking them. Perhaps epitomizing this state of academic balkanization, the sociology of religion has historically operated as an especially isolated sub-discipline. Until 1994, for example, when an American Sociological Association Section on Religion was first launched, sociological analyses of religion were "housed" primarily by three independent and disconnected organizations that published their own specialty journals.[3] As a consequence of this "insulation and isolation of the sociology of religion" (Beckford 1985; also see Ennis 1992), any interesting social-movement studies produced over the years by students of religion had minimal chance of influencing social movement scholars. Potential intellectual "cross-pollenization" was structurally impeded. So, social-movement scholars—with the notable exceptions of John Lofland and David Snow, who, even so, have focused primarily on insights from religious conversion theory—seem to have gleaned little from the sociology of religion.

Yet another possible reason for religion's neglect in social-movement studies relates to important developments in social-movement theory itself. The 1970s saw a major break in the social-movement literature with earlier theories—e.g., mass society, collective behavior, status discontent, and relative-deprivation theories—that emphasized the irrational and emotional nature of social movements (e.g., Oberschall 1973; Gamson 1975; McCarthy and Zald 1977). There was at the time a decisive pendulum-swing away from these "classical" theories toward the view of social movements as rational, strategically calculating, politically instrumental phenomena. Since religion is typically understood by moderns as something irrational and emotional, it is not unlikely that, in the move to sweep irrationality and emotion out of social-movement theory, religion—bearing all of those associations—was also swept away with the classical theories. It would have made little sense to take religion seriously—presumably irrational and emotional—when the idea of irrationality and emotion in social movements was widely considered outdated and erroneous.

A fifth explanation for why religion has not received the attention it deserves in social-movement literature, is that religion did not seem to play an important role in many of the actual social movements that helped to provoke the pendulum-swing in theory described above. True, religion was front and center in the civil rights movement—perhaps the most politically and theoretically significant movement on the list. But besides that, very little religion appeared to be present in the anti-Vietnam war movement, the student movement, the women's movement, or the environmental movement. If anything, religion appeared to be a conservative force, resisting these movements. Thus, few of the actual, historical movements—those that prodded scholars in this time period to question the old theories and replace them with more analytically fruitful approaches—summoned these scholars to account theoretically for the role of religion. Understandably, when a factor seems absent from watershed events, those who retool to make sense of those pivotal events are unlikely to view that factor as theoretically significant. Thus, religion was generally ignored in the development of the social-movement theories that dominate the field today.

If these are some of the reasons behind the neglect of religion in social-movement studies, what might we say of them? Perhaps the most appropriate response is to say that they are understandable, but deficient reasons. That is, they do help explain religion's neglect, but they do not justify it. Traditional secularization theory has been seriously disputed, empirically and theoretically, over the last two decades. The old assumption that religion is in progressive decline toward a likely extinction is sufficiently simplistic and doubtful that we must not allow it to blind us to religion's ongoing social significance, including its frequent *de facto* presence in disruptive politics. Likewise, the influence of structural-functionalism's over-emphasis on religion's socially integrating and harmonizing function ought not to prevent us from seeing religion's equally-important disruptive, defiant, and unruly face.

Furthermore, the fact that the sociology of religion has historically been an organizationally isolated field of study is a problem, not a justification. With that sub-discipline moving increasingly toward greater connection with mainstream sociology, there is no reason why social-movement scholars cannot, or should not, take cues and glean insights from the sociology of religion literature on disruptive religion. Moreover, there is no reason why religion needs to be associated with the classical social-movement theories that were widely debunked in the 1970s. For one, religious believers and organizations can act just as rationally, strategically, and instrumentally as can more secular forces. Also, the theory-pendulum has lately swung back toward the center as more scholars see the need to better account for cultural, expressive, ideological, emotional, and symbolic aspects of collective action (e.g., Morris and Mueller 1992). Surely, greater attention to religious factors can contribute here.

Additionally, the fact that religion did not seem to play an important role in some of the social movements that helped reorient theory in the 1970s does not justify its neglect in analyses of social movements more generally. Besides the probability that there was actually greater religious influence in some of these movements than is commonly recognized, we ought also to remember that the peace, women's, student, and environmental movements are not the only movements to be studied. Indeed, one could argue that the great attention paid in recent years to these four "core" movements (Klandermans and Tarrow 1988: 17-23) has produced something of a counterproductive myopia in social-movement studies. There exist a multitude of cases of organized social disruption, historically and cross-culturally, that deserve our attention, and religion plays a significant role in many of them.

Thus, we see that there are many understandable reasons why the religious factor has been so under-explored by students of social-movement activism. But we see equally clearly that none of these reasons justifies that neglect. If the social sciences are to develop a full and insightful understanding of the dynamics of collective activism, we will need to take more seriously the important role often played by religion in the mobilization and deployment of social-movement disruption.

THE DISRUPTIVE POTENTIAL OF SACRED TRANSCENDENCE

Religious believers and organizations possess a variety of assets—which we will examine below—that are useful for the promotion of social-movement activism. These include organizational resources, shared identity, normative motivational systems, public legitimacy, and so on. But many other social institutions and organizations also possess these assets, yet rarely employ them for disruptive political activism. What makes religion different in some cases? What is distinctive about religion that, under the right conditions, disposes it to disruptive collective activism? To answer that question, we need to step back and examine more closely what, sociologically speaking, religion is.

From a sociological perspective, religion is a system of beliefs and practices oriented toward the sacred or supernatural, through which the life experiences of groups of people are given meaning and direction.[4] This understanding of religion regards human beings as meaning-craving creatures. For human beings, life cannot simply transpire as a series of aimless or unintelligible events. Rather, life must be made meaningful. Humans appear to be strongly predisposed to find intolerable an existence without purpose or significance. Something fundamental in the human creature and social existence seems to demand that birth, growth, struggle, suffering, achievement, love, conflict, beauty, finitude, and death have some purpose, direction, or significance.

The problem for human beings, however, is that meaning is not automatically and immediately available. Those "batteries" are not included, so to speak; they have to be acquired. To use a different image: when I buy a new computer, it comes with an operating system and software pre-programmed on the hard drive by the manufacturer. All I have to do is plug it in, flip the switch, and it is ready to operate. Human beings are not like that when it comes to meaning. We don't come pre-programmed with meaning systems. Purpose, significance, and direction are not "hardwired" into newborn babies. Neither do human beings find in the natural world readily packaged and available meaning-systems that they can simply "plug" or "program" into themselves.

This means that humans have to *construct* meaning-systems; they have to create patterns of purpose and significance by which to make their lives meaningful. These created meaning-systems are what we sometimes call "culture," that is, a social group's conglomeration of shared codes, norms, values, beliefs, and symbols that tell its members what to do with their lives and why. Culture gives life meaning. It orients people to the world they inhabit, providing a sense of direction and purpose.

Religion, viewed sociologically, is a particular kind of cultural meaning-system, oriented toward the sacred or supernatural. Religion affords groups of people meaning and direction by providing sets of beliefs and practices grounded not in the ordinary, mundane world, but in the divine, the transcendent, the eternal, the holy, the spiritual.

Religious meaning-systems operate with reference to supernatural beings, timeless truths, celestial realities. This is what sets religion apart from non-religious cultural meaning systems. Marxism as a meaning-system, for example, takes as its starting-point a society's structures and relations of material production. Nationalism is grounded in the temporal history and experience of a common nation of people, but religion is rooted in realities that are believed to exist above and beyond the temporal, mundane, material world that we observe empirically. Religion is characterized by sacred transcendence.

Religion's investing life with meaning through sacred transcendence gives it an initially and primarily conservative thrust. By helping to explain and give meaning to the world and life as it is experienced, religion helps to justify and sustain the world and life just as it *is* experienced. By endowing life as it *is* with significance and purpose, religion provides a legitimation for the world as it is. Why do earthquakes happen? Because the earth-god was angrily awakened from his sleep. Why are we poor and the landowners rich? Because our poverty is God's will and, if we suffer with faithfulness, we will be rewarded in heaven. Why did my daughter die of a disease? Because evil spirits attacked her. Why was I born into an outcast family? Because in a previous life I failed to live a life that would transport me into nirvana, so I was reincarnated into a person with this outcast status. Given this conservative character, it is no wonder, then, that religion has historically served to justify and legitimate all types of injustice and indignity. Thus, Machiavelli (1940: 150) astutely advised, "It is therefore the duty of princes and heads of republics to uphold the foundations of the religions of their countries, for then it is easy to keep their people religious, and consequently well-conducted and united." And the Confucian *Book of Changes* observes (quoted in Yang 1961: 145), "The sages devised guidance by the way of the gods, and the people in the empire became obedient."

But that is not the complete story. For religion's very sacred transcendence—with its conservative inclinations—also contains within itself the seeds of radical social criticism and disruption. Religion provides life, the world, and history with meaning, through a sacred reality that transcends those mundane realities. But in doing so, religion establishes a perceived objective reality above and beyond temporal life, the world, and history, that then occupies an independent and privileged position to act—through those who believe the religion—back upon the mundane world. That which is sacred and transcends temporal, earthly reality also stands in the position to question, judge, and condemn temporal, earthly reality. In this way, the ultimate legitimator of the status quo can easily become its ultimate judge. This dual potential lies precisely in the ultimacy and distance that characterizes sacred transcendence itself.

Take, for example, religion and the rule of an oppressive monarch. A king and his priests can employ religion to justify the king's oppressive dominion. By promulgating a doctrine of the divine right of kings, for example, the king can declare that a power bigger and more important than himself—God—has appointed him as the rightful earthly ruler. Nobody can defy his rule, because that would defy God's rule. But in the very act of grounding his authority in God's will, the king has confirmed a power and a will bigger and more important than his own—a sacred transcendence—that may not be defied, not even by the king. By the very act of establishing its legitimation through sacred transcendence, the otherwise absolute—though perhaps not fully legitimated—rule of the king relativizes itself vis-a-vis that sacred transcendence. The king is no longer absolute—God is. That creates a higher standard by which the king may potentially be judged, a transcendent source of potential criticism that the king cannot repudiate without delegitimating himself. So, if the king's citizens come to believe that their oppressive earthly king is violating their righteous heavenly King's standards of good kingship, the earthly king's rule suddenly becomes illegitimate. For no one, not even a king, can deny or defy the will and law of a heavenly King.

We see, then, that those who garner submission through the gods, must themselves submit *to* the gods. And since the behavior of many such people is often quite ungodly, they can easily come to be viewed as standing under the judgement *of* the gods. Perhaps better—from the perspective of the ungodly—to have left the gods out of the picture. For the sacred transcendence that originally served to legitimate and justify returns to judge and condemn. In more abstract terms, the attempt to absolutize the relative—the social status quo—through association with the absolute—the divine—has the inescapable latent consequence of underscoring the relativity of the relative in contrast to the absoluteness of the absolute.[5]

That sacred transcendence possesses the potential to challenge as well as to legitimate a social order is a fact that should worry not only oppressive kings. All actors and sectors of a society in which religion is operative may potentially be evaluated and condemned by the sacredly-grounded normative standards of that religion. Economic structures and outcomes, patterns of race relations, military institutions and practices, family structures and customs, educational organizations, the character of gender relations, housing patterns, political systems and regimes, and even religious institutions and practices themselves are all susceptible to the evaluation, critique, and condemnation of a religion's sacred transcendence, mediated through the believing, religiously faithful. In this way, religion can serve not only to support and justify, but also to critique and disrupt the social status quo.

NEITHER MONOCAUSAL IDEALISM, NOR MATERIALIST REDUCTIONISM

It would be misguided to think that disruptive social movements in which religion has figured prominently are exclusively religious conflicts, disconnected from matters of material production and distribution, politics, and social status. Few disruptive social conflicts are simply battles over religious belief and practices alone. Religion itself is a socially constituted reality that always exists in a social context that shapes and is shaped by religion. For this reason, in explaining social movements, it is simply impossible to separate the religious factors of belief and practice from more mundane matters of wealth, power, and prestige. All of these elements of social existence interact dynamically and mutually, and can have combined and reinforcing effects in generating disruptive social conflict.

It is common, therefore, to find that religion is one of a complex of factors that propel and facilitate social movements. Oftentimes, religious cleavages align with class-, political-, and status-cleavages. The results are social movements that involve an amalgamation of religious, political, status, and social-class grievances. The conflict in Northern Ireland, for example, is not merely a controversy about Catholic versus Protestant beliefs and practices. It is also a struggle over the political rule of a geographic territory. The same is true of the "Religious Wars" fought between European Catholics and Protestants in the sixteenth and seventeenth centuries. Likewise, conservative Christian activists in the contemporary United States' pro-life movement are driven not only by religious doctrines about the "sanctity of life" and "humans made in God's image." Many of them are also fighting to defend an entire traditional way of life, involving a particular conception of motherhood and family, that is rooted in a specific social experience and status location (Luker 1986; Hunter 1991). Similarly, the insurgency of Islamic militants in Egypt does not merely reflect their passion to follow the Koran with greater purity, but it also expresses the frustrations of aspiring lower-class young adults for whom education has not produced expected upward mobility, as well as cultural resistance to the threatening, penetrating process of Westernization.

The observation that religious, political, class, and status interests often interact, align, and mobilize activism could similarly be made of the Iranian revolution of 1978; the South African anti-apartheid movement; the American abolition movement of the early nineteenth century; China's Taiping Rebellion of the 1850s; the contemporary liberation theology movement in Latin America; India's late-nineteenth century Hindu nationalist movement; the U.S. black civil rights movement; the 1986 Philippines revolution against Ferdinan Marcos; the seventeenth century English Civil War; the Know Nothing and Native American movements of nineteenth century America; twentieth century Melanesian Cargo cults; the American prohibitionist movement; the Burmese militant Buddhist-nationalist movement of the 1920s and 30s; the United States Central America peace movement of the 1980s; the East German "resistance church" in the 1980s; the American Social Gospel movement of the turn of the twentieth century; Ghandi's Indian independence movement; the contemporary United States Christian Right; Native American Ghost Dance movements in late- nineteenth century America; the Polish Solidarity movement; the nineteenth century American Christian Labor Union and Knights of Labor movements; the Maccabean Revolt in second century B.C. Palestine; the variety of nineteenth and twentieth century White Supremacy movements in the United States; the "German Christian Church" and the "Confessing Church" in 1930s and 40s Germany; the "popular church" in the Nicaraguan revolution of 1979; United States nineteenth century religious communitarian movements; and the Shi'ite and Hezbollah insurgencies in Lebanon in the 1980s, to name just a few (Smith 1996; Lewy 1974; Lincoln 1985; Goldberg 1991; Goeckel 1990; Findlay 1993; Kleiver 1987; Nielsen 1991; Moen and Gustafson 1992; Kanter 1972; Craig 1992; Oliner and Oliner 1988; Munson 1988; Worsley 1968; Pipes 1983; Walzer 1965; Martin 1991). When it comes to social movements, even ones where religion plays a prominent role, religion is rarely, if ever, the exclusive bone of contention.

Having said that, however, we must also acknowledge that it would be equally misguided to think that these kinds of social movements are not "actually" about religion, but are "really" only about the more mundane—read substantive and important—matters of acquiring wealth, power, and status. To argue that religion serves as a mere epiphenomenal cloak for essentially material or political interests is simplistic and erroneous. That kind of reductionistic analysis serves merely to obscure the actual complexity of social-movement dynamics that very much need to be better understood.

In fact, in the multiple cases we have cited, the stuff of religion has helped to constitute the very substance of these social movements' grievances, identities, organizations, and strategies. Pro-life activists, for example, *are* struggling to defend a socially-located, traditional way of life. But they *also* are genuinely propelled by religious convictions, are mobilized through religious institutions, share a trans-denominational religious identity, and are strategically constrained and informed by religious ideology. Likewise, liberation-theology activists in Latin America *have been* struggling to resist human-rights abuses and to alter the distribution of material resources in their countries on behalf of the poor. But, in doing so, they have *also* been genuinely activated and guided by theological and spiritual commitments, have found resources and space to organize within religious organizations, and have benefited from the popular legitimacy and political protection that the Latin American Church enjoys (Smith 1991). We would be foolish, therefore, not to recognize that religious worldviews, interests, traditions, structures, and practices themselves really do matter in shaping the mobilization, struggles, and outcomes of a multitude of social movements. We turn now to examine more precisely the variety of ways in which they can do just that.

RELIGIOUS ASSETS FOR ACTIVISM

If and when religious believers or organizations initiate or become caught up in a collective mobilization for disruptive activism, what attributes or assets do they embody or possess that can help to constitute and facilitate that action? Here I explicate a number of distinct, though closely related, religious properties and resources, grouped under general headings, that can and do serve as important assets for social-movement activism.

TRANSCENDENT MOTIVATION

All social movements confront the problem of motivating their participants to make and maintain a commitment to the collective cause, especially when the activism is costly for participants. Religion offers some important and sometimes unique solutions to this problem of motivation.

Legitimation for protest rooted in the ultimate or sacred

Perhaps the most potent motivational leverage that a social-movement can enjoy is the alignment of its cause with the ultimacy and sacredness associated with God's will, eternal truth, and the absolute moral structure of the universe. People can compromise, in the end, on wage increases and job security; they can pragmatically negotiate their best political advantage on many public-policy issues. But God's will is something apart—it is not up for grabs or negotiable. What is sacred is sacred. What is absolute is absolute. What is eternal is eternal—at least that is how reality can be constructed under some conditions. The social activism of religious "true believers," therefore, often reflects an uncompromising and tenacious certainty and commitment that sustains activism in the face of great adversity.

"We must obey God rather than men," declared the apostle Peter flatly to the authorities who were preparing his murder to stop the rapidly-spreading Jesus movement (Acts 5: 29-33). In a similar spirit of divinely-steeled tenacity, under tremendous pressure at his trial at the Diet of Worms to recant and reverse his religious movement, the reformer Martin Luther (quoted in Bainton 1950: 144) defied his antagonists:

> My conscience is captive to the Word of God. I cannot and will not recant anything.... Here I stand. I cannot do otherwise.

Seeing the zeal that faith-based activism can produce explains why one seventeenth century English writer (quoted in Wolterstorff 1983: 9) professed, "I had rather see coming toward me a whole regiment with drawn swords, than one lone Calvinist convinced that he is doing the will of God."

The point is not that religion is inherently or necessarily fanatical and absolutistic. The point, rather, is that, for many religious believers, the overwhelming intractability of the world as it is can, in some circumstances, melt into pliant transience before the face of the holy, the sacred, the eternal. Divine imperative does not merely raise the stakes of the game; it can, under some conditions, infuse the struggle with non-negotiability, and relativize what might otherwise seem insurmountable. Human preference and choice can be supplanted by divine compulsion. Such a motivational wellspring can be a tremendous asset for many social movements.

Moral imperatives for love, justice, peace, freedom, equity

Social movements emerge, in part, when people come to define their situations as needlessly unjust and susceptible to change. Scholars have labeled this situation-redefining process variously as adopting an "injustice frame" (Gamson et al. 1982), "cognitive liberation" (McAdam 1982), and the development of "insurgent consciousness" (Smith 1991). However labeled, the essential idea is that people determine that something about their world so egregiously violates their moral standards—of what is right, just, fair—that they must engage in collective action to correct it (Smith 1996). Determining this, of course, requires possessing a set of fundamental moral standards against which the status quo can be judged. In most societies, religion has served as a major source of those kind of moral standards.

Religion not only attempts to tell us what ultimately is—Yaweh reigns sovereignly over the universe, there is no god but Allah and Mohammed is his prophet, reality is an endless succession of birth, death, and rebirth. Religion also aspires to tell us what, therefore, *should be*, how people *must* live, how the world *ought to* operate—thou shalt not murder, love your neighbor as yourself, honor the spirits of the dead, and so on. The meaning and direction for life that religion provides is inextricably tied to the ethical systems it advocates. In religion, the *is* and *the* ought, the true and the necessary assume and reinforce each other.

Where one finds religion, therefore, one also finds some system of moral imperatives and values that compels the allegiance of the faithful. And whether they be the command to love others, to keep holy days, to establish justice, to curb intemperance, to revere the earth, to speak the truth, to work for peace, to repudiate debauchery, to defend freedom, to make a pilgrimage, or to protect the poor, these moral imperatives contain the inherent capacity, if not propensity, to evaluate and judge actual reality as immoral, unjust, unacceptable. "You have been weighed in the scales and found wanting," read Yaweh's writing on the wall, condemning king Belshazzar's sacrilege and idolatry and ending his rule over Babylon (Daniel 5:27). By possessing rich storehouses of moral standards by which social realities can be weighed in the scales and found wanting, religion can, has, and does serve as a principal source of a key element that generates the insurgent consciousness driving many social movements.

Powerfully motivating icons, rituals, songs, testimonies, oratory

Religion not only can help to generate and define the grievances that breed disruptive collective activism, it can also supply the symbolic and emotional resources needed to sustain that activism over time. A wealth of empirical research shows that social-movement participation is induced and sustained by much more than the simple motive of obtaining an end-goal benefit. All along the way, ideological, expressive, and emotional factors facilitate and sometimes constrain that motive and the activism it propels. *Homo oeconomicus*, in other words, is often joined, carried, and sometimes overridden by *homo ritualis*, *homo affectus*, *homo significans*, and *homo symbolicus*.

The significance and direction for life that religion provides is not only intimately tied to the ethical systems it advocates, but also to the expressive ceremonies and iconic images it embodies. In religion, worldview, ethics, and expressive practice together compose the coherent meaning system. All religions, therefore, incorporate established traditions of ritual, symbols, and narrative expression that represent the worldview, express devotion, and inspire and instruct the faithful. Often these expressive and iconic traditions are elaborate, sophisticated, emotionally powerful, and imbued with the authority of centuries, if not millennia, of historical observation.

Social movements need symbols, rituals, narratives, icons, and songs. They use these to construct their collective identities, to nurture solidarity, to express their grievances, and to draw inspiration and strength in difficult times. Religion, as a major creator and custodian of powerful symbols, rituals, icons, narratives, songs, testimonies, and oratory, is well-positioned to lend these sacred, expressive practices to the cause of political activism. The solidarity, inspiration, articulation, and education that these sacred expressions generate can then become channeled into political mobilization. The songs and sermons of black churches across the American South, for example, are renowned for the energy and hope they generated for civil rights activists in the 1950s and 60s (McAdam 1982). Likewise, the sermons, prayers, and marches of many mideastern Islamic militant groups—such as Lebanon and Palestine's Islamic Jihad and Hamas—help to sustain their commitment and sacrifice in the face of tremendous opposition and uncertain prospects for success. Similarly, many of the rituals of the Polish Catholic Church nurtured the life of Poland's Solidarity movement throughout the 1980s. Such symbolic, iconic, ritualistic, and narrative resources possessed by religion can, have, and do serve as vital assets, directly and indirectly, for a variety of social movements.

Ideologies demanding self-discipline, sacrifice, altruism

One major practical and analytical problem for social movements and those who study them concerns how and why individuals can be motivated to sacrifice their own personal well-being for a collective good. Why *has* aunt Helen devoted her entire life to the elimination of nuclear weapons? A world in which individuals only act to secure divisible rewards for themselves would be one devoid of social movements. For sustainable social movements require that some, perhaps many people, take risks, set examples, and pay prices on the movement's behalf, the personal costs of which are rarely fully repaid, even if the social-movement succeeds. This is especially true in early phases of movement mobilization. Movements need people who will sacrifice a great deal of time, money, energy, security, emotional resources, alternative opportunities, and sometimes even their lives in order to build the momentum and organization necessary to mount significant political challenges. Where does that kind of self-sacrifice come from? It can come from many places, of course, but an important source of such a self-sacrificial orientation is religion.

Most traditional religions engender in their followers an orientation of self-restraint (Bell 1976). They regard human persons not as complete and unblemished beings that ought to follow and express freely whatever desire, thought, and feeling passes through their stream of consciousness. Rather, they view humans as in some way incomplete, unenlightened, or lost, and therefore in need of completion, enlightenment, or salvation—and these are not generally regarded as coming naturally or easily. Completion, enlightenment, and salvation have to be struggled for, pursued single-mindedly, sought after like valued treasure. To achieve them, one has to learn self-discipline, self-sacrifice, self-abandonment, or self-control. Whether it is obeying the Torah, pursuing the Noble Eightfold Path toward nirvana, taking up one's cross and following Christ, struggling in the paths of Allah, pursuing the three Hindu paths to the emancipation of moksha, or renouncing one's own righteousness and trusting only in the unmerited grace of God, religious faithfulness requires some expression of self-restraint or self-denial. At its extreme, it requires psychic or literal self-obliteration.

While some may consider these views as distastefully anti-humanistic, for our purposes, the kind of personal self-sacrifice that many religions foster can be tremendously useful for social-movement mobilization. Faith-based self-sacrifice can help to generate a critical mass of participants early on, even when the cause is idealistic, unrewarding, and unpromising. It can encourage individual self-expenditure for what is believed to be a higher good—whether that be world peace, a better way of life for one's grandchildren, or the repeal of widespread, burdensome taxes. In short, self-sacrifice helps to transcend the "free rider" problem. And that is no small accomplishment.

Legitimation of organizational and strategic-tactical flexibility

Strong social movements need to manage organizational, strategic, and tactical flexibility; they need to be able to devise organizations, strategies, and tactics that are appropriate for the peculiar political and cultural environments they face; and they need to be able to adjust their organizations, strategies, and tactics as the struggles within which they are engaged develop, particularly as the strategies and tactics of their antagonists evolve (McAdam 1983). In many cases, to the extent that religion becomes a motivating factor in social-movement activism, it may aid in that organizational and strategic-tactical flexibility.

The sacred texts of all major religions are sufficiently ambiguous that they may be interpreted in disparate directions (see Hart 1992: 124). It is possible, therefore, for faith-based activists to find in their sacred texts—perhaps especially when important political interests are at stake—legitimations for a variety of political, organizational, and tactical approaches that may satisfy their movement's needs. A movement for whom violence commends itself as a useful element in its tactical repertoire, for example, can find legitimation for such violence, if it so desires, in the New Testament, the Torah and Prophets, the Koran, the Mahabharata, the Shu Ching, and so on (Lewy 1974: 11–54). Jesus said, "I have not come to bring peace, but a sword" (Matthew 10: 34). However, a movement dependent on a strategy of non-violent resistance can likewise find legitimating support for that strategy in the very same sacred texts. For Jesus also said, "Put your sword back in its place; for all who draw the sword will die by the sword" (Matthew 26: 52).

The same observation can be made about religious legitimations for organizational hierarchy and centralization versus egalitarian decentralization; the authority of charismatic leadership versus democratic consensus; the aggressive assertion of identity and political demands versus the strategic willingness to endure the blows of the enemy; the adoption of a reformist versus a revolutionary strategy; the embrace of the latest technologies and discourse versus the maintenance of a countercultural purity of rejection; and so on. The point is not that people of faith are generally spiritual mercenaries who expediently manipulate the content of their sacred texts to fit the political needs of the moment. The point is that the religious authority of sacred texts generally exhibits an openness and flexibility that can often facilitate the legitimation of a variety organizational and strategic-tactical forms, as social movements may need them.

ORGANIZATIONAL RESOURCES

Social movements require more than compelling motivations, moral judgement, symbols, self-discipline, and flexibility to generate political disruption. Movements also need a variety of organizational resources by which to mobilize and through which to channel their energy. Organized religion is well-equipped to provide, when it so desires, these key resources to social movements.

Trained and experienced leadership resources

Successful social movements require capable leaders who can inspire commitment in movement participants, plan strategies and tactics, coordinate insurgent actions, resolve internal conflicts, and articulate grievances to outsiders. Whether a movement is organized as a centralized hierarchy or a decentralized network, high-caliber leadership is indispensable.

All established religions—by definition collective phenomena—take on some kind of organizational form that, like social movements, necessitates the operation of active leadership. Well before any social-movement in need of resources appears, religious organizations have already established functioning systems of leadership. In many cases, the religious leaders are specialists, formally or informally educated, trained, and experienced in interpersonal communications, group dynamics, and collective-identity construction. Typically, these religious leaders also enjoy influence among their followers, linkages with their colleagues, relative autonomy and flexibility in their daily schedules, and extensive contacts in their broader communities. All of these are invaluable potential assets for a burgeoning social movement. Thus, when a social-movement in need of resources *does* appear, if the religion is sympathetic to its cause, it stands capable of lending its already-functioning leadership resources to the movement. Rather than having to build its leadership from scratch, then, the movement is able to import or build directly upon these fully-operational leadership resources. The central roles, for example, that black church ministers played in the civil rights movement, that militant Islamic clerics played in the Iranian revolution, and that Protestant and Catholic church leaders played in the South African anti-apartheid movement exemplify the great potential value of religious leadership for social-movement mobilization.

Financial resources

Two decades of resource-mobilization theory have clearly established the importance of the flow of financial resources in the fate of social movements. Money may not determine the outcome of collective action, but it certainly shapes it. It takes money to pay organizers, rent office space, print flyers, make telephone calls, send direct-mail appeals, construct banners and placards, transport protesters to protests, bail demonstrators out of jail, attract the attention of the media, consult lawyers, and offset the costs of boycotts, strikes, and sanctions. All other things being equal, for movements, more money buys more power.

Organized religion often possesses extraordinary financial resources that it can—if it so chooses—funnel, directly and indirectly, into social-movement activism. In the United States, for example, Protestant and Catholic churches each year collect from their adherents more than $39 billion in tithes and other contributions (Statistical Abstract 1994: 72). Furthermore, multiple para-church and other religious organizations raise additional hundreds of millions of dollars annually. If and when a religious organization judges that a political-activist cause falls within the bounds of its legitimate religious mission, it often possesses significant financial resources that it can contribute to the cause. Instances of movements obtaining funding from religious organizations—as diverse as Pat Robertson's Christian Coalition, the Unitarian Universalist Service Committee, and the Reverend Moon's Unification Church—abound.

Congregated participants and solidarity incentives

Besides leaders and money, of course, social movements need deployable rank-and-file activists to implement their strategies. Grass-roots participants are needed to strike, boycott, collect signatures, write letters, stuff envelopes, recruit new members, lobby, contribute money, protest at demonstrations, and fill the jails. The larger the numbers of participants, the better, for larger numbers of grassroots activists helps to spread work out, reduce the expected costs of high-risk activism, and boost activists' perceptions of political efficacy.

Organized religion is well-equipped to expand the ranks of grassroots activists by providing ready-made opportunities for network- and bloc-recruitment of new members into movements. Movements rarely recruit new members individually, straight "off the streets." Rather, movements typically recruit new participants through existing relational and organizational networks that "feed" their members into activist organizations (Smith 1996; McAdam, McCarthy and Zald 1988: 707–708). Religious organizations—which comprise in the United States, for example, the largest share of all types of non-profit, voluntary organizations—can represent a veritable "field ripe for the harvest" for movement recruiters whose issues resonate with religious actors. Viewed in reverse, religious leaders committed to mobilizing disruptive activism have at their disposal ready-made, extensive recruitment networks and organizations. So, for example, in the Sanctuary, civil rights, and pro-life movements, and in the Nicaraguan, Salvadoran, and Iranian revolutions, entire congregations of churches and mosques were drawn *en mass* into disruptive activism, helping to rapidly expand the growth of these movements.

Furthermore, when a movement recruits members through religious networks and organizations, along come the well-established structures of solidarity incentives imbedded in those networks of relationships. The movement can then rely less on selective incentives and the promise of public goods to induce participation, since the new activists now participate, in part, because other members of their religious networks are participating and expect or encourage them to participate. The camaraderie, shared experience, and collective affirmation of moral commitments and personal and group identity all become rewarding in and of themselves, beyond what the movement may or may not achieve.

Pre-existing communication channels

Social movements require not simply an abundance of warm bodies; they also need the ability to coordinate the actions of participants, to get them thinking and acting in unity. Movements require the capacity to deploy their forces with strategic coordination, to get participants meeting, lobbying, and protesting together. The fundamental issue here is the problem of communication: social movements need mechanisms to transmit streams of information from knowledge and decision-making sources to dispersed participants regularly, efficiently, and accurately. That is no easy task.

Just as organized religion is well-positioned to loan its leadership, financial, and personnel resources to social movements, so, too, it can lend its pre-existent communications systems. In effect, the religion's established communications infrastructures—its newsletters, bulletins, weekly announcements, telephone directories, magazines, television and radio programs, address lists, journals, synods, presbyteries, and councils—that normally transmit information related to the religion's spiritual mission, become employed or are coopted to transmit information related to political activism. The synagogue telephone-tree is used to announce a rally; the worship service bulletin includes a notice about an organization's need for volunteers and donations; the denominational newsletter publishes an article about a social injustice and organizations working to respond; the Imam announces details of a planned protest at the end of Friday prayers. In each case, by piggybacking on the pre-existent communication structure, rather than creating its own structure *ex nihilo*, the social-movement is able to spend energy and resources it otherwise would have devoted to organizational self-maintenance, on direct political engagement instead.

Pre-existing authority structures and deviance-monitoring mechanisms

Social movements, like any human organization, must deal with issues of authority, decision-making, and deviance. The questions are: Who in a social-movement holds legitimate power, for what purpose, and within what bounds? How are the movement's decisions to be arrived at and implemented? And how are violations of the movement's norms to be discouraged and sanctioned? Constructing from scratch cultures, routines, and systems that satisfactorily settle these questions can consume much time and energy, especially when movement participants do not share a common identity or moral worldview.

When social movements acquire the leadership, members, and communication channels of organized religion, however, they also often simultaneously acquire the pre-existing authority structures, decision-making routines, and deviance-monitoring mechanisms embedded in the functioning religious organizations. The propensity to respect the views of the pastor, rabbi, monk, or Imam; the familiarity with or commitment to consensual decision-making or the representation of elders; the complex of formal and informal positive and negative sanctions that encourage compliance with group norms within a religious group: all of these are readily transferable from the religious context to the movement-organization context. And like the organizational resources noted above, this transfer can help movements pay less attention to internal organizational maintenance, so they can pay more attention to their external political struggles.

Enterprise tools

The organizational work of social movements is greatly aided by the availability of equipment and facilities that expedite information communication and storage. These basic but important "enterprise tools" (Smith 1991: 61) include typewriters, telephone lines, office space, desks, photocopy and mimeograph machines, computers and software, internet access, fax machines, e-mail accounts, bookshelves, office supplies, file cabinets, secretarial help, and legal advice. Especially in movements' formative stages, quick and easy access to these tools can make a critical difference in the speed and extent of mobilization. Organized religion typically possesses many of these enterprise tools, and can greatly aid the mobilization of political activism by making them readily available to budding social movements.

"Movement midwives"

Oftentimes, newly emerging or resurging social movements are facilitated by the help of supportive, pre-existent organizations. These antecedent organizations intentionally foster movements by helping to organize new movement organizations, without ever actually themselves becoming social-movement organizations. These kinds of organizations we may call "movement midwives," in recognition of their deliberate efforts to help in the "birthing" of movements, while retaining identities distinct from the movements whose births they assist. Just as nurse midwives do not actually conceive nor bear the children they help to deliver, yet play a vital role in their delivery, these trans-movement and meta-movement organizations neither actually "cause" nor "become" social movements per se, yet play absolutely indispensable roles in facilitating movements' emergences and resurgences (see Smith 1996).[7]

Religious organizations can and often do act as movement midwives. In the United States, for example, the Fellowship of Reconciliation, the American Friends Service Committee, *Sojourners* magazine, Clergy and Laity Concerned, New Jewish Agenda, the National Council of Churches, the Catholic Worker, and a host of other denominations, divinity schools, and para-church organizations have, over the years, worked to help spawn a number of disruptive social movements, without themselves becoming directly identified with the movements (Zald and McCarthy 1987: 73–76). These kind of organizations can, have, and do offer invaluable start-up resources for mobilizing social movements.

SHARED IDENTITY

The so-called "new social movements" theorists—Alberto Melucci, Alezandro Pizzorno, Alain Touraine, Jurgen Habermas (see Cohen 1985)—have argued persuasively that social movements face an essential task besides merely mobilizing and strategically deploying organizational resources. Social movements must also construct and maintain collective identities that signify to themselves and the world who they are, what they stand for, and what kind of society they hope to create. Movements lacking coherent shared identities are likely to be culturally and politically ineffectual. Constructing and maintaining collective identities entails a significant amount of "identity work," whereby groups, through a process of lived experience, draw on available cultural codes, ideologies, worldviews, values, symbols, and traditions to develop and sustain a meaningful sense of their own character and purpose vis-a-vis their social environments. In addition to the inherent expressive and solidarity functions they serve within movements, coherent socially-constructed collective identities also enhance movements' instrumental capacities for effective organizing, issue-framing, and political struggle. Religion, as a pre-existing collective identity that can be conferred upon or coopted by a movement, represents a valuable resource for the task of collective identity construction and maintenance.

Common identification among gathered strangers

At the micro level, religion can provide a basis upon which strangers can work together with relative ease in common purpose. Learning that others one meets for the first time—at a street march, an organizer's meeting, or in jail—are, like oneself, also Catholics, Muslims, or Jews, can immediately foster a sense of ease, trust, and loyalty that greatly facilitates group communication and solidarity. Especially in the relatively ambiguous, fluid, and emergent situations that often surround disruptive activism, religious identity can greatly expedite the process of coming to a shared "definition of the situation." Religious actors employ their standard "recipe knowledge" (Schutz 1971) and "typificatory schemes" (Berger and Luckmann 1966) to define others who share their religious identity, in order to socially define a workable situational "reality." The actors then know better what assumptions to make about the others, what rhetorical style to employ, which values and symbols will resonate, and so on. They know which songs to sing, which authorities to cite, what moral commitments they ought to uphold.

The "overground railroad" of the 1980s Sanctuary movement, for example, that transported Central American refugees to safety, initially expanded rapidly among a letter-linked network of Quakers who shared the common heritage of Quaker activism in the nineteenth century "underground railroad" that transported black slaves to the safety of the North (Davidson 1988). This kind of readily-available common identification through religion can greatly enhance the capacity of activist groups to execute effective collective action.

Shared super-identities nationally and cross-nationally

At the macro level, religion can provide the basis for common identification and mutual cooperation between otherwise quite different groups of people. Most religions are national and transnational by nature, and therefore create common bonds between people of differing national and global regions, races, and classes, which can transcend and defy more proximate loyalties. So, for example, one critical factor helping to generate the 1980s United States Central America peace movement against President Reagan's policy in El Salvador and Nicaragua was the common religious bond felt between North American Christians and their counterparts in Central America. This mutual identification engendered a sense of moral responsibility among the North American believers to stop the United States-sponsored wars in Central America. Without the influence of this pre-existent transnational religious identity, that movement would certainly have been much smaller and less politically significant (Smith 1996).

Evidence also indicates a more recently-developed religious super-identity in the United States that is shared not only within religions but also *between* religions. James Hunter (1991) suggests that traditional religious cleavages in the United States are undergoing a momentous shift, so that the most important contemporary antagonisms are no longer between Protestants, Catholics, and Jews. Rather, they are between the "orthodox" and "progressive" moral worldviews that attract and divide Protestants, Catholics, and Jews alike. Hence, a conservative Baptist today may share in common more cultural and political assumptions, values, and aspirations with a traditional Catholic or Orthodox Jew, than with a liberal Protestant. Pat Robertson's Christian Coalition's recruitment of sympathetic Roman Catholics, Jews, and black Christians is evidence of this transformation (Birnbaum 1995: 33). Overall, the capacity of these religious and inter-religious super-identities to create solidarity and facilitate communication among faith-based activists can and has served as a tremendous identity resource for mobilizing social movements.

Unifying identity against outside threats

Finally, religious identities can serve as the unifying symbolic rallying point for groups mobilizing to defend themselves against outside threats. In so doing, religion provides a uniting catalyst of solidarity around which activists can mobilize resistance. The religion of many native American tribes, for example—including the Sioux, Delaware, Creek, Yamasee, and Powhatan—became the basis of resistance to and revolt against the European invasions from the seventeenth to the nineteenth centuries (Martin 1991). Similarly, native Melanesians expressed resistance to European colonialization through "cargo cults" and other religious millenarian movements (Worsley 1968). Likewise,

June Nash demonstrates in her chapter in this volume that religion has provided the grounds upon which native Bolivian tin miners have mobilized resistance to their economic oppressors. Similar observations could be made about Catholicism in Poland's Solidarity movement, the anti-Catholic movement of nineteenth-century United States Protestants, Ghandi's Indian independence movement, and many others.

SOCIAL AND GEOGRAPHIC POSITIONING

The social and spacial distribution of activists in a society can be an important variable helping to shape the fate of social movements. Religion often enjoys social and spacial characteristics that can promote the strength of social movements.

Geographical dispersion

In some cases, it can be a strategic advantage for the activists of a social-movement to be spread out over the geographical regions of a state or country, as opposed to concentrated in only one region or urban center. Presuming that the movement enjoys a well-functioning communications infrastructure that links and coordinates the widely-scattered activists, and that the movement does have some kind of identifiable leadership "center," geographical dispersion of participants can facilitate movement strength in many ways. It can extend recruitment efforts to larger numbers of potential participants; it can reduce public and state perceptions that the movement represents a narrow or small constituency; it can increase the number of political representatives to whom the movement has access; and it can make repression of the movement by the state or a counter-movement much more difficult.[8]

To the extent that a religion is geographically dispersed, as is often the case, and that its members participate in a social movement, that movement automatically benefits from these advantages of geographical dispersion. The fact that the faith-based United States Sanctuary movement, for example, rapidly spread through links with religious organizations from its origin in Arizona throughout the entire country, enabled it to carry out more effectively its task of protecting refugees and protest United States immigration policy, and to withstand state opposition (Davidson 1988). Similarly, the United States Central America Peace movement was able to defeat multiple administration requests for military aid to the Nicaraguan Contras precisely because it had committed activists lobbying hard in every region of the country (Smith 1996). Hence, the geographic dispersion of religion can translate into strategic strength for social movements.

Social diffusion and cross-cutting associations

Perhaps more valuable for a social-movement than geographical dispersion is the social diffusion of activists throughout many levels and sectors of society. Movement constituencies, alliances, and coalitions that cut across social class, occupational, racial, and ethnic lines can in some—though not all—cases and ways significantly strengthen a social movement's chance of success. For example, support from middle-class and business interests appears to be one of the most important determinants of the triumph or failure of revolutionary insurgencies in Latin America (Wickham-Crowley 1989).

Although religion is always conditioned by the stratifying forces of human inequality, religion can and sometimes does nonetheless cut across class, occupation, and racial lines in ways that link people together who would otherwise remain isolated. Therefore, when religion, in those cases, lends itself to an activist cause, the social-movement automatically benefits from the advantages that these cross-cutting social associations bring. M.M. Salehi's chapter in this volume, for example, shows that the fact that Islamic militants who eventually overthrew the Shah of Iran were located in all corners of society made it impossible for the Shah's proficient security forces to crush their insurgent organization.

Transnational organizational linkages

We have already noted the transnational nature of many religions in our discussion of common religious identities. The same fact—that most religions are socially positioned in a way that bridges together leaders and adherents from many nations and world regions—can provide social movements many organizational and ideological benefits. For example, numerous transnational religious organizations—such as the World Council of Churches, Pax Christi, and the Jesuits—have played key roles in fomenting political activism in many nations (Smith 1994). Tristan Borer's chapter in this volume, for instance, reveals that the World Council of Churches played a critical role in con-vening many South African religious leaders to organize a powerful church-based oppo-sition to apartheid. Similarly, the emergence of the liberation theology movement in Latin America resulted, in part, from a series of educational, ideological, and institu-tional transfers between Europe and Latin America, mediated through the structure of the Roman Catholic Church hierarchy (Smith 1991). By providing resource-bridges between actors from different nations, these kinds of religious transnational-organiza-tion linkages can help social movements transcend some of the restrictions and limita-tions they may encounter within their own national contexts.

PRIVILEGED LEGITIMACY

In many societies, organized religion enjoys a certain authority, legitimacy, and protec-tion not enjoyed by other social institutions and organizations. This is because religion deals with the sacred and the supernatural; and, perhaps, because in some situations, it may have a history or current status as a socially powerful institution. This authori-ty, legitimacy, and protection can be put to good use for the cause of social-movement activism.

Political legitimacy in public opinion

In many societies, and under certain circumstances, public opinion accords relatively greater authority to the voice of religion than to other voices. When a bishop, rabbi, ayatollah or other religious leader or teacher denounces an injustice, lodges a complaint against the government, or calls people to support a cause, it is often taken at least somewhat more seriously than the same declaration would be if spoken by a politician, business person, or secular activists. In the United States, the American public may view the voice of religion—especially grassroots religion and religion viewed as nor-mally nonpartisan—as politically naive, perhaps, but also generally as sincere and hon-orable. Therefore, when religious voices speak on behalf of social movements, they can lend a valuable extra force or earnestness to the movements' causes.

When, for example, the Reverend Billy Graham speaks against nuclear arms, San Salvador's Archbishop Oscar Romero denounces military repression, Tibet's Dhali Lama criticizes Chinese imperialism, Iran's Ayatollah Khomeni calls for uprisings in the streets, South Africa's Desmond Tutu condemns the apartheid regime, and Manila's Cardinal Sin demands the end of the Marcos dictatorship, people listen. At another level, when a local minister denounces violence against women, members of a religious congregation become visibly involved in a recycling campaign, or a group of rabbis march on behalf of racial equality, the public also takes notice. This is partly a product of abiding or latent public respect for religion; and partly a product of the media's desire to cover the novel and dramatic. In any case, religion can often capitalize on these factors to draw attention and lend credibility to activist causes, or undermine potential state or counter-movement charges that a social-movement represents marginal or extremist elements.

The protection of religion as a last "open space"

Sometimes, authoritarian political regimes, in efforts to crush the undermining autonomy of civil society, outlaw and repress all independent associations and voluntary organizations: labor unions, social clubs, student groups, neighborhood organizations, and so on. In many societies, however, even brutal authoritarian regimes are reluctant to ban and completely repress religious institutions. Sometimes religion is untouchable because it seems too influential to challenge; other times, authoritarian regimes consider religion—wrongly—to be "apolitical," and therefore exempt from repression. For whatever reason, in many authoritarian situations, religious organizations have become the only remaining "open spaces" in civil society.

Under these conditions, religious authorities will often feel morally obliged to allow political dissidents to operate within their religious institutions, if not to proactively champion the rights of the repressed people. This was certainly the case of the progressive church in Latin America during the 1970s (Smith 1991), of the South African churches during the 1980s (see Borer's chapter in this volume), and in Poland and East Germany at the end of the Cold War (Marullo and Meyer 1992). In these and similar instances, religion could use its relatively privileged position to help keep alive a remnant of autonomy in civil society, to sustain the voice of resistance, and to prepare the grounds for a broader social-movement opposition once the authoritarian regime begins to relent. This can be a valuable protection for repressed social movements.

INSTITUTIONAL SELF-INTEREST

Finally, in some cases, religion can aid the cause of a social movement, not so much through its privileged legitimacy, per se, but rather as a result of the purposeful defense of its institutional self-interest. The resulting positive effects for the social-movement may be felt directly or indirectly.

Institutional resistance to state encroachment

Sometimes, an established religion will begin to feel the State encroaching on domain it believes it "owns." For example, the State may take over a social function previously controlled by religion, such as education; it may ban religious symbols from public places and discourse; or it may actually attempt to eliminate the presence of religion altogether. In response, religious leaders will often begin to mobilize forces to defend and possibly win back pieces of "their territory." In the process, the religion will often develop a language and rituals of resistance, devote institutional resources to defiance of the State, and establish formal or informal alliances with other, nonreligious regime opponents. When this happens, the religious institution can itself become a center of anti-regime activism. And nonreligious movements also opposing the State can benefit from the religion's attitude, resistant rhetoric and rituals, institutional resources, and political alliances.

This process can develop in totalitarian situations. In East Germany, for example, the state increasingly impinged upon the affairs of the church. In defense of its own institutional autonomy and values, the churches and religious base communities became the center of resistance and mobilization. The Nikolai Church of Leipzig especially became a center of free speech and mass mobilization (Nielsen 1991; Goeckel 1990). Likewise, in Poland, the Catholic Church, in resistance to the Communist regime, helped lay the groundwork for the eventual rise of the Solidarity movement (Weigel 1992; see Osa's chapter in this volume). But this process of institutional resistance can also develop in more democratic situations. In the United States, for example, in recent decades, many conservative religious groups believe that the State has encroached on education by forbidding school prayer, denying meeting space to student religious groups, and by teaching "secular humanism" or "new age religion" in public schools. Others believe the State has overstepped its rightful boundaries by outlawing manger scenes on public property or by imposing equal-opportunity laws for homosexuals as employees in religious schools or churches. In many cases, religious leaders, sensing a threat to their own religious freedoms, have organized movements to counter what is perceived as illegitimate state infringement (Lienesch 1993; Hunter 1991).

WHAT FOLLOWS

The chapters that follow represent specific case studies of contemporary, important social movements in which religion has played a vital role. Each focuses on a specific aspect of religion's contribution to or influence upon the social-movement it analyzes. Together, the case studies reflect a wide range of ideological, geographical, and religious diversity.

The chapters by Aldon Morris and M.M. Salehi, on the black civil rights movement and the Iranian revolution, respectively, demonstrate the crucial role that preexistent religious organizations can play in mobilizing political protest. Maryjane Osa's chapter on Poland's Solidarity movement and June Nash's chapter on Bolivian tin-mining resistance highlight the ways in which religious rituals can serve to generate and sustain insurgent consciousness. The chapters by Sharon Erickson Nepstad on the progressive churches in Nicaragua and El Salvador and by Tristan Borer on the South African anti-apartheid movement examine the factors that draw religious groups into political activism and shape the ways in which they respond to repression. The chapters by David Sikkink and Mark Regnerus on the rise of the Nazis and by Rhys Williams and

Jeffrey Blackburn on Operation Rescue manifest how symbolic structures serve to construct identities in ways that both facilitate and impede political activism. Finally, James Aho's chapter on political extremism in the United States and Ron Pagnucco's chapter on faith-based peace organizations explore how religious ideologies influence social movements' tactical repertoires. I hope that, altogether, these chapters make an important step in the direction of encouraging social-movement studies to pay religion the analytical attention it deserves.

REFERENCES

Bainton, R. 1950. *Here I Stand: A Life of Martin Luther*. Nashville: Abingdon.

Beckford, J. 1985. "The Insulation and Isolation of the Sociology of Religion." *Sociological Analysis* 46: 347–354.

Bell, D. 1976. *The Cultural Contradictions of Capitalism*. New York: Basic Books.

Berger, P. 1967. *The Sacred Canopy*. Garden City: Doubleday.

Berger, P. and T. Luckmann. 1966. *The Social Construction of Reality*. Garden City: Anchor Books.

Birnbaum, J. 1995. "The Gospel According to Ralph." *Time*. 145:20 (May 15).

Cohen, J. 1985. "Strategy or Identity: New Theoretical Paradigms and Contemporary Social Movements." *Social Research*. 52.

Davidson, M. 1988. *Convictions of the Heart*. Tucson: University of Arizona Press.

Craig, R. 1992. *Religion and Radical Politics*. Philadelphia: Temple University Press.

Ennis, J. 1992. "The Social Organization of Sociological Knowledge: Modeling the Intersection of Specialities." *American Sociological Review*. 57:2. April.

Findlay, J. 1993. *Church People in the Struggle*. New York: Oxford University Press.

Gamson, W. 1975. *The Strategy of Social Protest*. Belmont: Wadsworth.

Gamson, W, Bruce Fireman, and Steven Rytina. 1982. *Encounters with Unjust Authority*. Chicago: Dorsey Press.

Geertz, C. 1973. *The Interpretation of Cultures*. New York: Basic Books.

Goeckel, R. 1990. *The Lutheran Church and the East German State*. Ithaca: Cornell University Press.

Goldberg, R. 1991. *Grassroots Resistance*. Belmont: Wadsworth Publishing.

Hart, S. 1992. *What Does the Lord Require?* New York: Oxford University Press.

Hill, C. 1972. *The World Turned Upside Down: Radical Ideas During the English Revolution*. New York: Penguin.

Hunter, J. 1991. *Culture Wars*. New York: Basic Books.

Kanter, R. M. 1972. *Commitment and Community*. Cambridge: Harvard University Press.

Klandermans, B. and S. Tarrow. 1988. "Mobilization in Social Movements: Synthesizing European and American Approaches." *International Social-movement Research: From Structure to Action.* Greenwich: JAI Press.

Kliever, L. (ed.) 1987. *The Terrible Meek: Essays on Religion and Revolution.* New York: Paragon House.

Lewy, G. 1974. *Religion and Revolution.* New York: Oxford University Press.

Lienesch, M. 1993. *Redeeming America: Piety and Politics in the New Christian Right.* Chapel Hill: University of North Carolina Press.

Linton, B. 1985. *Religion, Rebellion, Revolution.* New York: St. Martin's Press.

Luker, K. 1984. *Abortion and the Politics of Motherhood.* Berkeley: University of California Press.

Machiavelli, N. 1940 [1517]. *The Prince and the Discourses.* Book I. New York: McGraw-Hill.

Martin, D. 1969. "Notes Toward a General Theory of Secularisation." *European Journal of Sociology.* December.

Martin, J. 1991. "Before and Beyond the Sioux Ghost Dance." *Journal of the American Academy of Religion.* 59:4 (Winter).

Marullo, S.and D. Meyer. 1992. "Grassroots Mobilization and International Politics: Peace and the End of the Cold War." *Research in Social Movements, Conflict, and Change.* Greenwich: JAI Press.

McAdam, D. 1982. *Political Process and the Generation of Black Insurgency.* Chicago: University of Chicago Press.

_____. 1983. "Tactical Innovation and the Pace of Insurgency." *American Sociological Review.* 48 (December).

McAdam, D., J. McCarthy and M. Zald. 1988. "Social Movements." in Neil Smelser (ed.). *Handbood of Sociology.* Newbury Park: Sage.

McCarthy, J. and M. Zald. 1977. "Resource Mobilization and Social Movements: A Partial Theory." *American Journal of Sociology.* 82:6 (May).

Moen, M. and L. Gustafson. 1992. *The Religious Challenge to the State.* Philadelphia: Temple University Press.

Morris, A. 1984. *The Origins of the Civil Rights Movement.* New York: The Free Press.

Morris, A. and C. Mueller (eds.). 1992. *Frontiers of Social-movement Theory.* New Haven: Yale University Press.

Munson, H. 1988. *Islam and Revolution in the Middle East.* New Haven: Yale University Press.

Nielsen, N. 1991. *Revolutions in Eastern Europe: The Religious Roots.* Maryknoll: Orbis Books.

Nottingham, E. 1954. *Religion and Society.* New York: Random House.

Oberschall, A. 1973. *Social Conflict and Social Movements.* Englewood Cliffs: Prentice Hall.

Oliner, S. and P. Oliner. 1988. *The Altruistic Personality: Rescuers of Jews in Nazi Germany*. New York: The Free Press.

Parsons, T. 1963. "Christianity and Modern Industrial Society." (33-70) in Edward Tiryakin (ed.). *Sociological Theory, Values, and Socio-Cultural Change*. New York: Free Press.

Pipes, D. 1983. *In the Path of God: Islam and Political Power*. New York: Basic Books.

Schutz, A. 1971. *Collected Papers: The Problem of Reality* (Vol. 1). The Hague: Martinus Nijhoff.

Smith, C. 1996. *Resisting Reagan: the U.S. Central America Peace Movement*. Chicago: University of Chicago Press.

_____. 1991. *The Emergence of Liberation Theology: Radical Religion and Social-movement Activism*. Chicago: University of Chicago Press.

Smith, J. 1994. "Organizing Global Action." *Peace Review*. 6:4. Winter.

Statistical Abstract. 1994. *Statistical Abstract of the United States: 1994*. Bureau of Census.

Walzer, M. 1965. *The Revolution of the Saints: A Study in the Origins of Radical Politics*. Cambridge: Harvard University Press.

Weigel, G. 1992. *The Final Revolution: The Resistance Church and the Collapse of Communism*. New York: Oxford University Press.

Wickham-Crowley, T. 1989. "Winners, Losers, and Also-Rans: Toward a Comparative Sociology of Latin American Guerrilla Movements." in Susan Eckstein ed. *Power and Popular Protest*. Berkeley: University of California Press.

Wilson, B. 1966. *Religion in Secular Society*. Baltimore: Penguin Books.

Wolterstorff, N. 1983. *Until Justice and Peace Embrace*. Grand Rapids: Wm. B. Eerdmans.

Worsley, P. 1968. *The Trumpet Shall Sound: The Study of "Cargo" Cults in Melanesia*. New York: Schocken Books.

Yang, C.K. 1961. *Religion in Chinese Society*. Berkeley: University of California Press.

Zald, M. and J. McCarthy. 1987. "Religious Groups as Crucibles of Social Movements." in Mayer Zald and John McCarthy (eds.). *Social Movements in an Organizational Society*. New Brunswick: Transaction.

PART ONE

PRE-EXISTENT ORGANIZATIONS
AND LEADERSHIP

1

The Black Church in the Civil Rights Movement: the SCLC as the Decentralized, Radical Arm of the Black Church

Aldon Morris

The black church functioned as the institutional center of the modern civil rights movement. Churches provided the movement with an organized mass base; a leadership of clergymen largely economically independent of the larger white society and skilled in the art of managing people and resources; an institutionalized financial base through which protest was financed; and meeting-places where the masses planned tactics and strategies and collectively committed themselves to the struggle.

Successful social movements usually comprise people who are willing to make great sacrifices in a single-minded pursuit of their goals. The black church supplied the civil rights movement with a collective enthusiasm generated through a rich culture consisting of songs, testimonies, oratory, and prayers that spoke directly to the needs of an oppressed group. Many black churches preached that oppression is sinful and that God sanctions protest aimed at eradicating social evils. Besides, the church gave the civil rights movement continuity with its antecedents in the long-standing religious traditions of black people. Finally, the black church served as a relatively autonomous force in the movement, being an indigenous institution owned and controlled by blacks.

Scholars of the black church have consistently argued that it is the dominant institution within black society. It has provided the organizational framework for most activities of the community—economic, political, and educational endeavors as well as religious ones. The black church was unique in that it was organized and developed by an oppressed group shut off from the institutional life of the larger society. Historically, the institutions of the larger society were of very little use to blacks. Blacks were never equal partners in those economic, political, and cultural institutions and in fact were systematically excluded from their decision-making processes. This institutional subordination naturally prevented blacks from identifying with the institutions of the larger society. In short, the larger society denied blacks the institutional access and outlets necessary to normal social existence.

The black church filled a large part of the institutional void by providing support and direction for the diverse activities of an oppressed group. It furnished outlets for social and artistic expression; a forum for the discussion of important issues; a social environment that developed, trained, and disciplined potential leaders from all walks of life; and meaningful symbols to engender hope, enthusiasm, and a resilient group spirit. The church was a place to observe, participate in, and experience the reality of owning and directing an institution free from the control of whites. The church was also an arena where group interests could be articulated and defended collectively. For all these reasons and a host of others, the black church has served as the organizational hub of black life.

The urban church, by virtue of its quality of religious services and potential for political action, developed into a more efficient organization than its rural counterpart. Even by the early 1930s urban churches had become significantly more powerful and resourceful than rural churches. Urban churches were better financed, more numerous, and larger in membership. Urban ministers usually received more formal education and earned higher salaries than their rural counterparts. Stable leadership emerged as higher salaries led to a lower turnover rate among ministers, allowing them to become full-time pastors. The urban church was able to offer its congregations more activities and programs, which meant more committees and other formal bodies to run them, and greater organized cooperation within the church.

The great migration of blacks from rural to urban areas between 1910 and 1960 was responsible for the tremendous growth of the urban church throughout that period. Newly urbanized Southern blacks established close ties with the institution they knew best—the church. Numerous problems attended the major shift from rural to urban life, and the church facilitated the transition by offering valuable friendships and social networks through which the migrants could assimilate into urban life. Moreover, the Southern urban church was similar to its rural counterpart in that it provided an institutional alternative to, and an escape from, the racism and hostility of the larger society. Behind the church doors was a friendly and warm environment where black people could be temporarily at peace with themselves while displaying their talents and aspirations before an empathetic audience. For these reasons the urban church, like the rural church of the South, continued to function as the main community center. However, the great migration made it possible for the urban church to function on a scale unattainable in rural settings.

The urban churches of the South became organizations of considerable social power. The principal resource of the church was its organized mass base. The church not only organized the black masses but also commanded their allegiance. The fact that the church has been financially supported by its economically deprived parishioners clearly demonstrates that allegiance. Furthermore, the black community has always contributed the voluntary labor necessary to meet the church's considerable needs in its role as the main community center. These activities emerged from an elaborate organizational structure.

The typical church had a well-defined division of labor, with numerous standing committees and organized groups. Each group was task-oriented and coordinated its activities through authority structures. Individuals were held accountable for their assigned duties, and important conflicts were resolved by the minister, who usually exercised ultimate authority over the congregation. A strong work ethic existed in the church, where individuals and groups were routinely singled out and applauded for their contributions. This practice promoted a strong group identification with the church as members were made to feel important and respected, an experience denied to blacks by the institutions of larger society.

CHARISMA AND THE BLACK CHURCH

Another source of the black minister's power is charisma. The black church, a well-established institution, produced and thrived on charismatic relationships between minister and followers. Churches, especially the prestigious or leading ones, demanded ministers who could command the respect, support, and allegiance of congregations through their strong, magnetic personalities. Furthermore, the majority of black ministers claimed to have been "called" to the ministry directly by God or at least by God's son through such agencies as dreams, personal revelation, or divine inspiration. Once such a call was accepted, a minister continued—in his own perception and, usually, that of his congregation—to have a personal relationship with God. Clearly, the congregation's belief that such individuals enjoyed a direct pipeline to the Divine served to set them off from the rest of the population.

Charisma, however, is based not so much on the beliefs held by charismatic individuals or their followers as on performance. Experience is often crucial to performance, and most ministers who became charismatic civil rights leaders brought a great deal of experience into the movement. Most of them had grown up in the church and understood its inner workings. They knew that the highly successful minister developed a strong, magnetic personality capable of attracting and holding a following. Many of the ministers were college graduates with considerable training in theological studies. It cannot be overemphasized that much of these ministers' training occurred in black colleges and universities under the direction of leading black educators and theologians of the day. They were taught and counseled by such men as Dr. Benjamin Mays, C.D. Hubert, and S.A. Archer. The Reverend C.K. Steele, one of the early leaders of the movement, remarked (1978): "These are strong men and you could hardly sit under them seriously and sincerely, without being affected." He states further that these educators and theologians, who themselves had struggled to get an education, stressed such values as human dignity, personhood, manhood, and courage. These became core values of the civil rights movement.

During this period black universities and colleges were closely linked to the black church. Thus, a significant number of the leading professors were also ministers or closely attached to the ministerial profession. It was not unusual for the students to be required to attend daily or weekly chapel services, during which these influential cultural figures, expert in public speaking and the art of dramatic communication, attempted to imbue the students with certain values. In college as well as in the church, the future leaders of the movement were exposed to and taught the excitement and art of stimulating, persuading, and influencing crowds by individuals who had mastered the art of charisma.

The black church combines the mundane (finance of buildings, maintenance services, committee meetings, reports, choir rehearsals) and the charismatic (strong face-to-face personal relationships that foster allegiance, trust, and loyalty, and give rise to a shared symbolic world that provides an interpretation of earthly affairs and the anticipated afterlife). The charismatic element requires no allegiance to man, the government, the "city fathers," or traditional norms of behavior. For example, when Birmingham's blacks began to boycott buses, the Southern Conference Educational Fund reported (SCEF n.d.: 3):

> The city's famous police commissioner, Eugene "Bull" Connor, issued a decree that no Negro minister should urge his people to stay off the buses. Mr. Shuttlesworth's response was typical: Only God can tell me what to say in the pulpit. And I'm going to tell my people to stay off those buses if I have to go to Kilby prison....

Students of charismatic leadership have persuasively argued that if individuals are to be recognized as charismatic leaders, they must personify, symbolize, and articulate the goals, aspirations, and strivings of the group they aspire to lead. The ministers who were to become the charismatic leaders of the movement occupied strategic community positions which enabled them to become extremely familiar with the needs and aspirations of blacks.

The black minister, because of his occupation, listened to and counseled people about their financial woes, family problems, and health problems, as well as problems stemming from discrimination, prejudice, and powerlessness. By the same token, the black preacher was the figure who witnessed the resiliency, pride, and dignity that resided in what Dr. W.E.B. DuBois had characterized as the "souls of black folk." The ministers listened to the educational and occupational aspirations of countless black children, along with the pleas of their parents that God and the white man give their offspring the chance to have it better than they had had. Part of the minister's job was to single out for praise those individuals in the congregation who landed impressive jobs, were admitted to colleges and universities, or made any other personal stride.

Thus the black ministers of the 1950s knew black people because they had shared their innermost secrets and turmoils. They were happy when blacks progressed, and, with their fellows, they recoiled in shock when a member of their race was tarred, feathered, and lynched while a white mob drank beer and assembled for "show time." The minister was firmly anchored in the center of the ebb and flow of the social and cultural forces of the black community.

Specifically, the words and actions of such leaders as Martin Luther King, Jr., Fred Shuttlesworth, and C.K. Steele seemed to radiate the qualities required to jar loose the tripartite system of domination that paralyzed the black community. Their displays of courage, dignity, integrity, and burning desire for freedom earned the approval of the black masses, because such values were deeply embedded in the social fabric of black society. Moreover, these ministers, with their oratorical talents and training, were able to instill in people a sense of mission and commitment to social change. The words they used were effective because they symbolized and simplified the complex yearnings of a dominated group. This is one of the reasons blacks in the movement showed little hesitation in accepting such personalities as their charismatic leaders.

THE COLLECTIVE POWER OF CHURCHES

It was and is common for black ministers in a community and even in different communities to have personal relationships among themselves. They met at conventions, community gatherings, civic affairs, and the like. At times they exchanged pulpit duties and encouraged their choirs to sing at the churches of colleagues. Furthermore, black ministers in a community were linked formally by either a city ministerial alliance or an interdenominational alliance, through which they were able to debate and confer on issues important to the black community (Mays and Nicholson 1933: 158).

Within the ministerial alliances were to be found ministers of the poor, the educated, the unemployed, professionals, laborers, housemaids—indeed, the entire spectrum of black society. If these ministers, through their informal and formal bodies, could be persuaded to support protest activity, each could then mobilize his own slice of the community. The National Baptist Convention, one such body, operates on the national level with a membership of more than five million.

Scholars of the church have consistently noted how rapidly and efficiently information is transmitted to the black community from the pulpit. This reliable channel for disseminating information greatly enhances the possibility for mass action. The minister can deliver any type of message to the congregation; his salary is paid by the church, which frees him from white economic pressures. Moreover, with their disciplined workforces churches are able to act collectively. Once a plan of action is agreed on by a number of congregations it can be implemented systematically and thousands of dollars can be raised by a number of churches in a short time to finance a concerted plan.

THE SCLC

Scholars of social movements have been concerned with the important issue of how movements become forces in a society. Some theorists suggest that movements gather their strength by breaking from existing social structures, while others take the opposing view that movements draw their strength from preexisting organizations and social networks. In the case of the civil rights struggle, the preexisting black church provided the early movement with the social resources that made it a dynamic force; in particular, leadership, institutionalized charisma, finances, an organized following, and an ideological framework through which passive attitudes were transformed into a collective consciousness supportive of collective action.

But a new political dimension was needed to mobilize those church resources on a wide scale and commit them to the active pursuit of social change. The SCLC, because it was a church-based movement organization, supplied the political dimension that pulled churches directly into the movement and made it a dynamic force.

By 1957 local movements were under way in a number of Southern cities. They were often vigorous movements that engaged in nonviolent confrontations. In early January 1956, for example, seventy-two blacks, mostly students from Xavier University in New Orleans, were held in jail for defying segregation on a city bus. The local movement center in New Orleans was led by the Reverend A.L. Davis—an ideal man for mobilizing protest because he headed the New Orleans Interdenominational Ministerial Alliance. In March 1956, at a mass meeting called by the alliance and attended by five thousand blacks, Davis (NYT 1956) urged blacks to "rise up and let White Citizens' Councils know the time is out for segregation." After continuous protest action, New Orleans buses were finally integrated in the summer of 1958.

The New Orleans struggle typifies the local protest movements prevalent in the South during the middle and late 1950s. Many of the confrontations were not directed by visible movement organizations, nor did the protesters receive notoriety for their unprecedented efforts. But the clergy and the black church were at the center of the conflicts. Movement participants were meeting on a systematic basis, planning strategy, collecting funds, encouraging protest, and confronting local white power structures. For their efforts, many were paid off with bombed homes, burnt crosses, threats, and beatings. Nevertheless, the local movements endured because they were organized and rooted in community institutions.

The organizers of the various local movements usually maintained informal contact between localities and sporadically provided mutual support. At mass meetings of the New Orleans groups in 1956, $3,000 was collected for the MIA to assist the Montgomery movement (NYT 1956). A "talking relationship" existed among many local movement leaders throughout the South before the formation of SCLC. Such informal contact existed among Dr. King of Montgomery, the Reverend Joseph Lowery of Mobile, and Reverend Shuttlesworth of Birmingham. The three Alabama leaders would meet to discuss their local movements and to coordinate activities on a state level, previously the task of the outlawed NAACP. The Alabama group discussed formalizing contact among the various movements. Lowery, leader of the merging movement center in Mobile and president of the Mobile Interdenominational Ministerial Alliance, has recalled (1978) that in the informal meeting before the SCLC was organized, "we saw this need to get together and then we just talked about how we ought to broaden it to include Steele, Jemison, and the other guys."

In the meantime, Bayard Rustin, Ella Baker, and the white attorney Stanley Levison, all living in New York, were continuously analyzing and supporting the local movements. During the Montgomery bus boycott, Levison, Rustin, and Baker formed an organization in New York called "In Friendship." Its purpose was to financially assist movements in the South and to inform the Nation about racial injustice (Walder 1978). A. Philip Randolph was closely associated with "In Friendship" and gave his support. Then, according to Reverend Steele (1978), who at the time was deeply involved in the Tallahassee bus boycott, "I was called one night...and asked if I would call a meeting of the Southern leaders who were involved in these various tension points in the South...I discovered later, I think, that that person was Bayard Rustin."

Ella Baker, one of the most significant and unheralded leaders of the civil rights movement, adds (1978): "The idea [SCLC] grew out of our [Baker's, with Rustin and Levison] discussions...the suggestion was made that there needed to be an organization." Finally, Stanley Levison (1979) pointed to the collective effort that gave rise to the SCLC:

> It would be very difficult to single out one individual as the originator of the SCLC idea. Many discussions by Dr. King and other leaders such as Fred Shuttlesworth, C.K. Steele, Ralph Abernathy, Mrs. King and with Northern

figures who were consultants such as A. Philip Randolph, Bayard Rustin, Ella Baker, and myself were held. In brief, it arose out of a great deal of collective discussion, and if there was one individual who clarified and organized the discussion it was unquestionably Dr. King.

After the call from Rustin, Reverends Steele, King, Shuttlesworth, and Jemison issued a call to black churchmen and leaders across the South urging them to meet at the Reverend M.L. King, Sr's, Atlanta church early in January 1957 to form an organization to coordinate the local protest movements. As a result black leaders representing eleven Southern states converged on the historic Ebenezer Baptist Church in Atlanta.

It is no surprise that nearly all the participants were black (Walker 1978: 32; Fairclough 1977). Glenn Smiley (1978), a white friend and colleague of Dr. King and Rustin, has recalled: "Bayard Rustin had called together a group of labor leaders, churchmen, and so on, a select group. They were all black. I was not invited to the meeting and they set up the SCLC." From the outset the black leaders established a pattern whereby white groups could contribute to the movement through their organizational, individual, and group channels rather than occupying leadership roles in the SCLC. From its inception the SCLC was led by indigenous black leaders.

The first meeting of what was to become the SCLC was held in Atlanta on January 10 and 11, 1957. The title of this meeting, "Southern Negro Leaders Conference on Transportation and Integration," highlights the role the bus grievances played as a central organizing focus for the local movements and for the conference. Indeed, the discussions of the meeting centered on the dynamics and outcomes of the mass bus boycotts. Seven working papers, written in advance by Bayard Rustin, attempted to distill the importance of the local movements and were used to focus the discussions and chart a course for the new organization.

The first working paper addressed the role of the bus grievance in the protest movement. It pointed out (SCLC 1957a), "The people *knew* that in bus segregation they had a just *grievance*. No one had to arouse their social anger." It was recognized that a preexisting shared grievance facilitated rapid mobilization. The working paper further argued (SCLC 1957a): "These protests are directly related to *economic survival*, since the masses of people use buses to reach their work. The people are therefore interested in what happens in buses." Rustin's insight suggested that grievances vital to the masses were the ones that triggered organized collective action.

The working papers made it clear that the local protest movements broke from the legal strategies of the past and initiated the new period of mass confrontation. Working paper no. 7 acknowledged the break (SCLC 1957c):

> We must recognize in this new period that direct action is our most potent political weapon. We must understand that our refusal to accept Jim Crow in specific areas challenges the entire social, political and economic order that has kept us second class citizens since 1876.

The method of nonviolent direct action was stressed. It was contended (SCLC 1957c) that "nonviolence...makes humble folk noble and turns fear into courage." The working papers also insisted that nonviolent direct action was a tactic that immediately thrust power into the hands of every individual desiring to strike out directly against oppression. The tactic of direct action was conducive to mass protest. Moreover, it allowed the very bodies of blacks to become potential power instruments in the sense that ordinary people could organize together in masses and boycott, crowd the jails, march, and nonviolently create the crisis of social disruption. Indeed, throughout the turbulent protest years that followed, the familiar question asked of activists was, "Have you put your body on the line for the struggle?" The battle had shifted from the courtrooms to the seats of power in local communities.

The institutional base of the local movements was the next issue addressed by the working papers, which disclosed what the conference participants already knew: the protest movements grew out of an institutional base and culture rather than erupting spontaneously. Statement five of working paper no. 1 unequivocally stated (SCLC 1957a, emphasis in original), "The campaign is *based on the most stable social institution in Negro culture—the church.*" This document summarized the important role of the church in producing *community sharing* through mass meetings, collective giving of economical assistance and other contributions, and a *community spirit* that generated enthusiasm and promoted group pride (SCLC 1957a). The working paper argued that these dynamics were generated in normal community functioning even before the boycotts. Yet it was maintained that during the direct action movements, it was the church that harnessed these dynamics and gave them the form and momentum necessary for the effective organization of car pools, mass meetings, and organized protest.

The working papers also stressed that the white power structure was not homogeneous. In working paper no. 4, entitled "The Relationship of Community Economic Power Groups to the Struggle," Rustin wrote (SCLC 1957b):

> The bus protest has clearly revealed certain economic facts. (1) The Negro's dollar is a factor in the economic organization of the community, (2) his refusal to ride had a catastrophic effect on the economics of the bus companies, and (3) the unintended but nonetheless direct effect of the protest on downtown merchants is real, indeed.

These statements document the fact that these conference participants were being exposed to how economics could be used in terms of strategy. Indeed, the bus protest taught these leaders that the white community was not a monolithic entity but a heterogeneous one with an array of interests. They came to learn that the basic concern of the business community was money, while other groups, such as elected political leaders, were preoccupied with political power. The conference participants were thus beginning to realize that the movement had a greater chance of success if it could divide the white community along the lines of its diverse interests.

In short, the documents of the first organizational meeting of the SCLC stated that (1) the church had functioned effectively as the institutional base of protest movements; (2) aggressive nonviolent action by blacks was necessary if the system of segregation was to be overthrown; (3) an organized mass force was needed to supplement the activities of the NAACP, which was under fierce attack throughout the South; and (4) movements could be generated, coordinated, and sustained by activist clergy and organized black masses working in concert.

The working papers also contained definite plans to be implemented by the new organization. Foremost among them were the propositions that additional bus protest movements had to be initiated and developed; new protest movements focusing on voting, but modeled after the bus movements, had to be organized; and there was a pressing need to create an organization to unify the Southern movements. Thus the conferees made plans to attend subsequent meetings, a number of which followed in various Southern cities. After those meetings terminated, the group that began as the "Southern Negro Leaders Conference on Transportation and Non-Violent Integration" transformed itself into the "Southern Leaders Conference" and finally the Southern Christian Leadership Conference. The Reverend T.J. Jemison (1978), a founding member of SCLC, vividly points out why the name "Southern Christian Leadership" was adopted:

> Since the NAACP was like waving a red flag in front of some Southern whites, we decided that we needed an organization that would do the same thing and yet be called a Christian organization...We said Southern Christian Leadership Conference, so they would say, well, that's Baptist preachers so they didn't fear us, but they didn't bother us...The Negro minister only lost his place in the sun with whites when he started leading boycotts, and trying to tear down their social structure.

STRUCTURE: POLITICAL ARM OF THE CHURCH

Ministers who were in the process of leading local movements became leaders of the SCLC. Indeed, the criteria for leadership in SCLC proved to be movement experience and stature. After the initial organizing meetings of the SCLC, nine men emerged as its leadership: the Reverend Dr. Martin Luther King, Jr., leader of the Montgomery bus boycott, president; the Reverend C.K. Steele, leader of the Tallahassee bus boycott, first vice-president; the Reverend A.L. Davis, leader in the bus protest of New Orleans, second vice-president; the Reverend Samuel Williams, leader in effects to desegregate Atlanta buses, third vice-president; the Reverend T.J. Jemison, leader of the first mass bus boycott in Baton Rouge in 1953, secretary; the Reverend Fred Shuttlesworth, leader of the mass direct action movement in Birmingham, corresponding secretary; the Reverend Ralph Abernathy, a leader in the Montgomery bus boycott and confidant of Dr. King, treasurer; the Reverend Kelly Miller Smith, local NAACP President and activist of Nashville, chaplain; and Lawrence Reddick, a scholar at Alabama State College and an activist of the Montgomery bus boycott, SCLC historian.

All but Reddick were clergymen. They were all educated, having completed their undergraduate training in black institutions. They were all males. Except for Reverends Williams and Davis, they were all young, averaging approximately thirty years of age. They were all black and Southerners.

An examination of the Executive Board, which included the officers listed above, is instructive. What is striking is that of the sixteen remaining board members, thirteen were clergymen. Among the other three were a dentist, a pharmacist, and an attorney. All of the board members were black, and they came from eleven Southern states. The geographical residency of the board members highlights the fact that in the beginning the SCLC was first and foremost a Southern organization. The early SCLC needed board members from across the South so that access to many Southern communities could be ensured. The majority of the board members were direct action-oriented people. Many had been key organizers in the various bus movements of the day. Others were directly involved with direct action projects or had been in the past.

The SCLC was a church-related protest organization and the overwhelming majority of the SCLC's original leadership were ministers. The original SCLC had thirty-six formal leadership positions, including the Executive Staff, Administrative Committee, and Executive Board. Only four of the thirty-six were filled by non-clergymen. Most of the SCLC's decisions, therefore, were made by activist clergymen. Indeed, the important decisions of the early SCLC were made by the Administrative Committee, comprising thirteen individuals, eleven of whom were ministers.

Thus, the SCLC was anchored in the church and probably could not have been otherwise. For it was these activist ministers who became the leaders and symbols of the mass bus boycotts, controlled the resource-filled churches of the black masses, had economic independence and flexible schedules, were members of ministerial alliances that spoke the same spiritual and financial language whether in Brooklyn or Birmingham, and who came to understand that there is power harnessed in an organized group. So central was the church to the SCLC that Reverend Lowery, one of its original founders, stated (1978): "[The SCLC] was really the black church, that's what it was. It was the black church coming alive. It was the black church coming together across denominational and geographical lines."

AFFILIATE STRUCTURE

To understand the SCLC one must abandon the idea that it was one formal movement organization located in Atlanta. Another erroneous assumption often found in studies of the civil rights movement is that the SCLC was not a real organization at all, but simply the shadow of Dr. King (see, e.g., Clark 1966: 612; Walker 1978: 63; Fairclough 1977: 38). This assumption is usually asserted without any in-depth analysis of the SCLC's affiliates. The SCLC's Southwide affiliate structure, in fact, was one of the central factors responsible for its power. A prime reason why SCLC affiliates' structures had power lies in the fact that they were often mass-based.

The view that the SCLC had a mass base during this period departs from previous research. Oberschall (1973: 223), relying on data presented by J.J. Clarke in her early study of the MIA and the ACMHR, concludes that these organizations "were heavily middle class in membership." However, Clarke's findings suggest something very different from this conclusion. Clarke found that 49.6 percent of the members of the ACMHR and 44.7 percent of the MIA's membership were in unskilled or semiskilled occupations (Clark 1962: 37). She further found that the mean annual family income of the ACMHR membership was $3,715 and the corresponding mean for MIA was $3,094. Clarke also studied the Tuskegee Civic Association during this period and found that the mean family income of its members was $7,477 (Clark 1962: 37). This sharp difference in family income can be attributed to the fact that the majority of blacks in Tuskegee have historically been highly educated and have held jobs at Tuskegee Institute. Pointing to the mass base of the MIA and the ACMHR, Clarke wrote (1962: 27) that "the membership of the MIA is drawn from all the Negro social strata within Montgomery, but the largest number of members are middle-aged females and elderly men from the lower strata. Roughly the same membership characteristics prevail in ACMHR."

Clarke also pointed out (1962: 65–66) that the MIA and ACMHR use of sermons, prayer meetings, or devotional periods is an adequate way to attract the lower-class elements of the Negro communities, and "In Montgomery and Birmingham, the decisions seem to be to attract the lower class elements; this is after all, where the masses of Negroes are to be found." SCLC movement centers across the South operated largely in the same manner as the MIA and the ACMHR. In this regard, Dr. Simpkins of the UCMI claimed that at least 90 percent of the black communities in which they worked supported them. According to Simpkins (1978), "the [black masses] felt very much a part of it, not only in Shrevesport, but the whole area, I mean, the whole North Louisiana area."

Piven and Cloward have promoted the view that the SCLC did not have a mass base. Relying on a brief article written by Kenneth Clarke (1966), Piven and Cloward (1977) maintain that SCLC was "amorphous and symbolic" so that the large numbers of people drawn to its demonstration were not members." What they overlook is that the SCLC functioned as the decentralized arm of the mass-based black church. That mass base was built into the very structure of the SCLC.

The SCLC was not an individual-membership organization. Only other organizations, such as churches or civic leagues, could become its affiliates. Here we see the impact of the MIA and the other local "organizations of organizations," which had demonstrated that community resources could be mobilized by uniting the various community organizations. Indeed, it was known that the Montgomery boycott had endured more than a year because the Women's Political Council, the Progressive Democrats, the NAACP, the Citizens Coordinating Committee, and dozens of churches coordinated by the MIA provided it with the necessary organizational networks and resources. The founders of the SCLC reasoned that it would organize a large Southwide mass movement if it were able to mobilize and coordinate community organizations across the South. The SCLC was to be a Southwide organization of organizations.

Although the SCLC was officially incorporated to function in sixteen Southern states, it was clear from the beginning that the black community outside the South had an important role to play. Thus, the SCLC bylaws (SCLC n.d.) stated, "the magnitude of the problem calls for the maximum commitment of resources of all institutions in Negro life, North and South...." To gain the support of the national black community it was decided that the SCLC affiliate structure would comprise community organizations whose aims and methods were closely akin to those of the SCLC. Community organizations became affiliates of the SCLC by paying a twenty-five-dollar fee and signing a charter committing them to organize their communities to engage in direct action protests.

It was the local movements that created the need for the SCLC. Local movement centers already in existence provided the SCLC with its initial affiliated structure. Thus, the MIA, the ICC, the ACMHR, the Mobile Civil Association (MCA), and similar organizations became the early affiliates. Moreover, ministers from across the South who attended the SCLC's organizing meetings were encouraged to affiliate their churches. The action of the Reverend Kelly Smith, local president of the Nashville NAACP, typifies the response of many of these ministers (1978):

> After the [SCLC organizing] meeting and after the discussion that we had and all that, it became clear to me that we needed something in addition to the NAACP. So I came back and I called some people together and formed what we named the Nashville Christian Leadership Council in order to address the same kind of issues that the SCLC would be addressing.

Some of these ministers formed new direction action organizations, while others affiliated their churches with the SCLC.

Indeed, during the late 1950s the SCLC held numerous meetings across the South where various community groups, including some nonreligious organizations such as Black Masons, lodges, and labor organizations, became affiliates. But it was the churches and church-related organizations, including Interdenominational Ministerial Alliances and local Baptist Conferences, that constituted the bulk of SCLC affiliates. The churches and related organizations constituted the crucial internal organization enabling the SCLC to mobilize community resources. They were so central that SCLC leaders called them the "invisible hand of God." Thus Dr. King was not merely a symbolic leader created by the mass media. His power, like that of other important leaders, stemmed from the fact that he and his colleagues were able to mobilize a variety of resources through community organizations.

It is useful, therefore, to think of the SCLC of that period as the decentralized political arm of the black church. The SCLC's leaders did not attempt to centralize the activities of its affiliates, because it was felt that centralization would stifle local protest. Rather, the role of the SCLC's affiliates was to organize local movements and address grievances salient in local communities. Speaking of local leaders, the Reverend Wyatt Walker (1978), who affiliated his Gillfield Baptist Church of Petersburg, Virginia, with the SCLC, explained that "they knew their communities better than anyone else could ever know them." Reflecting local diversity, some affiliates organized around bus boycotts; others focused on voting drives, still others concerned themselves with school integration. The role of the SCLC was to coordinate and strengthen these efforts by linking the various leaders so that they could share resources and experiences. Finally, affiliation meant that local groups were organizationally linked to a charismatic leader, Martin Luther King, Jr.

THE SCLC AND CHARISMA

At the heart of the SCLC's organizational structure was a charismatic center. As in the black church that spawned it, institutionalized charisma was an important resource of the SCLC. It cannot be overemphasized that the SCLC's power grew out of a dynamic combination of organizational strength and charisma. Without the church base, it is unlikely that King would have become a great organizer and symbol of an effective mass movement. Being at the center of a church base allowed King to use his charisma as a mobilizing force. In the church community it is customary for black churches to conduct revival services once a year. The purposes of a revival are to convert new souls for Christ, increase church membership, and raise money for the host church. Seldom will the church's pastor preside at the revival. The common practice is to invite a renowned and often charismatic minister from outside to present a series of sermons. The renowned charismatic minister was important for the revival, because his presence attracted large numbers of people who provided the needed resources.

Most of the community meetings and rallies sponsored by the SCLC and its affiliates resembled the revival. Dr. Martin Luther King became the centerpiece of these gatherings, because his presence attracted people and resources.... Reverend Walker (1978), who became Executive Director of the SCLC in 1960, maintained that when local groups needed to raise money or were engaged in difficult struggles,

> they wanted Martin and Ralph [Abernathy] to come. 'Cause they knew they could get the folk; you can't do anything without folk. And, Martin and Ralph could get up the folk....Charisma plays a great role. Martin Luther King's great leadership came from the fact that he was able to get more warm bodies in the street at one time than anybody else we've ever seen in American history. That's what gave him his tremendous influence and power.

Ella Baker (1978), the SCLC's first Associate Director, its second Executive Director, and a critic of charismatic leadership in general and of Dr. King's in particular, admits: "The charismatic figure has value certainly—because it's like having a basis for calling people together. They responded to his call. People will come." The Reverend James Lawson, who organized in numerous communities with King, arrived at a similar conclusion (1978):

> It was the nature of the struggle at that time, that [King] was the single overwhelming symbol of the agitation and of the struggle....He gave the black community an advantage the black community has never had, and has not since his death. Namely, that any time King went to a community, immediately the focus of the nation was on that community. And the people were prepared to start coming, and they may not have come otherwise. Many of them didn't. He had the eyes of the world on where he went. And in the black community it never had that kind of person.

Thus, a movement organization with a charismatic leader rooted in a mass-based institution is more likely to mobilize masses of people than a movement organization without such a leader. Charismatic leaders of this type play a crucial role in the mobilization process and the building of an internal organization.

THE SCLC AND THE LOCAL COMMUNITY

The newly organized local movements evolved in conflict-ridden settings. Black protest groups were up against an opposition that included white terrorist organizations, the courts, Southern governments, and police departments that deployed attack dogs, high-powered rifles, and policemen who were not reluctant to use intimidation and violence against people they referred to as "niggers." The dangers encountered by protest groups often went unchecked in the late 1950s because the Eisenhower Administration, reluctant to intervene, was promoting the politically expedient line that Southern problems had to be worked out by Southerners. That left black protestors in local communities to confront a vicious opposition largely alone. The moment Revered Abernathy reflected on this situation, his jovial mood turned into melancholy. He (1978) characterized those early protestors as the ones who traveled "out there on that lonely road."

The formation of the SCLC made a great contribution to the local struggles by creating deep social bonds among these "lonely protestors." At early SCLC meetings and conventions it was important for protest leaders to engage in meaningful face-to-face social interactions. Abernathy, as he recalls those early meetings (1978), quickly recaptures his joviality and states:

> But, every now and then you get together with members of the household of faith, and you get a sort of camaraderie. You get strengthened, backed, and supported because you see a Kelly Miller Smith from Nashville and C.K. Steele from Tallahassee and T.J. Jemison. We shared at our conventions.

Abernathy explained that during these meetings an hour was set aside for mutual sharing, when participants would give reports from the field. Aaron Henry, an SCLC board member from Clarksdale, Mississippi, told of difficulties resulting from his affiliation with the movement, while others experiencing similar problems across the South listened. According to Abernathy (1978), problems that seemed insurmountable to one's local movement were placed in perspective through comparisons with problems of other movements. Face-to-face interactions among local protest groups diminished the opposition's effectiveness by minimizing the potency of its tactics.

The formation of the SCLC also contributed to local struggles by strengthening their internal organization. Jemison stated (1978) that the Baton Rouge movement was helped by joining the SCLC: "People would feel that you [the local SCLC leader] were tied to the whole thing, so they didn't mind following their leadership locally because you were one of the ones that was leading it all over the South." It was very important politically for local black communities to be linked symbolically and organizationally to the larger movement. When asked, "What did it mean to be affiliated with SCLC?" the Reverend C.T. Vivian, a local leader in Nashville during the late 1950s, responded (1978):

> If you ask it that way, it meant Martin Luther King. It also meant a central focus. It meant that there was something outside of ourselves which gave one a certain sense of security. Though you didn't know what it was...it meant that

you had a national symbol. It meant you had a spokesman. That you had forces outside yourself working. It also meant you had a success in Montgomery.

In Shreveport, Louisiana, C.O. Simpkins, a dentist who became a local SCLC leader and affiliated his direct action organization with the SCLC in 1957, said (1978) the affiliation meant "that you would enlarge your contacts and knowledge of what was going on, and we would get support on a national level for our efforts." Reverend Shuttlesworth, when asked what effect the early SCLC meetings had on local movement bases, answered (1978): "In one word, elevating and lifting, because it's always lifting and moving to know that something that is moving has just come to your area. I think that people were inspired to ask for more, seek more, and try to get more." Every local SCLC leader interviewed for this study stressed the importance of the support and national context the SCLC provided for their local movements. In Reverend Lowery's words (1978), affiliating with the SCLC helped,

> 'cause it gave you a national backing. This is very significant—and the white folks in the community knew that when you spoke, you didn't just speak for yourself, that you had some supporters around the South and around the country.

Finally, the SCLC played a direct role in producing among local community people the mental attitudes conducive to protest. The SCLC promoted "consciousness raising" by engaging in the politics of agitation and refocusing black religion. Indeed, SCLC officials brought direct action workshops, voting clinics, and mass rallies to many local communities across the South. Community leaders, students, and young people usually attended the daytime meetings and workshops, because they had flexible schedules. It was at night that the adults came out to hear the singing and oratory about this desired thing called "freedom." According to Steele (1978), at the nighttime meetings, "people filled up the auditorium." The Reverend Kelly Smith recalled:

> The meetings always had mass meetings attached to them that people came out to hear and just to be spurred on...and to be reminded of what needs to be done and how badly we're being treated, and how we can do things to overcome. That was in the public meetings—that was done.

In some periods, members of an oppressed group who appear docile are rapidly transformed into active protestors. While the transformation process is crucial to understanding a protest movement, it remains largely unexplained. Some light can be shed on how this mental transformation occurred in the civil rights movement. The point is that people's attitudes are heavily shaped by the institutions with which they are closely affiliated. This is especially true of such institutions as schools and churches, whose primary purpose is to interpret social reality and make moral pronouncements regarding the "right" relationship for people with the world around them. These institutions provide the cultural content that molds and shapes individual attitudes. Therefore, fairly rapid transformation of those attitudes may be accomplished by refocusing the cultural content of the institutions engaged in defining social reality. Changing attitudes by refocusing the cultural content of institutions can be much more effective than changing the attitudes of separate individuals, because institutional refocusing enables organizers to reach large numbers of people simultaneously.

For the first half of the twentieth century most black churches taught that the meek would inherit the earth; that God would judge the oppressor according to his wicked deeds; that God loved the dispossessed and would provide them with just rewards after they had fought the long Christian fight; and that a good Christian was more concerned with perfecting his or her spiritual life rather than with material well-being. These messages were expressed through elaborate and eloquent rituals of song, prayers, and sermons. It was a religion of containment, the opiate of the masses, a religion that soothed the pains of economic, political, and social exploitation (Mays and Nicholson 1969: 7).

But a new message crept into the "revival" and began refocusing the cultural content of a significant number of churches. King carried the new message (1958: 36):

> But a religion true to its nature must also be concerned about man's social conditions....Any religion that professes to be concerned with the souls of men and is not concerned with the slums that damn, the economic conditions that strangle, and the social conditions that cripple them, is a dry-as-dust religion.

A refocusing of the cultural content of the church was required to operationalize King's view of religion. This "militant" view of religion has always existed in the Black church, as is attested by the fact that such leaders of slave revolts as Nat Turner and Denmark Vesey adopted it. This view of religion guided the effects of Frederick Douglass and Harriet Tubman as they fought the slave regime and transported slaves through the underground railroad. This religious view became institutionalized through songs, sermons, and the literature of the church. Dr. Benjamin Mays, an authority on black religion and a minister who taught King and many other civil rights leaders the militant view of religion, maintains that "the Negro was selective in his preaching. He usually selected Biblical passages which emphasized that all men are children of God." Mays pointed out that such a position suggests equal treatment and social equality. Thus Mays concluded (1978) that black ministers "preached a revolution but in disguise." In addition, the view of religion as a dynamic force for social change was a cornerstone of the "social gospel" movement. A significant portion of the SCLC's leadership was familiar with the main doctrines of the "social gospel" movement, and King studied them while in graduate school (Bennett 1965: 196–97). Even though this view of religion was institutionalized, it was not usually the aspect emphasized. However, refocusing black religion was made easier for King and his counterparts because they were activating a religious view latent in the church rather than creating it from a vacuum.

The SCLC represented the emergence of an organized force across the South, dedicated to refocusing the cultural content of the religion of the black masses. This discussion has focused on Dr. King because he was regarded as the master of this refocusing process, but he is also important for having served as a model for activist clergymen across the South. King was able to succeed in "refocusing" black religion because by any criterion he was a Christian minister, and the masses regarded him as that. It would surely have been difficult for an "outsider" to tamper with the sacred religious beliefs and practices of a people. King's power was enhanced by his image among blacks as a respectable man, the "Reverend Doctor King," who practiced what he preached. In Reverend Walker's words (1978), King was a hero who would go to jail, confront redneck racists, and speak boldly before them without hating them and taking a club to them, or trying to shoot back. Finally, King's oratorical abilities aided him in refocusing the cultural content of black religion. Septima Clark, a great grassroots organizer of the period, said of King (1978): "As he talked about Moses, and leading the people out, and getting the people into the place where the Red Sea would cover them, he would just make you see them. You believed it." Mrs. Clark maintained that King's speeches made people feel that if they worked hard enough, they really could make justice roll down like water, and righteousness like a mighty stream.

Thus, by giving contemporary relevance to familiar Biblical struggles through spellbinding oratory and by defining such religious heroes as Jesus and Moses as revolutionaries, King had begun to refocus the content of black religion.

The issue, of course, is whether this refocusing process actually worked. There is evidence that it did. For instance, in assessing Dr. King's role in the Albany, Georgia, movement, the attorney C.B. King maintains (1981) that Dr. King,

> was a catalyst for mass involvement because he made a very significant difference in terms of how the masses of people were willing to interpret this opiate. King served up religion in a rather unique fashion as a militant force for the first time. King was using religion as a key to inspire a perception which moved the masses in what could be conservatively considered the direction of revolution.

Yet it was not an easy task. For example, Reverend Shuttlesworth required members of his church to register and vote. He explained that when he asked deacons to register, they immediately fell to their knees and uttered long prayers. They were substituting the opiate for direct action. Shuttlesworth (1978), practicing the militant religion, demanded they stop wearing out the knees of their pants and personally took them to register. In short, during the late 1950s the SCLC leadership began preparing members of the black community to participate in protest activities by systematically introducing them to direct action workshops, movement literature, and a familiar religious doctrine that had been significantly altered to encourage protest. In this context a "good Christian" was one who actually sought to change "sinful" social conditions.

REFERENCES

Baker, E. 1978. Interview. August 28. New York.

Bennett, L. 1965. *Confrontation: Black and White*. Baltimore: Penguin Books.

_____. 1970. "When the Man and the Hour Are Met" in C. E. Lincoln (ed.), *Martin Luther King, Jr.* New York: Hill and Wang.

Bevel, D. N. 1978. Interview. December 14. Chicago.

Clark, K. 1966. "The Civil Rights Movement: Momentum and Organization." *Daedalus.* 95 (Winter).

Clark, S. 1978. Interview. November 17. Charleston, S.C.

Clarke, J. 1962. *These Rights They Seek.* Washington, D.C.: Public Affairs Press.

Fairclough, A. 1977. "A Study of the Southern Christian Leadership Conference and the Rise and Fall of the Nonviolent Civil Rights Movement." Ph.D. dissertation, University of Keele.

Jemison, T.J. 1978. Interview. October 16. Baton Rouge.

King, C.B. 1981. Interview. August 7. Albany, Ga.

King, M. L. 1958. *Stride Toward Freedom.* New York: Harper & Row.

Lawson, J. 1978. Interview, October 2 and 6. Los Angeles.

Levison, S. 1979. Letter to Aldon Morris. March 21.

Mays, B. and J. Nicholson. 1933. *The Negro Church.* New York: Arno Press.

Meier, A. 1970. "The Conservative Militant" in C. Eric Lincoln (ed.), *Martin Luther King, Jr.* New York: Hill and Wang.

NYT. 1956. "Trial of Negroes for Montgomery Bus Boycott Opens." *New York Times,* March 20. p. 1.

Oberschall, A. 1973. *Social Conflict and Social Movements.* Englewood Cliffs: Prentice Hall.

Piven, F. F. and R. Cloward. 1977. *Poor People's Movements.* New York: Vintage Books.

SCEF. n.d. "They Challenged Segregation at Its Core." Southern Conference Educational Fund.

SCLC. 1957a. "The Meaning of the Bus Protest in Southern Struggle for Total Integration." January 10-11. Atlanta: Southern Christian Leadership Conference.

_____. 1957b. "The Relationship of Community Economic Power Groups to the Struggle." January 10-11. Atlanta: Southern Christian Leadership Conference.

_____. 1957c. "The Role of Law in Our Struggle: Its Advantages and Limitations." January 10-11. Atlanta: Southern Christian Leadership Conference.

_____. n.d. *Constitution and By-Laws of the Southern Christian Leadership Conference.* Atlanta: Southern Christian Leadership Conference.

Shuttlesworth, F. 1978. Interview, September 12. Cincinnati.

Simpkins, C.O. 1978. Interview. October 25. Merrick, N.Y.

Smiley, G. 1978. Interview. October 1. Los Angeles.

Smith, K. M. 1978. Interview. October 13. Nashville.

Speed, D. 1978. Interview. October 11. Tallahassee.

Steele, C. 1978. Interview. October 12. Tallahassee.

Vivian, C.T. 1978. Interview. December 7. Philadelphia.

Walker, E. 1978. "A History of the Southern Christian Leadership Conference, 1955-1965: The Evolution of a Southern Strategy for Social Change." Ph.D. dissertation, Duke University.

Walker, W. 1978. Interview. September 29. New York.

2

Radical Islamic Insurgency in the Iranian Revolution of 1978–1979

M.M. Salehi

The 1978 political turbulence that put an end to the millennium-old monarchy in Iran has become known as the "Iranian Revolution." Officially, it is called the "Islamic Revolution," a notion emphasized by the new sovereigns and their loyal supporters in order to justify the rule of the Shiia clergymen and their Islamic Principles.

The "Revolution" replaced the existing political order with a theocracy, a development incongruent with trends prevalent elsewhere in contemporary history wherever there has been a revolution. The incongruency is apparent not merely because a revolution had taken place, but because it had occurred under the leadership of a traditionalist Muslim clergy who were striving to materialize their long-term objective: the establishment of a theocracy.

In fact, it is surprising to note that until the early 1970s Iran was undergoing a transition toward a more secular society, with the role of religion diminishing in regard to political affairs. The outspoken revolutionary and reformist opposition forces were mainly secular in their orientation. Their domain of influence was expanding, making them a likely candidate to replace the existing regime. Then, in the 1970s, a renewed Shiia revitalization movement began. This movement gained momentum and penetrated almost every segment of the population. It conquered certain social territories that had been the stronghold of the former secular political groups. Simultaneously, it strengthened and expanded its influence among the lower classes and rural people.

This movement even found access to those members of the middle class who were better educated than most other Iranians. It was a great success for the proponents of Islamic rule, for now they had easy access to the group with the most significant political potential in the country—the urban middle class. This stratum included most of Iran's politically hotheaded college students, younger white-collar employees, and young officers in the administration of Iran's growing industrial system. These groups included most of Iran's long-time opponents of the regime who were thoroughly experienced in radical activities under repressive rule. They were people with the knowledge and skills of political persuasion. It was not, therefore, the size of this stratum that was significant, but its political potential.

It became increasingly apparent that a redirection of the national struggle was in process and that events were moving in favor of Islamic activists. Building upon this movement, different Muslim groups were encouraged to expand their activities, both in political and nonpolitical affairs. Some groups attempted to appeal to all classes with their political objectives and demands for a national uprising against the regime. As the struggle proceeded, during 1977–78, the Shiia groups under Ayatollah Khomeini's leadership managed to unify the major opposition forces over the objective of pushing the Shah out of office. This objective brought nearly all the opposition groups under a single leadership. As a result, the leading clergy who commanded the alliance of the insurgent masses rose to the position of leader of the opposition groups, speaking with a national voice. This promotion was not only political; simultaneously, it imposed the clergy's objectives and preferences upon the people.

Such activities at the leadership level were complemented by the entrance into the movement of millions of people who had very little previous political experience. A power was created that could easily crush any resistance, could silence any other alternative suggestions, and was obedient to the clergymen who had established themselves as the leaders of the uprising. The contribution and power of the small, but highly influential, new middle class was becoming insignificant compared to that of the urban lower class and the rural people. These earlier activists found themselves powerless to exert any determining influence upon the new course of social change. The energies that now moved the masses were beyond the control or command of the new middle class. The slogans, for example, during the early wave of the uprising in the winter of 1978, were "Freedom and Independence." By the end of the year, they had become "Freedom and Independence, and the Islamic Republic...." The original political demands, for which the secularists had fought for years and to which they had tried to educate the populace, were fading away in the uproar of escalating revolution. Those demands were overstepped by an Islamic fundamentalist revitalization movement that had attracted millions of newcomers to the realm of revolutionary politics. Ideologically, the secular group found themselves to be like a gust of wind lost in a hurricane.

In this phase, the demands of nearly all political forces that did not belong to the clergy-led groups were either removed from the agenda or pushed down on the list. Very little opportunity remained for secular demands, even if they were made by Muslim intellectuals. The revolution of the secular groups and the consequences of the earlier activists' efforts were swallowed up by the Shiia revitalization movement. The immense national power was not invested in a clerical leadership. Millions of devoted Shiia Iranians listened eagerly to these leaders as both political commanders and religious authorities; millions of others obeyed them, at least as a political leadership. In this way, it was possible for the Shiia activists to elevate Ayatollah Khomeini to a leading position as a personification of the "People's Revolution," as both its spokesman and commander. Thus, a theocracy was born.

INSURGENCY BY SYMBOLIC MEANS

In a little over a year, from 1977 to 1979, the Iranian people began a variety of protest attempts that eventually escalated into a nationwide uprising. What is intended here is to show the pattern of the escalation, and specifically, how and why it favored the dominance of religious parties. The issue is how people finally managed to develop a successful strategy leading to a national uprising and why this strategy relied heavily on religious and symbolic means.

A close study of the history of the Iranian struggle against the regime, and the limitations of their earlier style of resistance and insurgency, may reveal some facts about why Iranians rose up under the banner of religion. There is a logical connection between the conditions of struggle against the regime of the Shah and the people's choice in their strategies of revolt. It seems reasonable to claim that insurgency through religion was not simply their only choice, but the only effective option left to them.

Ever since the beginning of the twentieth century, Iranians had attempted to alter the rule of their dictators. After the Constitutional Revolution of 1906–1909, they had fought continuously against the reemergence of a dictatorial rule. Radical groups occasionally attempted to uproot the monarchy. One such attempt was the uprising known as *Jasmgglies*, in the 1920s, headed by Kuchick Kan, which managed to establish the Republic of *Gilan* in Gilan province. Also included in this category are the events that lead to the royal-CIA coup of 1953. In their struggles, as recently as the last couple of decades, opposition groups had put into operation almost every strategy known to modern radicals—the attempt to assassinate the Shah, mass demonstrations, a sustained state of unrest, Cuban-style armed efforts, and urban underground armed movements, to name a few. Their attempts were counterbalanced through the boosting of the security forces and the subsequent evolution of the regime into one of the most oppressive police states in the region.

Also, in the 1970s, despite the economic development and improvement of living conditions for certain classes of people, a state of unrest prevailed within nearly all classes of society. Obviously, this unrest was something that had the potential to be manifested in action. Sporadic small-scale acts of opposition were frequent, but they were not strong enough to alter the political system. The source of tension, therefore, remained unchanged.

It was not necessary to politicize the masses of people further in order to make them dissentive. They were already quite prepared for an uprising. The question one would hear in private circles was *how* was it to happen. Political groups were also deeply concerned with the question of strategy. Their underground documents reflect how much they were involved in discussing the issue. No one expected a simple answer. They had learned by experience that the system was quite alert and was well prepared to crush any opposition movement.

As early as the mid-1960s, some political activist groups who were convinced that nothing could be accomplished without an armed movement established armed underground movements. Such armed movements had different origins and objectives. Some Marxists youths, disappointed with the past strategies and the experiences of the Iranian leftists, became pioneers in this new phase of the struggle. They formed small groups of highly dedicated, well-trained fighters who occasionally engaged the security forces of the regime in bloody battles. Some of them tried a guerrilla movement, similar to the Cuban experience. A group using underground tactics but Islamic in its rationale and objectives emerged to prove itself also quite effective. There was even the assassination operation of Prime Minister Mansour (1965), executed by *Fa da eian* Islam, a group of fundamentalist Shiia elements that had been active for decades. But none of these attempts seriously challenged the regime (Abrahamian 1985). They merely maintained the state of tension. Likewise, severe manpower limitations prevented the armed groups from becoming a major revolutionary armed force. In order to grow, they eventually needed a fixed base where they could set up their headquarters and supplies. Iran's military forces, specially trained and equipped for local warfare and anti-insurgency operations, were both large enough and strong enough to easily crush any such attempts. It was well known that the regime's anti-insurgency strategy was designed to kill the armed opposition's action in "embryo."

When the struggle finally entered the stage of armed movements, the security forces intensified their punishments of active opposition groups. Underground fighters came to expect no less than the death sentence. Stories of torture and beatings in the political prisons had intimidated citizens to the point that many dared not get involved. They muttered against the regime in their own private circles, but such minimal dissent was not considered enough to require action. Any organized activity was sure to be crushed immediately; consequently, the people were divided into two groups. A few had risked their lives and were active against the regime, and a larger number were against the regime but would not take any action. If there was to be a successful strategy, it was imperative that those who were active find some way of activating the masses of people. A significant number of the active members needed to be willing to risk their lives in order to inspire the masses toward commitment. They hoped that this would prove to the masses that the regime was not made of steel, that it was vulnerable, and that united, the people could themselves alter their political situation.

The underground groups, however, even though they were quite small, did manage to achieve some change, but for these basically psychological conquests, they had to pay a heavy price. Some members carried cyanide pills. If they were arrested, they might bite the pill and within a few minutes be dead. This type of suicide prevented the regime from extracting information from them by torture. For large numbers of militant youths, these sacrificial soldiers became idols, ideological references, symbols of the resistance, and inevitably, examples to be followed. Although such psychological gains were crucial in boosting the people's morale, there was still no guarantee that such a movement would grow to form a large-scale revolutionary army able to alter the regime. There had to be a simultaneous engagement occurring throughout the country in order to loosen the security forces' grip on the people's minds and lives. At that time, these forces were focused merely on a small group of active elements. The strategy was to force the regime to spread its forces across a wide front, thereby weakening its potential strength.

Such a massive engagement would require a specially organized team to further train large numbers of revolutionaries. These trained revolutionary forerunners of the campaign would take their stand on the front line, risk their lives, and send out the rallying cry to their comrades. Such soldiers required an ideological training that would instill a deep level of commitment to the cause. Mere dissatisfaction with the regime was not sufficient to inspire people to want to risk their lives. A strong commitment was essential to downplay any attachment to fear that had ordinarily prevented people from joining the movement.

It is only in the light of the above facts that the significance of transforming millions of devoted Muslims, almost overnight, into political activists can be understood. An army of well-disciplined protesters came into existence, many of them volunteering for the most dangerous acts. Some of the clerical leaders made the protest a religious obligation by subjecting the political situation to religious definitions and interpretations. The security forces quickly found that they were no longer dealing with the same disciplined demonstrations with which they were familiar. Throughout the country, a giant was awakening. The features that distinguished this new insurgent wave of Shiia-dominated followers was that they enjoyed a number of advantages that other groups had not. This foretold the formation of significant power. The advantages were as follows:

1. The Islamic groups had thousands, even hundreds of thousands, of fully devoted individuals under their command. These were the type of individuals who could be directed to undertake the most dangerous tasks. Some of their members were equal in Islamic ideological commitment to the underground fighters. They dared to face the armed forces of the regime in a struggle that was, to them, the equivalent of a holy war. To them, death meant martyrdom, a concept that had become an internalized ideal. Their leading organization could function more openly now because of the invested commitment of these followers. It was religious training that had created these activities, and religious training was the one thing not forbidden in the country.

2. They did not have to create an underground organization because they already had a highly disciplined one through the line of religious authority.

3. Their members were stationed in every corner of the society. The security forces knew only the hierarchial religious leaders. These leaders were untouchable, unless the government was prepared to face large and immediate riots. The followers were mostly from the business class and lower class, and rural people who were unknown as political opponents to the security forces. They came from the ranks of the apolitical faceless masses on whom no detailed files had been created in the data banks of the political police. The security forces had focused mainly on the college community, civil and military servants, the large industrial organizations, and other middle-class people who were politically concerned. These new activists were not only unknown to the authorities, but there was additionally no way to cut their line of communication. Their organization was, therefore, uncrushable.

4. They had their fixed bases—the mosque and other religious centers. The city of Qhom, the seat of the high clergy, was the main headquarters of the new phase of opposition. It was a large city, and a sacred one, housing one of the holiest shrines in Iran. Sacred also was the city of Meshad. A number of places where less important shrines were located were also seats of powerful clergy leaders. Each day thousands of pilgrims would travel to Qhom or Meshad, and return with the new messages. It was impossible to arrest the spread of turbulence from these centers to the rest of the country.

5. The clergy numbered in the tens of thousands and had close relations with the lay people. They had close and informal ties with a variety of people from nearly all classes, so when each chose to support the movement, he would become a central figure for the opposition.

6. Muslim groups had had valuable experiences in mass demonstrations. These experiences originated in Islamic teaching and history of the rise of Islam.

ESCALATION OF PROTESTS

Prior to the autumn of 1977, sporadic protests were typical on college campuses, and occasionally would also break out elsewhere. These protests would primarily begin under the cover of a nonpolitical grievance. However, once it had transformed itself into emotionalized actions, the security forces would intervene. Then, the protest would take a more political overtone and could even become violent. From the autumn of 1977 onward, however, the nature of these protests began to change. The change was mainly in the form of the extension of the protest from its center of origin (from a college campus into the streets) and the outbreak of protests from different sources, as though all those who opposed the system had begun a round of well-orchestrated open activism.

All of the reasons for such expanding protests from a wide-range of groups are not clearly known. However, in early 1977, there were rumors that Americans, fearing the further growth of leftist movements, were pressuring the Shah to relax his strong-handed rule and to let other alternatives to the leftist extremism have a chance to emerge. To what extent such a rumor was founded on truth is not clearly known either. Undoubtedly, the growth in size and the frequency of underground armed actions was a serious concern of the regime and its American patrons, as was the relaxation of repressive actions. In fact, the elevation of the level of opposition from verbal attacks and small protest gatherings to modern-style urban guerrilla warfare had made the former look insignificant. Therefore, its toleration was reasonable, because the regime had to utilize its security capacities and manpower to counter the underground armed units of the militant groups, and let less challenging actions pass unguarded. In practice, this meant that the regime intended to tolerate some degree of opposition.

The first major sign of change of policy was an unexpected permission granted for a reading by dissentive poets (Green 1982). They were permitted to read their poems to the public at the Cultural Center of the German Consulate in the north of Tehran. A number of poets, who were Marxists, Islamics, or independents, read their political poetry to an audience that numbered in the tens of thousands. It was an outdoor gathering of people, most of whom were college students and among the poets were those who had served long-term prison sentences for political actions. It was an extraordinary event because up until a few months earlier, not even a single line of these poems could have been made available to the public. The audience was amazed and could not believe what their ears were hearing or their eyes were seeing. The news of the gathering spread all over the country. The next night, the number of those who attended was multiplied so greatly that the crowd filled all the streets and alleys surrounding the German Cultural Compound.

Outside the compound the police were present in a capacity similar to the guides of a convention, mostly helping with the traffic. Unlike the usual scene, there was no sign of any riot police on combat units or anti-protest police. Those who were there that night were very polite and acted as though they had been given orders not to agitate anyone and not to interfere with what was going on. For the Iranian youths, who were mostly in their teens and early twenties, it was a unique experience because they had never had a chance to attend a gathering in which the regime was criticized but the security forces did not attack the gatherers. After the first night, when the people had made sure that there seemed to be some degree of freedom in the air, their numbers increased. The next few nights witnessed tens of thousands of attendants, some even coming from faraway provinces.

The center of this new round of dissensions resided in the organs and places frequented by the better-educated people. Included were long-time activists who had had the earlier experience of two decades of party politics. Once again, some of the former political parties were returning to the scene. Not all such activities were completely tolerated. The regime might still react violently, but probably not as severely as it had in the past. For example, the National Front held a social gathering of its leading elements in a suburb of Tehran. SAVAK had organized a group of plain-clothed agents to break up their gatherings and to beat them. The association of Iranian lawyers, dominated by radicals and democratic-oriented elements, was trying to freely choose its officials (Green 1982). In the past, all the syndicate officers would be picked up through SAVAK influence and approved in rubber-stamped elections. Previously, anyone arrested in the demonstrations was dealt with by special courts under the charges of revolting against the security of the state. These were, directly or indirectly, military courts. Then there was a change of policy allowing civilian lawyers to defend these demonstrators as civil disobedients, changing the whole definition of dissension and, therefore, the regime's reaction to it.

Up to this point, the winter of 1978, secular-oriented opposition activists were still in the lead in initiating the opposition action, and would be the most visible people in the demonstrations. This situation was changing rapidly, however, and with dissensions being voiced in the holy city of Qhom, attentions were diverted toward clergy-led opposition actions.

REACTIVATION OF SHIIA POLITICS

This new round of dissentive activities was also building up in other religious centers. The protests of the clergy-led groups, however, were originated and masterminded in Iran's most influential Shiia clerical school, *Fay-z-yeh*, located at the holy city of Qhom (Green 1982: 154). Meanwhile, Ayatollah Khomeini, who had earlier led a violent demonstration against the Shah's "White Revolution" reforms, was spending a term of exile in Iraq. From there he was organizing and overlooking the secret activities of his supporters in Iran. These activities were various forms of dissension as well as the formation of secret religion-based organizations with political-religious intents. Finally, in the winter of 1978, the clerical hierarchy who opposed the regime began to unleash their followers into the streets to protest. The strategy of the religious groups was not too complicated, utilizing the cultural and religious institutions to organize, politicize, and then lead the people to uprising. Their objectives were to stage a rather peaceful demonstration in order to win over the manpower that the regime had employed to run its military and bureaucratic machine. These people worked in the country's industries, especially in the oil industry, which provided the main funds for the government's budget and they intended to isolate the autocrats, to prevent any confrontation within the populace, to unite everyone in a national uprising against the Shah, and to force him out of office.

Other objectives gradually emerged as their influence expanded. The factor that increased the size of the demonstrations was the push the people received from the Shiia clerical leaders. Gradually, the mosques became centers of opposition that sometimes attracted thousands to preaching services or other special ceremonies. In line with tradition, politically minded clergymen would preach emotionally and fearlessly, delving into issues that people would otherwise not have dared to discuss in public. Some such congregations turned into demonstrations. Other convenient events were the burials of those killed in the above demonstrations or the ceremonies normally performed on the fortieth day after death—an Islamic tradition held with much enthusiasm. These demonstrations would, in turn, breed further demonstrations seven or forty days later. One riot would conceive even larger riots.

The ice of political passivity was melting. People could now gather more easily: In their homes, they could hold small political gatherings; in demonstrations, they could sing slogans that even a few months earlier they would not have dared to whisper in the privacy of their homes. It was obvious that a revolution was finally erupting; demonstrations and rebellion were growing like avalanches. Drawing from nearly all classes, this was the tip of the iceberg beginning to show as the early phase of the national uprising began.

Within two months, in the summer of 1978, the regime found itself facing an increasingly hostile crowd in all its cities. By September of 1978, tanks were stationed in the streets of most cities and martial law was in effect in nearly every major metropolis. The demonstrations escalated to a final revolutionary stage after the early September massacre, thereafter referred to as Black Friday (Nobari 1978). The event began as a peaceful demonstration and was broken up by soldiers. No one has ever been able to determine how many people were killed, but it is generally believed that the deaths were in the hundreds or even thousands. Eyewitnesses reported that many truckloads of dead or wounded were taken from the streets. Until this point, college students, secular political forces, and long-term political activists still had some influence upon the trends of the uprising. Afterward, there occurred a noticeable shift toward the clerical leadership, as masses of lower-class and rural people began to join the movement.

As the movement escalated into daily disturbances, a general strike, and mass defiance of martial law, the people themselves began to innovate new and effective tactics of resistance. For example, in order to sing slogans at night, starting usually at nine p.m. when curfew hours began, they would go up on the roofs of their homes. They could not be either seen or shot at by the security forces because Iranian buildings have flat roofs. In this manner the demonstrations could continue utilizing the advantage of the dark and the protected roof. The security forces could not stop them and the people would increasingly express their opposition in religious language—in terms of beliefs that would emotionalize them.

The main strategy was to isolate the autocrats who ruled the country and to prevent civil war. They would, for example, give flowers to the soldiers who had been ordered to shoot the people. They would tell them, "You are our brothers. We will give secure hiding, food, and money to any who will flee from the barracks." They asked the people to preach to their relatives who served in the military, especially those in the security forces, asking the soldiers to quit their positions. Simply put, these were revolutionary people utilizing whatever means they saw as necessary in order to alter an oppressive regime through symbolic methods.

Both lines of opposition action—from the secularist side and the religious side—were expanding their domain of activities independently. However, the spread of these actions to the masses would bring them into inevitable contact and cooperation. The first phase of this culmination was the uprising in the historic city of Tabriz. It took the form of a large-scale political riot, forcing the regime to put the city under a state of martial law.

The events of Tabriz had rocked the entire political and security structure of the regime. It was a mass movement, including nearly all strata of the society, and differed from the earlier actions that occurred in certain organizations or on college campuses. With the uprising of Tabriz, the opposition actions escalated to a new phase. The demonstrators could no longer be accused as a single small, political, or ideological group, nor as agents of foreign influence. They were the people of the nation itself, from all walks of life and ideological affiliations. The demonstrators had attacked and damaged certain key organizations of the regime. They had destroyed official cars, and in effect the city had been given the appearance of a war zone. As a consequence of this successful riot, the security forces were proven ineffective in preventing mass protests; people began to see them as paper tigers capable only of dealing with small-scale group actions.

From then on, a more important development was the specific structuring of the protests that would guarantee the continuation and periodic occurrence of these events. The protest attempts were therefore no longer random occurrences, but happened quite precisely on schedule. The protestors were organizing themselves to fit the shaping of a new chain of events. With each of these events, the timing of the next one would automatically be set. Such linkage and timing had originated in Islamic practices and beliefs which were, to an extent, masterminded by the Muslim organizers. They had promised that protest attempts would grow into a nationwide mass movement against the regime. The mechanism of such systematization centered around the burial ceremonies. With Iranian Shiia Muslims, as previously mentioned, it is a common practice to observe some ceremonies on the first, third, seventh, and fortieth days after a family member's death. A large and highly emotional gathering takes place at the graveyard when the deceased person is buried. An even larger gathering takes place afterward. The later ceremonies are in the home of the deceased and the close relatives. A clergyman preaches and sings a sad sermon that makes the attendants highly emotional. If the person has been a public or top religious figure, there may be some official ceremonies arranged by the state. In cases of notable figures, these ceremonies may take place in a number of cities where the person had had economic, political, ethnic, or some other form of great influence.

The best political use was made of these ceremonial practices in order to structure the ongoing protests of 1977–78. It was becoming a common practice to hold large gatherings to commemorate those who had been killed in the demonstrations. This was taken even more seriously if they had lost their lives in demonstrations led by Islamic groups, for then the clergy, having influence upon the laity and Bazaaris, would invite the public to attend and ask the shops to close down in protest. As a practice, the seventh and fortieth commemoration of those killed in one city was organized to be held in another city—they were to be held quite elegantly, with thousands attending.

In such a gathering, people would typically be made aware of the reason why these persons had lost their lives, and the preaching would become quite political. Then the demonstration would again turn into an open protest against the regime, breaking into confrontation with the security elements. More people would get hurt and killed, providing the ammunition for the next round of gatherings in the next few days and weeks.

The uprising of Tabriz was an occasion of one such commemoration ceremony for those who had earlier lost their lives elsewhere. The organizers would intentionally hold these commemorations for those killed in one place at some other location, therefore, spreading the dissentive actions nationwide and eventually arousing the masses all over the country.

After Tabriz, Isfahan, the second largest metropolis of Iran, was put under martial law. Yazd, another provincial capital, was the scene of a bloody demonstration. With such events repeated in a chain, escalating in magnitude and spreading all over the country, it was quite clear to everyone that these demonstrations were not the work of a few "traitors" as the regime would have liked to call it. Moreover, it was also clear that the escalating movements were not going to cease and vanish unless some major changes took place in the country. In other words, it was quite clear that a revolution was on its way, and it was not something that could be stopped by the police or a detachment of a few units of the military forces.

To confront a nation of demonstrators, the utilization of large-scale military forces was required. It was toward the end of the spring of 1978 that regular combat troops were brought in and stationed all over the capital city and in some other cities that were hot spots. The presence of these forces was a horrifying scene, with soldiers sitting on the top of tanks and armored vehicles, manning the guns that were pointed at the crowded streets and squares. It made the entire place look like a war zone. The presence of combat-ready troops facing empty-handed citizens was then undermining the claims of the Shah who hoped to pose as a popular modernizer. Instead of intimidating the people, the presence of these troops gave them further reason to think that the opposition must be powerful. Otherwise, there would be no need for such elaborate preparation in order to confront them.

As the religiously sacred month of Ramadan (the month of fasting) was approaching, the regime was getting more nervous. In Shiia Iran there exist two months of the year in which intensive ceremonial practices and mass gatherings normally occur. Ramadan is one of those months, especially during its nineteenth to twenty-first days, which coincide with the anniversary of the martyrdom of the first Shiia Imam, Ali. It is in these months that the clergy finds a chance to address millions of Iranians with their fiery preaching. Mosques, and other religious centers, become jammed with attendants who more than anything else are there to hear the clergy address them in lengthy sermons. During these gatherings, the audiences are emotionally prepared to follow the clergy's suggestions. In the turbulent year of 1978, the month of Ramadan made the clerical leadership the center of attention. The organizers of the ceremonies had also taken a role similar to that of the party officials, who had planned and managed a party campaign gathering, for more than anything else the content and intention of the ceremonies had become political.

All these conditions favored the religious groups in assuming the leadership of the ongoing mass protests. During this month, people gathered in mosques in large and unprecedented numbers. The preachers were excited to see the young educated crowd among their audience, who in the past had been influenced away from the mosques. Large numbers of people had to stand on the sidewalks of the surrounding streets, listening to the preaching that was broadcast through loudspeakers. With mosques formed into gathering-centers, the Islamic leadership had a chance to integrate the opposition's potential into a united, citywide, and (to an extent) nationwide effort. The two opposition groups—the secularists and the religious—were furthermore merging into one. It needs to be mentioned that in Iran many of those who may have aspired to a secular polity were themselves religious people. Therefore, no matter what their political ideals were, their attendance at these ceremonies would iron out some of their differences of view on the immediate issue of fighting the Shah's regime.

BLACK FRIDAY

The first manifestation of this merger happened in the last days of the month of Ramadan and the following Friday, which later became known as "Black Friday." It is an Islamic tradition that on the last day of the month of fasting, people celebrate. It is a celebration all over the Muslim world. In Iran, on this day and early in the morning, all the people in the town or city gather in one large congregation to perform a special prayer. Ordinarily, this prayer takes place in the open fields or on the outskirts of the city. One reason for gathering outside of town is because the crowd is usually very large, and could therefore not be accommodated in one mosque. In this particular year, it was announced that this prayer would take place in a large, wide-open piece of land in the center of Tehran. The site was close to the upper-middle-class and upper-class residential areas.

Following the prayer, which had attracted well over one-hundred thousand people, the participants formed long lines to march into the city, shouting political slogans. Some police officers who had cooperated with them were raised and held above the people's heads as an Iranian way of showing their gratitude to someone special. People had hugged some armed soldiers, kissing them, installing flowers on the tips of their guns and telling them, "We are brothers." It was, apparently, the first time that the Shah was openly referred to by name and cursed by the demonstrators. It was apparent that the revolution was advanced enough to create an atmosphere of open expression of dissent. The march ended with a rendezvous set for the next Friday, when everyone would meet again in a square located right on the border of the lower-middle-class and lower-class residential areas of Tehran.

On Friday, beginning in the early morning, people gathered in the square in large numbers. By nine a.m., one could not even get within a half-mile of the square; people from all walks of life were jammed in the surrounding streets. They were not from a single ideological grouping, but had come no matter what their feelings or associations. They all had one thing in common—opposition to the regime for one reason or another. Earlier in the morning, it had been announced on the radio that Tehran was now under martial law, but it did not seem to matter to the people. Later on in the day, trying to disperse the demonstrators, the security forces opened fire, killing and wounding an unknown number of them. It is believed that those killed numbered in the thousands although the official count was less than one hundred. Some of the wounded were carried into the nearby residential areas for first aid. No one dared to take the wounded to hospitals for fear that the secret police would detain them along with the wounded person. In a large neighborhood region, people were going from house to house gathering sheets to use for taking care of the wounded comrades. Seeing the brutality used against the unarmed demonstrators, some people began to call relatives and friends all over the city and country. In a matter of hours, a national multitude had learned about the details of the massacre. There was nothing that the regime could do to stop the spread of the news and its exaggerated versions. That night, when the curfew began at nine p.m., international radio stations such as the BBC broadcasted the details of the massacre. It was quite clear to everyone that the confrontation the regime had been preparing for had begun.

Apparently it was a massacre that turned the page of contemporary Iranian history. A new phase of the uprising had begun, a phase that was to bring masses of people onto the scene, escalating the protests from simple political opposition by certain groups to a revolutionary uprising by the whole nation. From the following day onward, people all over the city were displaying open anger and talking against the regime quite explicitly. The general theme of their arguments ran as follows: after Black Friday, the people no longer intended to compromise with the regime. In their view, it was no longer a political but a criminal matter when the regime could shoot down thousands of unarmed people who were simply peacefully showing their political viewpoints.

The incident of Black Friday set the people's uprising in a new direction and gave another perspective to the opposition actions. It reinforced and contributed to the unification of a pluralistic opposition force. However, following the events of the sacred month of Ramadan, the religious leadership had found a more active role. It was more or less a matter of fact that even secularly-oriented groups had inclined to yield to this leadership, not because they necessarily saw them as the authority, but because in them they could more properly see the capacities necessary to move the masses. The objective of removing the police state was so important that the ends seemed to justify the means. The clergymen were able to call on the masses, they held the mosques, and they were entitled to the privileges of preachers. Why should the opposition have hesitated to support them since they intended to remove the Shah? This was the general outlook of those who sincerely cooperated with the clergy, even though they themselves were secular-minded. It probably never occurred to them that a theocratic totalitarian regime might replace the Shah's police state. Such a strong sense of solidarity was developed that it severely undermined any stratifying factor.

At the end of summer, Ayatollah Khomeini, whose supporters were becoming a major opposition group, was asked to leave Iraq where he was spending a term of exile.

He went to Paris where he was to establish the headquarters of command of his loyal forces in Iran (Green 1982: 159). In Paris, he was easy to reach through the international mass media and he could not be arrested by the Shah's security elements. Therefore, the city was for him a sanctuary and a place from which he could openly address the Iranian people through radio broadcasting or tapes sent home. Quite rapidly, he emerged as the leading element of the opposition movement and the spokesman of the revolution. Such a leadership was further reaffirmed when the National Front representatives met with him in Paris and accepted his terms to ally with him. With that move, he not only commanded the religiously committed followers, but he also commanded a good segment of the secularly oriented political modernists.

The situation, in the minds of the people, was being set up as a dichotomy of the people versus the armed soldiers. At least during this stage, it was not in the form of a class struggle with the poor against the rich and workers against managers. The military forces came to symbolize the backbone of the regime. As more people joined the movement, including government employees, the military people were the only ones that remained on the Shah's side. This, however, did not reflect the will and wishes of the individual soldiers and officers, but was due only to the way that the military organizations were commanded and functioned.

The strategy of the opposition was to talk the manpower of the regime's organization into neutrality and possibly desertion, to transform its organizational machinery, and to turn it into an empty shell. They would accommodate soldiers (if they deserted), would demoralize the public employees in order to stop their work, and would prevent any action that might persuade individuals or groups to side with the Shah. It was like an expanding spiral; as the movement advanced, its social base of support was expanded more and more. It was at this stage that the revolution entered the phase of general strikes, especially in the vital organs of the state.

The era of crippling the system began with the postal employees going on strike, which would gradually spread to all other organs. The Iranian administrative and service sectors were quite advanced in terms of their division of labor, but with strikes crippling certain key sectors the whole system would become dysfunctional. The consequences of the crippling of the public sector were reinforced by that of the several-months-old strike of the Bazaar and the industrial sector. A strike of the oil industry was the most vital, because it would stop the flow of dollars. This would not only make the Shah a useless ally of the West, unable to sell them oil or to buy from them, but would also make the regime incapable of paying the manpower that manned its machinery of state.

As strikes were slowing down the economy and stopping the service sectors from functioning, daily confrontations were being reported. These confrontations took the form of sharply unequal contests between empty-handed citizens and heavily armed soldiers. They left scores dead or wounded, further antagonizing and emotionalizing the people. In the autumn of 1978, the regime was in a defensive position. The organizers of the demonstrations had the initiative, could plan for demonstrations, had full command of millions of supporters, and could more properly control these demonstrations. Part of this management involved designing slogans and suggesting to the participants which slogans should be shouted, as well as when and where it should be done. To the earlier slogan of "Freedom and independence" they added the "Islamic Republic."

When the machinery of the state was almost at a standstill due to the large-scale strikes, the opposition began to form volunteer units to take care of their abandoned tasks. A network of organized groups were emerging that were on the side of the revolution and functioned as a special service organization. For example, because of the strike in the oil industry, people had difficulty in receiving fuel. Lines at fuel stations were over a mile long. Volunteers would oversee the distribution in such a way as to ensure that no one was left without a minimum of their necessities and no profiteer was able to exploit the situation for his own greedy objectives. Such management of public affairs was initiating community-based volunteer groups, which had begun to emerge as a more permanent administrative organ. Being in a revolutionary state, such groups would be quite sincerely devoted to their tasks and would attract popular support. They were the groups who, later on when the regime had eventually broken down, emerged as the occupants of the revolutionary organs. Their headquarters were mostly in the mosques, and they were therefore in close cooperation with the clergy. The formation of such groups, as well as the organization of the mass demonstrations, was providing the leadership of the Revolution with its own system of control and administration. With their enthusiastic presence on the scene, the country was not headed for uncontrollable chaos. As the authority and administrative capacities of the regime began to fade away, the opposition's system was set to replace it. In the new order, command was more or less in the hands of certain clergymen, most of whom were strong supporters of Ayatollah Khomeini.

It was under such conditions that by the end of the autumn, 1978, the regime was also reaching the end of its rope. With Moharram, the first of the sacred months of the Shiia calendar, the clergy once again had a chance to consolidate its leadership, expand the movement to larger segments of the population, and put into operation the Shiia instruments of mass politicization.

It was during this month that the Islamic group managed to bring onto the scene millions of the so-called silent majority. During Moharram, eleven days in a row are marked by unusually intensive ceremonies with mass participation. In each community, a number of halls are temporarily decorated and used for mass assemblies to mourn the martyrdom of the Imam Hosein and his associates who died at Karballa in seventh century A.D. The organizations responsible for these ceremonies are temporary ones, although each year essentially the same people are involved with the administration of the events.

In cities, such organizers are mostly petty business, the elderly in the community, faithful notables, and a large number of young people who took their orders to serve the participants. One reason why these temporary units are formed is because all of the marches are planned to go on for hours, and they pass through each mosque or assembly site created for the ceremonies. In each of these locations, marchers are to be served tea or some kind of sweet soft drinks. Therefore, even if a mosque had been chosen as the center, there would still be the need for some supplementary locations to complement it. To serve tea to approximately ten thousand visiting marchers in a matter of a few minutes requires a large, well-organized manpower unit, as well as well-prepared facilities. This type of visitation would go on for hours, with different marching groups arriving one after another. Therefore, these temporary locations would involve a good number of the residences of the community in the program. These ceremonies would strengthen community members' sense of solidarity, put them in a cooperative network, and undermine the differences in personal interest and ideology that otherwise would have separated the people. In Shiia villages, the whole population is invited and will participate. In cities, the Shiia population also participates in large numbers. In the capital city, where a traditional middle class, lower class, and upper class (Bazaaris) live, the bulk of the residents get involved in one way or another. The central figures of these ceremonies are the clergy, who in the late 1970s found a chance to speak out more freely than before.

Given the condition of the revolution and the regime's defensive position, the Moharram of 1978 was a time of freedom of speech, a freedom that people had forced upon the regime. The organizers of the ceremonies managed to attract millions of people to participate, especially for the street marches, which were taking a complete political form. Under the rule of martial law, they had a difficult time staging street demonstrations as freely as they would have liked. However, on the tenth of this month, when the street marches were ordinarily held during the day, all the marchers gathered in a few big spots to observe the final ceremonies. The revolutionary issues obviously overrode all other matters, and assembling for the ceremonies of Moharram was once again an excuse to get millions of people into a few spots in the cities to cast their oral vote against the regime.

It was on the tenth of this month that millions of people gathered in the *Azady* (freedom) square of Tehran, shouting their approval for the readings of the clergymen who had led the marches (NYT 1978). The statements that were read included a call for the establishment of the Islamic republic, which was followed by the then-popular slogan of "Death to the Shah." In Paris, Ayatollah Khomeini took the occasion to alert all governments that from now on, they should not deal with the Iranian regime because it had been voted out of office by the people themselves. From this moment on, it was quite clear that the clergy-led groups were the leading commanders of the demonstrations, and that they had established themselves as the political authority of the faithful, who otherwise would have been reluctant to take to the streets. The content of the slogans that they instructed the marchers to sing were quite religious, such as the highly emotional slogans that drew parallels between the events of the day and those of Imam Hosein's uprising. By shouting "Every day is Ashura and every place is Karballa!" they fed religious content into the political movement of the Revolution. The authority of Ayatollah Khomeini as the leader of the Revolution was already established. With a further intensification of the Revolution and an increase in the amount of its religious content, the Ayatollah was becoming elevated beyond the traditional rank of merely top clergyman, to the personality of *Imam*, or saint.

Following the religious-political street referendum of Moharram, the Shah was no longer in control. The organization of military forces was shaken by dissension, desertions, and demoralization. The government and industrial sectors were further crippled by the continuation of strikes. A civilian government was set up that was supposed to function in the absence of the Shah. Meanwhile, the Shah had no other choice but to get out of Iran for an undetermined length of time. It was a well-known fact that the civilian cabinet would only be a transitionary one for the post-Shah era. It was headed by Shahpour Bakhtyar, one of the Shah's long-time opponents from the secularist wing of the National—one of its leaders who had refused to ally with the Ayatollah. He tried to install a program that guaranteed freedom of expression and abolished the interference of SAVAK in the social and political life of the populace, as well as a wide variety of other democratic measures. If such a government had been formed much earlier, the Revolution probably would have never become so radicalized. It was too late now, however, for a secular government; the clergy-led groups were already in control of the country. In places where the functioning of the state agencies were crippled, they had established their command of the masses, securing the business sector and leaving little for this democratic-oriented government to administer. Very soon, in the capacity of the leader of the Revolution and on behalf of the "invisible Imam"—whose rule was an extension of the divine rule—the Ayatollah nominated Mehdi Bazargan as his own prime minister (NYT 1979).

There were now two prime ministers in the country. People were asked to demonstrate their support of the one chosen by the Ayatollah and once again, masses of people were in streets chanting slogans in support of the Ayatollah's choice, while lambasting the other with humiliating curses. In most government offices, the employees began to announce their loyalty to the man chosen by the Ayatollah. During this stage, the only resistance remained on the side of certain military commanders and certain officers who were still loyal to the monarchical regime. The martial law officers in Tehran made a decision to prolong curfew hours—an act interpreted by the Ayatollah as a sign of preparation for a military coup against the Revolution. He asked the people to stay in the streets in defiance of such a regulation. Up to this point, the integrity of the command of the military forces had not yet been shattered.

The final stage of the Revolution was terminated in an attempt made by a loyal unit of the Royal Guards to discipline the dissident elements of an air force unit. This attempt led to a military clash in which masses of people intervened. Films later shown on Iranian television and a general account by observers indicated that organized units of underground armed groups (both Marxist and Islamic) had played a significant role in the incident, helping to defeat the disciplinary attempt made by the guardsmen. The people managed to break into the depot of a barracks and take away arms and ammunition. With people armed all over the capital city, the military and police headquarters came under attack. The same pattern was duplicated elsewhere, with people surrounding the barracks and asking the military forces to surrender. By taking over the radio stations, the revolutionaries announced the fall of the regime and the victory of the Revolution on February 2, 1979.

REFERENCES

Abrahamian, E. 1985. "The Guerilla Movement in Iran, 1963–77" in H. Afshar (ed.), *Iran: A Revolution in Turmoil*. London: Macmillan.

Green, J. 1982. *Revolution in Iran*. New York: Praeger.

Nobari, A. R. (ed.). 1978. *Iran Erupts*. Stanford: Iran-American Documentation Group.

NYT. 1978. "Several Million Iranians March for Second Day." *New York Times*, December 12.

NYT. 1979. "Khomeini Appoints Mehdi Bazargan, 73, Prime Minister." *New York Times*, February 6.

PART TWO

RELIGIOUS RITUAL AND
INSURGENT CONSCIOUSNESS

Pastoral Mobilization and Contention: The Religious Foundations of the Solidarity Movement in Poland[1]

Maryjane Osa

In the mid-1950s, the world was engaged in a new Cold War defined by the division of nations into two superpower camps. Western observers perceived the Soviet Bloc as a monolith, a totalitarian power whose control over its satellites was absolute. After Stalin's death in 1953, the hegemony of Soviet control was challenged by the rumblings of discontent in the East: workers' riots in East Berlin and in Pozńa, Poland, and, especially, the Hungarian revolt of 1956. When Hungary withdrew from the Warsaw Pact and renounced the one-party system, Russian tanks rolled in to crush the Hungarian independence movement. The reimposition of repression in Hungary confirmed the West's view of tyrannical Soviet power.

In Communist Poland, Roman Catholic Cardinal Stefan Wyszyński, began a surprising—and politically provocative—program of national religious renewal. The Cardinal's undertaking, the Great Novena of the Millennium, promoted values and conceptions of community that were the opposite of those advanced in state socialist propaganda. The Church's ten-year-long renewal was intended to rededicate the Nation to the Blessed Virgin Mary, who was venerated as the Queen of Poland. Great Novena ceremonies centered on the iconic painting of the Black Madonna of Częstochowa, enshrined in the Pauline monastery at Jasna Góra (Bright Mountain).

A key element of this program was the peregrination, or "voyages," of a copy of the painting throughout Poland. The Black Madonna painting travelled throughout Poland during the years of the Great Novena, "hosted" by the dioceses; within dioceses, vistations of parishes were conducted. The reception of the painting representing "Holy Mary, Queen of Poland" was a major event, especially in the dreary working-class parishes. One such community was Holy Cross parish in Gdańsk, where the painting made its visitation on October 11–12, 1960. The days of visitation at Holy Cross were described in the parish chronicle:

> The enthusiastic parishioners did not spare any difficulty, labor, or expense for greeting the Painting of the Holy Mother. The church was adorned like never before. The throne [by the main altar] prepared for Mary, Queen and Ruler of the Polish Nation, was draped with a great royal purple cape, lined with ermine.

At the top of the cape, a queenly crown, handmade by a Marian devotee, was suspended and an inscription displayed which proclaimed Her thousand year rule over the Polish lands and people. The sounds of the wonderful intrada pierced the dark October evening. From the hearts and mouths of the believing Polish people (*lud*) rang out the powerful Jasna Góra Vows. Mary stood on the shoulders of the Catholic husbands, on an ornate dais, lovingly looking down on Her beloved people, who fell silent under her gaze. At the ringing of the bells...the honor guard of the Painting of Visitation and all the Catholic status groups (*stany*) slowly flowed around the church in a high ceremonial procession....At the moment when Mary was placed on her throne in the church, the kindergarten children recited a sincere declamation. The hearts of the ordinary believers, the simple, gray people, burdened with the difficulties of daily life, also wanted to speak to their Heavenly Mother and from thousands of breasts came forth the ancient melody, "Virgin-Mother of God".... Finally, the sad moment to part company with the Venerated Painting had arrived.... People were so moved, they had tears in their eyes. "Mother, do not leave us!" one heard the voices. The Painting must be transferred to the next parish.... The processession moved slowly along the streets.... People went along singing marian hymns, carrying candles, kneeling at the sight of the auto-chapel. And in this manner, the parish conducted the Holy Mother to the church of St. Anthony. It was an unforgettable sight, one which deeply implanted itself in the hearts of believers.[2]

The narrative, in its personalization of the painting of the Black Madonna, conveys the sense parishioners had of being in the actual presence of the Virgin. The Great Novena-ideology fostered the belief that the Nation was under Mary's special protection. The Virgin Mother was viewed as Poland's Queen in metaphysical terms that superceded ordinary, political concepts. Further, because of this posited relationship between the Polish people and their Heavenly Queen, the Nation was considered a primary form of attachment imbued with a transcendent spiritual significance. The relation between Nation and State, on the other hand, was seen as one of material necessity and of oppression. The forms of observance and the sentiments expressed during the parish visitations were those of a traditional peasant culture in which the marian cult was wedded to rural folk superstitions and practices. The novelty of the Great Novena observances was that these were not rustic festivals, but rather parts of a national program realized in local variations. Finally, the narrative seems to confirm the traditional view of an intensely religious, even primordial Polish Catholicism where the Church stands with the Nation and against the oppressive State.

To view another picture of oppositional Polish mobilization, we turn now to the Gdańsk shipyard and the founding of the Solidarity trade union in August 1980. That summer, workers across Poland responded with a wave of strikes to the communist government's decision to drastically increase food prices. Striking workers initially called for rescinding price hikes. Their demands then escalated to wage increases, and finally to the call for establishing trade unions independent of the communist party. A national workers' opposition crystallized around and was coordinated by the Inter-factory

Strike Committee led by strike organizers and their intellectual advisors in the Lenin Shipyards in Gdańsk. Despite the countermovement by the authorities—including the harassment of activists, threats of retaliation directed at family members, incarceration of strike supporters, and the telephone and communications blackout of Gdańsk—occupation strikes went on for more than two weeks. Workers subsequently won unheard-of concessions from the communist government, including the legalization of their union and other rights of limited free speech. On August 31, 1980, Lech Wałęsa, leader of the new Solidarity trade union, signed the Gdańsk Accords, using an oversized souvenir pen with Pope John Paul II's portrait emblazoned on it, and sporting a lapel pin of the Black Madonna of Częstochowa.

Herein lies the puzzle: what, if anything, connects religious mobilization begun in the late 1950s to working-class activism in 1980? It is clear that, because of the nature of the one-party state, both types of social mobilization threatened the communist party's hegemony over public life. Both are based on social solidarity, contain nationalist elements, and deploy traditional religious and historical symbols in their appeals. But the question remains: Is it possible that the mobilization of a religiosity based on traditional symbols and practices could become a political weapon powerful enough to theaten a coercive communist regime? How does the transformation from religious to political activism take place?

COMPETING EXPLANATIONS AND THEORETICAL DEBATES

The question of a causal connection between Church action and the emergence of Solidarity is a matter of ongoing debate. At one extreme, Lawrence Goodwyn takes the position that (Goodwyn 1991: 319; italics added):

> The Church could console;…it could provide a bedrock of ethical belief; but it could not provide the explicit strategic or tactical ideas that might move Poland toward a freer social life. Those ideas had to come from elsewhere.… The Church was reactively relevant. But *it was not a source of causation. It played no active role in the origins and development of the democratic movement.*

Goodwyn contends that Solidarity emerged from the development since 1970 of active working-class organization and culture. A contrary view is held by George Weigel, who argues that the moral leadership of Pope John Paul II taught the Poles "a new way of being partisan." Thus, "the Church…helped give birth to Solidarity" (Weigel 1992: 140, 143). Indeed, Weigel believes that what he calls "the resistance church" was involved in the collapse of communism generally. He contends that workers' consciousness was transformed by "the steady catechesis of human rights preached by the Church since the 1960s." This encouraged the working class to challenge "the vanguard claims of Marxism-Leninism" by shifting their attention from economic issues "to the higher plane of human rights and political participation" (Weigel 1992: 140; Garton Ash 1984: 68).

Debate is enjoined by many analysts who advance their preferred actors (Church, workers, intellectuals) as "the particular Poles who brought Solidarnosc [Solidarity] onstage" (Goodwyn 1991: xx). The "who done it?" dispute has been the focus of sometimes acrimonious arguments over the origins of Soldarity (Tymowski 1992; Goodwyn 1992; Kubik 1994b), the meanings of Solidarity, its nature as a social phenomenon, and its long-term significance (see Staniszkis 1984 and Goodwyn 1991). What seems so surprising in these accounts is the dearth of discussion of those causal variables which social-movement scholars have linked to movement emergence in other cases. For example, only Bunce (1989) refers to political opportunity structures, and only Kubik (1994) endeavors to unpack the highly elaborated symbolic code of opposition employed by Solidarity. There has been no systematic attention to collective action framing, tactical repertoires, and protest cyclicity—despite the fact that workers' protests in People's Poland (*Polska Rzeczpospolita Ludowa*—PRL) date back to 1956.

In this chapter, I will begin to address this weakness in the Solidarity literature by examining the long-term dynamics of social movement development in Poland. Recent social-movement theorizing has provided concepts and propositions that may be investigated through analysis of the Polish case. Does social-movement theory provide more convincing explanations and account for more of the empirical facts than "civil society" arguments, or explanations based on a single promulgator "who done it"? Also, how may we use this body of theory to bridge the gap between religion and politics? I will employ three concepts—repertoires of collective action, frame alignment, and cycles of protest—to help redirect inquiry away from the monocausal explanations mentioned above and to specify the links between religious and political mobilization.

First, in his research on the historical development of European states and capitalism, Charles Tilly introduced the notion of popular contention, "discontinous, contentious collective action," (Tilly 1986: 3) as a type of grassroots politics. As economic development and geopolitics put pressure on local populations, people banded together to protest, resist, or contend with rulers over the direction of change. Collective action takes certain forms (Tilly 1986: 390–391):

> Any population has a limited repertoire of collective action: alternative means of acting together on shared interests. In our time, for example, most people know how to…join or form a special-interest association,.., demonstrate, strike, hold a meeting…. These varieties of action constitute a repertoire…people know the general rules of performance more or less well and vary the performance to meet the purpose at hand. Every performance involves at least two parties—an initiator and an object of the action. Third parties often get involved; even when they are not the object of collective action, for example, agents of the state spend a good deal of their time monitoring, regulating, facilitating, and repressing different sorts of collective action. The existing repertoire constrains collective action;… That constraint results in part from the advantages of familiarity, partly from the investment of second and third parties in the established forms of collective action.

Tilly notes a significant change in collective action repertoires in the nineteenth century. In France, Tilly documents change from "old" parochial/patronized repertoires—e.g., local festivals, charivaris, grain seizures—to "new" national/autonomous repertoires—

e.g., election rallies, public meetings, street demonstrations—as capitalism advanced and as national states in Western Europe became more powerful (Tilly 1986: 390–404). In Poland, a country surrounded by powerful neighbors whose history is a demonstration of nation-state fragility, we should expect to see different repertoires and strategies of contention with rulers. Nevertheless, the end-point repertoires in democratic France and at the height of Polish Solidarity were the same: public meetings, strikes, street demonstrations, a social movement. The dramatic events on the Baltic coast in 1980, then, may be seen as a defining breakthrough in "the continuing struggle for power, [for] the changing structure of power as it has involved the fates of local communities and ordinary people" (Tilly 1986: 10).

A second conceptual tool comes from Sidney Tarrow's elaboration of cycles of protest. His work is an attempt to account for the temporal and spatial clustering of opposition activity. In discussing the connections between specific movements and cycles of protest, Tarrow states (1991: 4) that:

> Collective action…goes through phases of mobilization and demobilization…. The presence of a surrounding wave of mobilization helps to explain why, during some periods of history, resource-poor movements which would be suppressed or ignored in other circumstances can gain a hearing.

Analysis of the parabolas of popular mobilization has shown that protest cycles have differentiated and mediated effects on different population groups (Tarrow 1989; McAdam 1982). Thus, we would expect to find that workers and intellectuals become mobilized at different times in different ways according to political opportunities which are specific to their particular group. Joint action among various groups would occur at collective action peaks (Tarrow 1991: 47).

> Particular groups recur with regularity in the vanguard of waves of social protest (e.g., miners, students) but they are frequently joined during the peak of the cycle by groups not generally known for their insurgent tendencies (e.g., peasants, workers in small industry, women).

Protest cycles have several other important characteristics which include the unpredictable lengths and intensity of waves of action, collective action surges of heightened conflict across the social system, and specific diffusion patterns of tactics and resources (Tarrow 1991: 44–49). However, the most distinctive characteristic of cycles of protest is that they "produce new forms of collective action…. Cycles of protest are the crucibles within which new collective action frames are born, tested, and refined" (Tarrow 1991: 48). Thus, if we consider Solidarity as a collective action peak in a cycle of protest, we ask: What events initiated the protest cycle? What forms did contention take prior to Solidarity? Can these earlier forms be linked to the trade union movement? What were the factors that allowed the surge of mobilization to happen when it did and to take such a distinctive form? In short, why did the long post-war wave of popular contention peak in 1980, and why did the social opposition crystallize around the demand for free trade unions?

Third, the potential contribution of the Church to Solidarity's development can be reconsidered using the "frame alignment" theory articulated by David Snow and his colleagues (Snow et al. 1986; Snow and Benford 1988, 1992). They argue that social movement development inherently is signifying activity, or "agency and contention at the level of meaning construction" (Snow and Benford 1992: 136). Framing theory links ideology to participant mobilization through examining elements of values, beliefs, and the social construction of meaning. Diagnostic, prognostic, and phenome-nological dimensions of framing activity combine to create resonant ideological "pack-ages" that define problem situations and communicate action plans (Snow and Benford 1988). The resulting collective action frame is (Snow and Benford 1992, 137):

> an interpretive schemata that simplifies and condenses the 'world out there' by selectively punctuating and encoding objects, situations, events, experiences, and sequences of actions within one's present or past environment.... Collective action frames not only perform this focusing and punctuating role; they also function simultaneously as modes of attribution and articulation.

Snow and Benford present evidence from diverse social movements to show how frame resonance is positively associated with participant mobilization. This proposition pro-vides an alternative to the "engaged civil society" explanations that dominate the Solidarity literature. The weakness of the latter arguments is the postulate that civil society development in the 1970s potentiates social mobilization in 1980–81; they fail to account for the disappearance of social cohesion subsequently. Since "civil society" is a social structural variable, it cannot disappear overnight. If Solidarity's rapid expan-sion was due to a healthy civil society—relative to Poland's East European neighbors—why didn't this civil basis flourish after 1989, when party domination was lifted? Ironically, analysts of post-communism now lament the lack of a civil society upon which to build a democratic political culture.

To place Solidarity's emergence within a cycle of protest, it is helpful first to clearly distinguish between "master frames" and "collective action frames." Master frames are generic, paradigmatic; they set up a symbolic and meaningful universe in which con-flict is organized around certain themes. In other words, master frames "provide the interpretive medium through which collective actors associated with different move-ments within a cycle assign blame for the problem they are attempting to ameliorate" (Snow and Benford 1992: 139). They may also assert a collective identity, "a public pronouncement of status, in the classic Weberian sense" (Friedman and McAdam 1992: 157). Collective action frames, on the other hand, are movement-specific. They utilize ideological components of master frames, adopt or adapt what has already proved res-onant, and appropriate multivocal symbols. Snow and Benford (1992) put forward sev-eral propositions to theorize how master frames function in a cycle of protest. First, innovative master frames are associated with the appearance of a new cycle of protest. Second, early movements in a cycle of protest "are likely to function as progenitors of master frames that provide ideational and interpretive anchoring for subsequent move-ments within the cycle." Conversely, movements that appear later would find framing efforts constrained by the previously elaborated master frames. Finally, the elaboration of master frames also stimulates innovation in tactical collective action repertoires (Snow and Benford 1992: 143–146).

This theoretical exegesis of social movement dynamics underlies the argument in this chapter. To preview: I will argue that the Roman Catholic Church was crucial in the emergence and sustenance of the Solidarity movement. Pastoral mobilization that began with the Great Novena of the Millennium (1956–1980) preceded and laid the foundation for the political breakthrough and social mobilization of the Solidarity era. The Church elaborated master frames, provided organizational resources, developed co-optable social networks, and created a repertoire for strategic opposition. Its achievement was initially to shift the arena of political confrontation. While the state reigned supreme in the official sphere of coercive political power, in the realm of national symbols and historic authority, the Church was sovereign. The Church managed to relocate its confrontation with Leninism from the substantive ground of public policy to a higher plateau of symbolic politics, where the Church and society *could win* (Osa 1989, 1992, 1995).

MOBILIZATION AND CONTENTION

In this section, I will examine the patterns of contention in the post-war cycle of protest in Poland with special attention to their religious roots. First, I will discuss the critical events of 1956, which I argue initiated the long wave of social protest. Second, I will analyze the Church's pastoral mobilization, the Great Novena of the Millennium, begun in 1956; sustained and complex, the Great Novena had many effects that may be causally related to the later political mobilizations. One important consequence, which is beyond the scope of the present paper, was the expansion of parish social networks that integrated urban workers and intellectuals and rural factory workers and farmers into moral communities. The aspects of the Great Novena that I will examine are: (1) ideological formulations that were the basis for elaborated master frames; and (2) collective action repertoires that developed in the course of responding to state attempts at suppression of the religious movement.

THE CRUCIBLE OF 1956

The onset of a cycle of protest is characterized by heightened conflict across the social system. Ineffective responses to early demands of protesters demonstrate the vulnerability of the authorities. As divisions among the elite deepen, contention diffuses to other sectors, and further demands are made by other, usually passive groups. New movement actors engage with the previously mobilized groups, and in the process master frames are created. Master frames link the actions of disparate groups to one another, and foster increased mobilization of challengers and countermovement by the state. This is the political scenario predicted by the social-movement theory outlined earlier. The dramatic events of 1956 in Poland have all these elements. They mark the end of the Stalinist period and the beginning of the reassertion by Polish society of its autonomy from the Leninist state.

Several key contingencies allowed contentious collective action to take place in 1956. Unexpected political opportunities stemmed from Khrushchev's denunciation of Stalin at the Twentieth Party Congress in February, and the subsequent confusion and increased conflict within the Party—both the CPSU and the Polish United Workers Party [PUWP]. When Polish First Secretary Bierut died in Moscow shortly after the Congress, a power struggle for leadership ensued, leading to disarray in the PUWP as the party divided into camps that held differing interpretations of Soviet directives, especially concerning how far to go with reform.

The Poznań mobilization in June took advantage of this party disarray and a further opportunity: the presence in Poznań of hundreds of foreign visitors, including journalists, participating in an international trade exposition. Protesting under the eyes of foreign reporters, the workers could circumvent party censorship controls and get their message out to the world. The June uprising began when Cegielski factory workers sent a delegation to Warsaw, over the heads of the local party bosses, with demands for improved working conditions. The Warsaw party leadership threatened, stonewalled, and equivocated, but finally agreed to send a representative back to Pozna'n to meet the workers. Once there, the party boss made no promise to investigate conditions at the factory; rather, he relayed more threats and exhortations to go back to work. This infuriated the workers and led to a march to the city center. With crowds growing, protesters' demands escalating, and police provocations, the demonstrations finally turned violent. Protesters confiscated arms from the arsenal, the party building was stormed, crowds threw Molotov cocktails into the secret police headquarters, security police were beaten to death, records were destroyed, and the tall antenna at the state radio-television station that was blocking BBC and RFE broadcasts was torn down. After three days of street fighting, the party regained control with help of the security police and the army. There is no accurate figure on how many people were killed and wounded, but they most likely numbered in the hundreds. To the initial demands of the protestors—"Bread!"—were added "Freedom!" and calls for the release from house detention of the Catholic Primate, Cardinal Wyszyński (Goodwyn 1991: 54–101; Ladorski 1992).

The aftermath of the Poznań insurrection saw a dangerous rift within PUWP between stalinist hardliners—the Natolin group—and communist reformers led by Gomulka. This was accompanied by a serious threat of Soviet intervention that included the mobilization of Soviet troops stationed in Poland and the unannounced arrival of Khrushchev, Molotov, and Mikoyan in Warsaw in July. Eventually, the Soviets backed down and allowed the appointment of Gomulka as First Secretary to oversee reforms. By the fall, negotiations between Church and state were underway, the party agreed to establish workers' councils, censorship was eased, and agricultural collectivization was provisionally abandoned. Then, in late October, the Soviet invasion of Hungary and the restoration of a Soviet-approved regime there caused a chill felt in Poland. The reforms slowed down, and by late 1957, a degree of repression returned, as Gomulka consolidated his regime.

While workers rallied behind the idea of workers' councils in the fall of 1956, other groups also took opportunity of "the thaw" to organize. Numerous student and professional clubs, newsletters, and journals were set up. These included efforts of the left intellectuals around the journal, *Po Prostu*, and its editor, Leszek Kolakowski; the Club of the Crooked Circle; and Catholic intelligentsia active in the Znak group, *Tygodnik Powszechny*, *Więz*, and the newly formed Clubs of Catholic Intelligentsia (KIK). In addition, the Primate was released from detention after driving a hard bargain with the Party comrades. Wyszyński refused to leave his place of incarceration without guarantees that the authorities would allow legalization of the independent institutional activities of the Church (Wyszyński 1983).

In 1956, mobilization across the social and political spectrum intiated a cycle of protest. A subsequent repressive countermovement by the state was only partly effective because Cardinal Wyszyński had been able to secure some space for collective action that was free from state control. Party officials had in the Church an institutional rival that was much harder to supress than were isolated dissident intellectuals. The dissent and collective opposition begun in 1956 incubated over the next decade, kept warm by the institutional protection of the Church.

THE GREAT NOVENA OF THE MILLENNIUM

The grass-roots mobilizing potential of religious institutions is well established (Morris 1984; Zald and McCarthy 1987). In Poland, this potential was realized through the Great Novena of the Millennium (Phase I: 1956–1966, Phase II: 1967–1980). I contend that this religious movement was the early innovator in the post-war protest cycle which established a symbolic and tactical paradigm for contention. First, the ideological formulations of the Great Novena were important because they articulated a clear and purposeful statement of collective identity, one that was inherently opposed to the socialist identity promoted by the State. Second, during the first ten years of intensive pastoral mobilization, confrontations between local church communities and party bosses, and between party officials and clerical elites, evolved into a form of "symbolic politics" (Osa 1992; Kubik 1994a). Thus, the early development of master frames and repertoires stemmed from the Great Novena ideology and activities. A paradigm of confrontation was created: the solidary nation—possessing a national historic and religious tradition of which the Black Madonna was its primary symbol and the Church its defender—versus the atheistic, artificial, traditionless communist state. This interpretive axis provided a framework that made the initial public presentation of Solidarity in the Gdańsk shipyards in August 1980—with its crosses, flowers, religious pictures, masses—instantly comprehensible. Such religious/historical formats both enhanced Solidarity's potential for mass mobilization and constrained it in its move towards increasingly instrumental, less expressive, ends (Staniszkis 1984: 80-96).

Theology of the Nation

The ideology of the Great Novena was based on Cardinal Wyszyński's "theology of the nation." In this formulation, Wyszyński synthesized the various schools of Polish nationalism. Starting from a basis in neo-Thomist philosophy, he appropriated the Polish Romantic nationalists' glorification of the past and their nineteenth-century messianism; and he borrowed the integral Dmowskian nationalist ideas of future progress and the ethnic basis of the nation. The interweaving of philosophical, historical, and social elements is seen in the following definition (Lewandowski 1989: 20):

By "the Nation," the Primate understood: the precise natural social formation of human beings in an ethnic community, linked in its entirety, and establishing the personhood of the living, biological, historical and spiritual subject. The very existence of this community underscores the value of the personal world and the unity of historical experience. It is a social objectivity standing for the most important spiritual values.

The Cardinal's theological nationalism was precisely fitted to the church's situation in communist Poland. He was prepared to leave the arena of official politics in the hands of the party in order to ensure political stability. The Church, while conceding "politics" to the party, wanted to maintain its authority over private life: especially the family, individual morality, child-rearing, and religious education. Yet it also wanted to comment from the sidelines as the voice of morality in the public life of the community. Under the conditions of the post-war reality, Wyszyński emphasized the implicit but clearly understood premises of his argument: that the State represented "internationalism" (read: domination by the Soviet Union), but the Church represented national culture. In effect, Wyszyński created a new religious nationalism that was detached from party politics, a nationalism that made the very existence of the nation dependent on the church and her royal, divine Protectress, the Virgin Mary, Queen of Poland. The continuity of the Polish nation was inviolately linked to the persistence of the Church in the Polish lands. Meanwhile, this vision took on added significance because of the organized attacks on religion by the communists and the contemporary rewriting of Polish history from a vulgar Marxist perspective.[3]

The main impact of theological nationalism, however, was felt not in the realm of theory but of practice. Wyszyński's direct contribution was not only to intellectualize but also to adapt rural Marian traditions to the new post-war reality. Cardinal Wyszyński blended Polish legends, folklore and peasant mysticism with the intellectual products of the Polish Romantic poets and elements of Catholic theology to create a Mariological vision of the Nation and Polish history (Lewandowski 1989: 130–32):

> According to this thought, Mary is, next to Christ, an important factor shaping Polish history; she becomes a 'helping principle' 'in mystical perspective' in light of which the Catholic theologian may appropriately interpret that history.... Wyszyński was convinced that Polish history and the Marian devotion of Poles link with each other so precisely that one conditions the other.

Wyszyński's philosophical convictions and his ability to utilize cultural elements in novel combinations helped him to create a powerful ideological system according to which the events of Polish history take on a specifically Catholic meaning.

Pastoral Mobilization

Church leaders blamed the social unrest in 1956 on the PUWP's social and economic development programs. The episcopate's diagnosis was that state policies would inevitably be destructive of society because they were rooted in the party's atheism, secularism, and program of social atomization. The prognosis of the Church fathers was to undertake pastoral mobilization to intensfy religious culture and thus to counteract the destructive tendencies of state socialism. This problem-identification and proposed solution formed the basis for an "Us/Them" master frame that attributed society's hardships to regime exploitation and linked a solidary nation with Polish historical myths and the Church. Pastoral mobilization took the form of programs designed to strengthen the church-society link by involving believers in intensive religious activities. In addition, mass demonstrations carried forward the Catholic social agenda into the public domain. Manifestations, usually on dates of religious significance, showed mass sanction of "Catholic values." Public expressions of support for the Church in fact implied demands for political change to make social and political life congruent with Catholic morality. Pastoral mobilization was different from other organized collective action or political mobilization in that it lacked explicit political goals while it carried strong political implications.

A mass mobilization of Catholics in Leninist Poland was, of course, a provocative and difficult undertaking. Nevertheless, it was a goal to which Cardinal Wyszyński was committed; and the episcopate supported the Primate in declaring the revitalization of religion in Poland a pressing concern. Thus, the Great Novena of the Millennium began in 1957, as a nine-year program leading up to the church's celebration of one-thousand years of Polish Catholicism.[4] Its focal point was the annual pilgrimage to the shrine of the Black Madonna at the monastery of Jasna Góra and the dedication of the Nation to the Blessed Virgin. On the first Sunday after May 3—the feast day of the Blessed Mother, Queen of Poland—Church dignitaries led tens of thousands of pilgrims in the repetition of the Jasna Góra vows. On that same day, throughout Poland believers "gave themselves in servitude to Mary" by repeating the vows at celebrations in all the parish churches.

The Great Novena represented a departure from the organization of the inter-war pastoral mobilization, Catholic Action. Whereas the latter was bureaucratic and centralized, the Great Novena's organizing principles were temporal and spatial. This was a significant innovation which accorded well with the post-war, loosely-coupled ecclesiastical organization (Osa 1989: 295–298). First, the Great Novena's span, high points, and climax were determined by meaningful time. The nine years of the program anticipated the church's celebration in 1966 of "Poland's baptism." By claiming the rhetorical field early on, religious authorities prevented the politicians from defining Poland's millennium, which also marked the country's political founding, in strictly secular terms.[5] Church leaders emphasized the primacy of the Catholic faith in the history of the Nation. The myths about Mary saving Poland at key historical junctures— from the Swedes at Jasna Góra in 1655, and from the Soviets in 1920 with the famous "miracle at the Vistula"—played a large role in the Great Novena. Thus, the different anniversaries and feast days of the Blessed Virgin during the year were occasions for collective manifestations. Second, spatial organization involved not only the convergence of the faithful upon a central, holy point—the Pauline monastery at Jasna Góra— but also the peregrination of a replica of the icon throughout the country. The ceremonies and events surrounding the diocesan appearances of the Black Madonna complemented observances on the national level, linking the two.

Collective Action Repertoires

In the Great Novena pastoral mobilization, new repertoires of collective action developed that were based on expressive, symbolic activities which asserted a collective identity antithetical to that promoted by the State. No political demands were articulated and the protest dimension of pastoral activities was manifested infrequently, usually in response to harassment by political authorities. Nevertheless, the subtext of the Great Novena—with its assertion of "Catholic values" and Wyszyński's theological nationalism—contained an implicit negation of the premises upon which the political rulers' authority was based. Thus, a protest repertoire that was particularly adaptive and effective under the restrictive conditions of state socialism developed as an intended consequence of pastoral mobilization.

To illustrate this process, we will examine three episodes that show how collective action repertoires were the result of pastoral mobilization. All the following events involved religious and lay Catholic leaders, ordinary people, state and party functionaries, and police or security forces. A repertoire developed when these actors dealt with confrontational situations in a patterned way, where specific roles were adopted, and "scripts" followed a predictable plot. We begin mid-way through the Great Novena in Gdańsk.

The copy of the Black Madonna painting reached the archdiocese of Gdańsk on August 18, 1960. The icon first visited the outlying villages and parishes of the archdiocese, and arrived at the parish of The Immaculate Conception of Our Lady in Gdańsk on September 29, 1960. The parishioners and priests had been preparing for the Black Madonna's visit the entire month of August. The pastor preached sermons about the Our Lady of Częstochowa, how the Blessed Mother defended the monastery at Jasna Góra, and in different periods took the Polish nation under her care. Lay people participated in retreats led by religious brothers to prepare their souls for the visit. Parishioners also spent much time and money decorating the church with flags, banners, and flowers. Plans were made for the ceremonial greeting of the Black Madonna:

Permission was granted from the [local] authorities for removing the doors of the church in order to directly allow access to the church interior from the street. [Involved in their preparations], the parishioners demonstrated great ardor for church affairs.... This festive mood was spoiled by the subsequent prohibition of the governmental authorities regarding decorations of the windows of the apartment buildings along the processional path of the Holy Painting, and also the authorities' prohibiting the ceremonial greeting of the Blessed Countenance by the double rows of children with floral bouquets [in the street]. But this sad moment intensified the fervent commitment of the parishioners. The parish church, a former monastery chapel...had become [after the war] a parish church for 12,000 Catholics. It was impossible to accommodate such numbers of believers simultaneously, that is why the pastor had proposed that the children not enter into the church, but rather meet the Blessed Painting on the street, greeting Our Lady with bouquets of flowers, and that the windows of apartments should be decorated just as they are for [the feast of] Christ the King. Now (*otoz*) it was forbidden, and it was ordered [by the Party] to countermand the administration of the pastor!... In response to the prohibition of the authorities, the parishioners lavishly decorated the church interior with evergreens and throughout the entire night they remained in devotion, burning hundreds of small candles that they placed along the entire perimeter of the church grounds.... [The next day, as the Black Madonna took her leave] the songs of the believers flowed above the rooftops, the songs of the participants in procession clambered up to the windows of the bureaucrats as they returned from work to their homes.[6]

What does this story tell us about pastoral mobilization and symbolic politics? First, the pattern of action and response shown above is characteristic of the repertoire which developed during the Novena and which was manifested frequently during repressive periods—before 1980 and during martial law. Initially, what was intended as a religious occasion was interpreted as political by the Party and government authorities. These officials then responded with some effort at repression, frequently by means of petty harassments to beleaguer the religious leaders or to erect obstacles to mass participation. The response to the prohibition and other harassment was not outright opposition; rather the local Catholic community was able to "trump" petty bureaucrats by means of symbols. The sumptuous decoration of the church, the outline—that is, emphasis— of church boundaries with flickering candles, and forceful singing beneath the windows of government offices, all showed the unity of the people and the Church, the protection of Our Lady, Queen of Poland, and the moral purity and force of the participants' symbolic message, in contrast to the dirty material politics of the regime. Second, the annoying and arbitrary decisions of the local authorities increased commitment and led to a much greater turnout for these celebrations than would have been the case if they were allowed to fulfill a strictly religious agenda.

The Great Novena ceremonies were not confined to the grounds of individual parishes, nor were they primarily occasions for opportunistic quasi-political protest. The program was complex and well-planned, following lines set down by the episcopate. But every local church had autonomy to make decisions about how best to achieve the goals of the Novena. In the Gdańsk archdiocese, the Party authorities' attention to the Black Madonna's peregrination increased as the icon moved from the outskirts of the diocese—in the villages such as Pogorzala Wieś, Milorząd, Gnójewo—to the center of Gdańsk and neighborhoods of the large workers' hostels—such as Gdańsk-Stogi and Wrzeszcz. The festivities gained momentum and became occasions for building the solidarity of the Catholic community and for church networking.[7]

The next two narratives take us to Warsaw during the millenial year, 1966. The mild contention that had taken place six years earlier in Gdańsk adumbrated a much broader and more dangerous confrontation during the "central celebrations" in Warsaw's Old City. For some time, Church and State had been locked in tense competition concerning the status of the millennium: was it the celebration of one thousand years of Polish statehood, or a millennium of Christianity in the Polish lands? The capital was the site of important ceremonies representing the climax of the Great Novena's nine years of preparation—besides being the location of the Polish episcopate and the Communist Party headquarters. Pomp and ceremony were planned for the observances during June 21–26, 1966. This is what was supposed to happen: ceremonies were to begin on Tuesday, June 21 at 3 p.m., with the ceremonial greeting of the painting at the boundaries of the diocese in Nowy Dwór; a procession would then accompany the Black

Madonna painting to St. Stanislaw Kostka Church in the Zoliborz neighborhood—home to many workers and intellectuals; at 6 PM the Blessed Mother would be greeted at the church by the Primate, Cardinal Wyszyński, and all of Warsaw. On Wednesday, June 22, at 6:30 p.m., the painting was supposed to process through the streets from Zoliborz to the Cathedral in the Old City. This program had been established for a long time and had been communicated from all pulpits in the capital city. However, Party authorities were afraid of a large turnout; they wanted to diminish the scope of the activities and to harass church officials. So, they tried to preempt the opening ceremonies by "intercepting" the Black Madonna painting on its way to Warsaw. On the night of Monday, June 20, at about 9 p.m.,

> a Zuk sedan driven by functionaries of the state militia (MO) stopped in front of the cathedral on Canon St. The painting of the Black Madonna was in this auto accompanied by...[several high-ranking clerics]. Consequently, there was no doubt that this was the authentic Painting of Visitation. Despite the late hour, a crowd immediately began to gather. Flowers were laid down and someone intoned Marian hymns. A procession formed.... The painting was transferred to the canon's sacristy in the cathedral and placed in a barred window facing the street, appearing as if it were in jail.... [S]uddenly something changed in the mood of the people. It was felt that God's Mother unifies the nation, unites all hearts. She was the hostess of the Millennium.... "The Blessed Virgin Behind Bars," everywhere this was said of Her. One must compensate Her for Her incarceration. In what manner? Praying...massive pilgrimages. Despite the rain, day and night, without a break, people arrived, bringing flowers and candles.... Under [the barred] window grew a heap of flowers and burning candles.... This was the beginning of the Millennium in Warsaw's Basilica. [The "incarceration" of the Virgin] had a deciding influence on the character of the entire celebration—it mobilized the entire city of Warsaw.[8]

Once again, we see pastoral mobilization transformed into a collective statement of political resistance and contention. The "repertoire" of collective behavior plays out according to its established pattern: 1) church authorities and parishioners plan religious observances; 2) party and local officials interfere in planned activities—to diminish or attempt to suppress popular involvement and harass the hierarchy, frequently using police agents; 3) religious authorities and adherents respond by devising a public symbolic gesture which "trumps" or exposes the coercive maneuvering of the state; 4) this results in the increased salience of the events, strengthening the commitment of participants and attracting many less religiously motivated actors.

In the Warsaw confrontation, the church's trumping was particularly effective. By placing the painting "behind bars," the Cardinal sent a message: "Look at the evil perpetrated by the authorities: instead of allowing Poland's Queen, the Black Madonna, to greet her children in joy, with the respect befitting her, she is waylaid, detained by police, and kept from her subjects, resulting in sorrow and disappointment." "The Blessed Virgin Behind Bars" became the highly evocative slogan of the Millennial ceremonies. It engendered emotive, mobilizing responses. The Millennial ceremonies in

Warsaw, then, signified the struggle between God's Mother, the Church, and the Nation, on the one side—"Us," *my*—and the functionaries, police, repressors, and atheists—"they," *oni*—on the other.

The intensified rallying around the symbol of the incarcerated Virgin increased both popular mobilization and the counter-mobilization by the State. With such a high degree of tension, situations can easily cross the line from expressive collective action to contentious action and potentially violent demonstrations. Thus, on June 24, when the Black Madonna painting was "released" to take her proper place on the throne in the cathedral, in the presence of tens of thousands of believers, the stage was set for the next confrontation:

[When] the ceremonies of that day were over, the people left from the cathedral in the direction of the Royal Square (*plac Zamkowy*). It turned out, however, that the crossing towards the square was blocked by ORMO [riot police] and soldiers. The bishops went out through another street (*ul. Dziekan*) towards the Royal Square but they were detained at the end of the street. They stood for about fifteen minutes but the soldiers did not withdraw. Finally, the bishops changed directions and made their way towards...the Primate's Palace [on Miodowa St.]. The people's indignation grew with each minute.... With difficulty, the bishops had managed to reach Miodowa Street. Already an enormous crowd had gathered there...to show their gratitude and to acknowledge solidarity with the Episcopate. When the bishops entered the Primatial compound, the gate was closed. However, the crowd did not disperse but rather began to occupy the entire thoroughfare. The people prevented the buses and trams from moving. Despite the interventions of the the state militia, the officers did not manage to remove the people from the road. Then a group of militiamen on motorcycles, with their headlights shining, headed into the crowd. The crowd, however, did not withdraw but instead attacked; the militiamen were pressed by the crowd and forced to withdraw in the direction of Krasiński Square. Meanwhile, one of the militiamen turned over on his motorcycle and was nearly killed. This turned into a dangerous scene. Seeing this from his window, Father Jerzy Zalewski immediately ran down to the street and pleaded with the people to go back on the sidewalks and leave the trolley buses and autobuses to continue on their routes. The people listened to the priest and slowly began to flow towards Krakowskie Przedmieście St. The public transportation also began to move again. There, where the strength and threat of the militia had no effect, things were settled by the hand of one chaplain. Because this was a group returning from the Millennial ceremonies, people in whose ears had just rung the words of the Primate on love, peace, and forgiveness.[9]

Days of observances and rallying around the "incarcerated" Blessed Virgin had generated strong feelings of injustice and of unity among those thousands of attendees at the Millennial celebrations. Chafing from their symbolic humiliation by the episcopate, the Party responded with the blunt instrument of brute force to provide a dangerous spark. The street demonstrations recounted above could have turned into a bloody riot like that of Poznań, 1956. Yet, the Warsaw manifestations were constrained by their religious touchstones and the increased authority of the church representatives, in the eyes of the people, due to harassment of the latter by the authorities.

For Poland, the repertoire of contentious collective action that developed out of pastoral mobilization represented an historic break with earlier patterns of resistance. Bloody, violent, and unsuccessful uprisings against invaders—Swedes, Russians, Germans—had been the pattern from the seventeenth to the twentieth century. Consequently, the shift to nonviolent repertoires of collective resistance against political domination was significant. Solidarity's nonviolence in the face of government harassment and repression in 1980–81 was perplexing to many observers. We should rightly understand it, however, as a direct effect of prior pastoral mobilization and the adoption and adaptation by mobilized workers of Great Novena rhetoric, symbols, and tactics.

CONCLUSION

The symbolism of the Great Novena provided a vocabulary that was quickly adapted by strikers in the Lenin shipyards in Gdańsk. The Baltic workers' demands for work with dignity were couched in symbols that spoke to a national audience, not just to factory workers or Party chiefs. Solidarity's semiology connected the movement to Poland's Catholic mythology and the touchstones of the Great Novena: the Black Madonna, the suffering Christ, the Christian nation. Elaborate ceremonies and symbolic displays were as essential to Solidarity as the sit-down strike. Explicit reference to the beginning of this cycle of contention was set in stone when Solidarity activists in Poznań erected a monument to commemorate the 1956 workers' uprising (Kubik 1994, 214–16).

Yet the "Us/Them" master frame revealed its limitations when it came time to go beyond the listing of demands and the construction of memorials. Staniszkis observed the problems activists had in forming coherent programs to achieve concrete, pragmatic goals. She writes that the shift away from the expressive towards the instrumental generated serious internal conflicts within Solidarity in late winter 1980–81. Staniszkis (1984: 81–82) observes that:

> The politics of status seem to be more important than the politics of interest, and...the most expressive functions in the movement were monopolized by its middle-class members.... [T]he worker's leaders were infected by the virus of playing politics through symbols, so typical of the Polish intelligentsia. One example of this was a noticeable tendency after December 1980 for the activists to react strongly to any government decision perceived as a threat but *not* to follow the protest with any consequent course of action.

From November 1980, there was evidence that dramatic confrontations were an end in themselves. Radical demands were made, workers went on strike, the government agreed to demands—but nothing happened. The party reneged on its agreements with the union, yet Solidarity activists did not respond with a follow-through.

Here we see the limitations of the repertoire that developed in the post-war protest cycle: pastoral mobilization developed tactics that were good for the expressive asser-tion of collective identity and for symbolic confrontation. But the repertoire, condi-tioned by the limitations on collective action imposed by a repressive regime format, ultimately proved ineffective. Symbolic politics deflect instrumentality—"the politics of interest"—and diffuse activism by providing "symbolic," not actual, victories.

In this chapter, I have drawn on social-movement theory to refocus the investigation of Solidarity's origins examining the links between religion and politics in Poland. By situating the problem of collective contention in a cycle of protest and analyzing the framing work of the movement, we avoid the worker-intellectual imbroglio over its social origins. The results of the foregoing analysis suggest that Solidarity is more com-pletely understood as a late movement in the post-war cycle of protest that began with the Poznań uprising in 1956. Finally, the ideological and tactical innovations of the Great Novena set certain parameters for social movement development that facilitated rapid mobilization in August 1980, then constrained the movement from going beyond symbolic politics.

REFERENCES

Ash, T. G. 1984. *The Polish Revolution: Solidarity*. New York: Scribner.

Bendix, R. 1990–91. "State, Legitimation and 'Civil Society'," *Telos* 86: 143–152.

Berhnard, M. 1993. *The Origins of Democratization in Poland*. New York: Columbia University Press.

Brumberg, A., ed. 1983. *Poland: Genesis of a Revolution*. New York: Vintage Books.

Bunce, V. 1989. "The Polish Crisis of 1980-81 and Theories of Revolution," in Terry Boswell, ed., *Revolution and the World System*. New York: Praeger.

Friedman, D. and D. McAdam. 1992. "Collective Identity and Activism: Networks, Choices, and the Life of a Social Movement." in A. Morris and C. Mueller, eds., *Frontiers in Social Movement Theory*. New Haven: Yale University Press, 156–173.

Gellner, E. 1994. *Conditions of Liberty: Civil Society and its Rivals*. New York: Allen Lane/The Penguin Press.

Goodwyn, L. 1991. *Breaking the Barrier: The Rise of Solidarity in Poland*. Oxford: Oxford University Press.

_____. 1992. "Reply to Tymowski," Telos 91: 131–134.

Jowitt, K. 1978. *The Leninist Response to National Dependency*. Institute of International Studies Research Series, no. 37. Berkeley: Institute of International Studies, University of California.

_____. 1992. New World Disorder: *The Leninist Extinction*. Berkeley: University of California Press.

Kubik, J. 1994a. *The Power of Symbols Against the Symbols of Power: The Rise of Solidarity and the Fall of State Socialism in Poland*. University Park: Pennsylvania State University Press.

————. 1994b. "Who Done It: Workers, Intellectuals, or Someone Else? Controversy over Solidarity's Origins and Social Composition," *Theory and Society* Vol 23/3 (June): 441–446.

Laba, R. 1991. *The Roots of Solidarity: A Political Sociology of Poland's Working Class Democratization.* Princeton: Princeton University Press.

Ladorski, H. 1992. *Niepokonani Poznań 1956.* Zwiazek Powstańców Poznańskiego Czerwca 1956. Poznań: Druk. Pallottinum.

Lewandowski, J. 1989. *Naród w nauczaniu Kardynala Stefana Wyszy´nskiego.* Warsaw: Wydawnictwo Archidiecezji Warszawskiej.

McAdam, D. 1982. *Political Process and the Development of Black Insurgency, 1930–1970.* Chicago: University of Chicago Press.

Morris, A. 1984. *The Origins of the Civil Rights Movement.* New York: The Free Press.

Osa, M. 1989. "Persistence, Resistance and Change: The Transformation of the Catholic Church in Poland," *Eastern European Politics and Societies.* Vol. 3, No. 2 (Winter): 267–298.

————. 1992. "Pastoral Mobilization and Symbolic Politics: The Catholic Church in Poland, 1918–1966." Ph.D. Disertation, Department of Sociology, University of Chicago.

————. 1995. "Reorganizacja Struktur Kosciola, a Kultura Polityczna," [Ecclesiastical Reorganization and Political Culture]. *Polish Sociological Review* 3. Also in A. Suek and J. Styk, eds., *Ludzie i instytucje. Stawanie sie ladu spolecznego.* Lublin: Marie Curie University Press.

————. n.d. "Religion, Politics and Social Change: Beyond Church-State Relations in Eastern Europe," Manuscript.

Ost, D. 1990. *Solidarity and the Politics of Anti-Politics: Opposition and Reform in Poland since 1968.* Philadelphia: Temple University Press.

Raina, P. 1991. *"Te Deum" Narodu Polskiego. Obchody Tysiaclecia Chrztu Polski w wietle dokumentów Kościelnych.* Olsztyn: Warminskie Wydawnictwo Diecezjalne.

Seligman, A. 1992. *The Idea of Civil Society.* New York: The Free Press.

Snow, D, and R. Benford. 1988. "Ideology, Frame Resonance, and Participant Mobilization." In B. Klandermans, H. Kriesi, and S. Tarrow, eds., *From Structure to Action: Comparing Social Movement Research Across Cultures.* International Social Movement Research, vol. 1. Greenwich, Conn.: JAI Press, 197–218.

————. 1992. "Master Frames and Cycles of Protest" in A. Morris and C. Mueller, eds., *Frontiers in Social Movement Theory.* New Haven: Yale University Press, 133–155.

Snow, D., and E. B. Rochford, Jr., S. K. Worden, and R. Benford. 1986. "Frame Alignment Processes, Micromobilization, and Movement Participation." *America Sociological Review* 51: 464–81.

Staniszkis, J. 1984. *Poland's Self-Limiting Revolution.* Princeton: Princeton University Press.

Stinchcombe, A. 1979. *Theoretical Methods in Social History*. New York: Academic Press.

Szajkowski, B. 1983. *Next to God...Poland, Politics, and Religion in Contemporary Poland*. New York: St. Martin's Press.

Tarrow, S. 1989. *Democracy and Disorder: Protest and Politics in Italy, 1965–1975*. Oxford: Oxford University Press.

Tilly, C. 1976 [1964]. *The Vendeé*. Cambridge: Harvard University Press.

____. ed. 1975. The Formation of National States in Western Europe. Princeton: Princeton University Press.

____. 1978. *From Mobilization to Revolution*. New York: Random House.

____. 1986. *The Contentious French*. Cambridge Belknap Press/Harvard University Press.

Touraine, A., et al. 1983. *Solidarity: Poland 1980–81*. Cambridge: Cambridge University Press.

Tymowski, A. 1992. "Workers vs. Intellectuals in Solidarnosc," Telos 90 (Winter 91/92): 157–174.

Weigel, G. 1992. *The Final Revolution: The Resistance Church and the Collapse of Communism*. New York: Oxford University Press.

Wyszyński, S. C. 1983. *A Freedom Within: The Prison Notes of Stefan Cardinal Wyszyński*. New York: Harcourt Brace Jovanovich.

Zald, M. N., and J. D. McCarthy. 1987. "Religious Groups as Crucibles of Social Movements" in M.N. Zald and J.D. McCarthy, eds., *Social Movements in Organizational Society*. New Brunswick: Transaction Publishers, 67–95.

4

Religious Rituals of Resistance and Class Consciousness in Bolivian Tin-Mining Communities

June Nash

Primordial beliefs and rituals provide deep roots for people's sense of identity. Surviving from precolonial periods, they generate a sense of self that rejects subordination and repression. The cultural roots of resistance to alien control can generate social movements that restructure the society, influencing the choice of timing for political acts of protest as well as the place and form in which rebellion arises.

The people of the mining communities in highland Bolivia have resisted the attempts of conquerors, viceroys, governors, and populist leaders of the independence period to wipe out their own beliefs. Mining families relate to a superhuman world of saints, devils, deities, and enchanted beings with which they live in the mine, the encampment, and the region. They tend to encapsulate in a unitary worldview the widely disparate, apparently contradictory ideologies to which they have been exposed. This worldview includes primordial figures of the Quechua and Aymara-speaking population who work in the mines; the saints and diabolical agents that have been introduced by Spanish conquerors and missionaries; and Marxist, Trotskyist, and developmentalist ideologies that inspire the political and labor movements in which they have been involved since the early part of the twentieth century.

Miners have been credited with spurring the populist revolution in 1952 that ushered in the nationalization of the mines as well as land reform liberating the peasants. Miners in the large mines owned by the tin magnates prior to the revolution share a life experience that has given them a strong identity as a community and as a class. In almost a century of industrial exploitation of the mines, they have transformed themselves from a peasant population with a localized worldview into a proletariat aware of the world market in which they buy many of their consumer goods. Although they numbered only twenty-four thousand or two percent of the work-force before massive layoffs in 1986, they have had a profound effect on the labor movement of the nation. From the very beginning of industrial mining, these men and women—drawn from the agricultural valleys of Cochabamba and the *ayllus* (land-based kinship groups) of the altiplano to the mines—endured extremely hard working and living conditions. Whenever the workers joined in collective action to improve their lot, the army, quartered in barracks close to all the major mining centers, crushed their protest. The history of massacres as well as the murder and exile of their leaders have raised their consciousness of the need for political action in defense of their class interests. The imported ideologies of revolutionary action directed toward socialism have found receptive ground in the mines, where the thesis of the inevitability of class struggle and the ultimate victory of the proletariat are given meaning in the miners' present misery and their utopian visions of the future. Bolivia is one of the growing number of countries of the world where the once-repudiated Marxist thesis of the increasing misery of the working class can claim support from a measurable real decline in subsistence levels, not just a proportionate decline in earning power in relation to capitalist expropriation.

In the transition to modern industrial mining, contemporary ideologies of socialism and communism have been combined with primordial mythic forces in such a way that the people are not alienated from their cultural roots. Unlike workers in most industrial centers, they have not lost their sense of personal worth and their faith in human potential to bring about change. The Federation of Bolivian Mine Workers' Unions (FSTMB) includes leaders from all of the major ideological currents that have influenced the labor movement in the twentieth century, but it has had sufficient unity to influence national events. The FSTMB alliance with the National Revolutionary Movement (MNR) under Victor Paz Estenssoro helped turn it into a revolutionary movement by pressing for the nationalization of the major mines and workers' control with power in the management of those mines. The Federation gained the right to name and control the vice-presidency and several ministries during Paz Estenssoro's first term of office because of its help in bringing the MNR to power in 1952. It split with the MNR in 1956 when Paz's successor, Hernán Siles Zuazo, introduced an International Monetary Fund —a United States-backed stabilization plan that lowered miners' real wages in an attempt to reduce inflation. Some of the leaders of the Federation supported the coup by General René Barrientos in 1964. He betrayed his promises to the workers' movement by invading the mines in 1965, repressing the labor unions, and exiling and jailing their leaders. After his death in 1969, union democracy was revived during the brief terms of office of Alfredo Ovando Candia and Juan José Torres (1969–71) only to be repressed brutally when Colonel Hugo Banzer Suárez seized power in 1971. In 1978 a fast initiated by women in the mining communities, joined by hundreds of political opponents of the military regime, including Christian Democrat as well as left-wing parties, brought about elections and the victory of Hernán Siles Zuazo. He was prevented from taking power by a rapid succession of military coups. The brutal repression and rank corruption of these despots was brought to an end by a series of strikes in 1982, when Siles Zuazo returned to office, this time with the support of the labor movement he had opposed in the 1950s. Yet his political base withered, including that in the mines, as the economy deteriorated because of the heavy debt incurred by the military and the declining revenues from the mines. In 1985 he was succeeded by Paz Estenssoro, who returned to power as the candidate of the post-revolutionary bourgeoisie, not the miners whom he had championed three decades earlier. In the year following his re-election, Paz Estenssoro consolidated an alliance with Banzer's party, the Democratic National Action, and proceeded to dismantle the nationalized mining sector, where the major opposition to his neoliberal economic policies was mobilized.

Considering the chronic state of crisis and the political lability of Bolivia, it seems paradoxical that mining communities retain the rituals and beliefs that link them to their agricultural past. Yet when I did my original fieldwork in Oruro from 1969 to 1971, and upon my recent return to the mining centers in 1985, I found continuous recognition of Huari, a hill spirit who has become identified with Supay, or the devil in the mines. Oruro is the capital of the department of the same name, where the major mines that were nationalized in 1952 are situated. These include Siglo XX-Catavi, Huanuni, Uncia, and Colquechaca, as well as numerous small private mines. Reflecting the continued importance of preconquest beliefs, a major sacrifice was carried out by miners in the San José mine in Oruro in the summer of 1985 when an accident took the life of a miner. Some of those who organized the ritual had been in political exile until 1982. Clearly the significance has not been lost. The integrity of this worldview that maintains contact with the past while allowing full participation in contemporary struggles is explored below.

THE BELIEF SYSTEM AND THE SCHEDULING OF REBELLION

The ritual cycle in Oruro is structured on two axes, one dealing with agriculture, the earth, and the Pachamama (the time/space concept that is identified with Mother Earth in the hispanic tradition), the other with mining, the underground, and Supay (some-times called Huari, the spirit of the hills). The overlay is Spanish colonial and postin-dependence Catholicism, but the deeper structuring derives from preconquest agricul-tural rites concerned with preserving the fertility of the land and maintaining harmony with the supernatural. The miners fit their industry into the old structure, maintaining equilibrium by sacrificial offerings to Supay for the mineral they extract.

Ritual time relates to the preindustrial agricultural cycles and to the spirits of the earth and hills that the farmers propitiated. The warming-of-earth ceremonies in June, with the onset of the cold dry season; the preparation of the soil in August for planting in September; and even Carnival, the season for harvests and joy, relate to farming activities.

The rituals are carried out at the four compass points, where enchanted creatures are found. These creatures relate to a myth that miners tell about Huari, the lord of the hills and the underworld, who was incensed by the failure of the agriculturalists-turned-miners to render him the fiestas that were his due and sent out monsters to eat them. Each of the four monsters, a toad, a water serpent, a reptile, and a hoard of ants were turned to stone or sand by the intervention of an Inca princess to whom the peo-ple prayed.

In each quarter, there are shrines devoted to the monsters that threatened to destroy the population of Uru Uru, the preconquest name for Oruro, when they first entered the mines and forgot their rituals to Huari. These stand like sentinels at the four compass points of the city of Oruro.

A giant toad sculpted out of stone greets one at the northern entrance to the city. Behind it is the rubble of the original natural stone toad, which was a meeting place of dissidents during the unpopular Chaco War with Paraguay in the 1930s, when many local miners and peasants were drafted. A general blew up the previous natural stone image in an effort to repress anti-war protest. While he succeeded in destroying the material symbol, according to local lore, he succumbed to the powers of the toad, becaoming paralyzed and dying within a year. The toad is still given offerings on the Friday before Carnival when hundreds of Orureños gather at the statue and celebrate *ch'alla*, an offering of food and liquor to the Pachamama.

A rocky incrustation that looks like a reptile encircling a hill on the south side of town became the site of a chapel when the priests tried to capture the power emanating in this spot, but when people attend mass here during the fiesta of the Day of the Cross on the third of May, they bring offerings of liquor and sweets for the monster. The reptile is associated with fertility, and in the recent past, I was told, newly married couples used to come to seek its blessing.

A water serpent rises in the east from what is a lake during the rainy season. At the peak of its head is a tiny chapel that was also an attempt by the Catholic Church to co-opt the space and its power, but the graffiti on the wall inside include messages to the serpent as well as to the Christ figure ensconced in the church nearby. At the bottom of the water serpent is a black stain that people say is the image of a priest who fought the worship of the serpent and died of paralysis.

Acres of sand dunes to the west side of town are, according to legend, the remains of ants that were sent by Huari to devour the people when they failed to render homage with the customary ceremonials. Here, too, there is a chapel with a figure of Jesus Christ, said to be a brother of the Jesus Christ figure in the church near the water serpent.

All of these enchanted figures are worshiped during the ceremonies devoted to the Christian calendar, but beyond these shrines that the missionaries tried to encapsulate, rituals devoted to pre- and postconquest deities occupy a different space as well as time. While Tuesdays and Fridays are the preferred days for the worship of Huari, the condor, the toad, the reptile, the water serpent, and the hoard of ants, Sundays and saints' days are devoted to Christ the Lord, and the appropriate saints. The church and the plaza in front of it are appropriated by the saints, but the earth is devoted to libations to the Pachamama. Supay is the power that miners attend to below level zero, the entry level to the mines, where they never even swear in the name of the Christian saints or Jesus, although the entry to the mine has a small shrine to the patron saint of San José and a priest said a mass in the vaulted entrance during Carnival.

Although miners defer to Supay in their productive base within the mines, the cycle of Pachamama is still the most pervasive. A *ch'alla* is made to the Pachamama at all life-crisis ceremonies, inaugurations of new houses, work sites, and public buildings, as well as at most public gatherings. Alliance to the Pachamama relates the individual to life, while a contract with Supay, sometimes referred to as the devil, and more often as Tío (Uncle), brings luck and the chance windfall that might change one's circumstances but inevitably causes death in a short time. The Awicha, an old woman who lives in the mines, tempers the anger of Supay. When a thundering blast of dynamite shakes the underground and threatens a cave-in, miners call on the Awicha, who is their intermediary with Supay.

This complementarity of Pachamama and Supay is found along other dimensions of contrast. The Pachamama is a female force of continuity in subsistence production. Offering to her ensures continuity in the returns from crops and flocks. The offering of *chicha*, a fermented corn liquor sometimes mixed with alcohol, or, in some more elaborate ceremonies, the fetus of a llama, guarantees equilibrium in the productive and reproductive forces. Offerings to him are in the form of propitiation to gain his goodwill; they are not for maintenance of a status quo, but for enrichment from the hidden treasures of the hills. A live white llama is sacrificed and its heart interred in the mines to gain his goodwill twice yearly, during Carnival and on 21 July, the eve of the month of Supay. It is both an offering to satisfy his voracious appetite so that he will not eat the men who work the mine, and a request that he yield to the workers some of the riches of the mine.

While celebrations of the preconquest deities are separated in the weekly calendar, the annual cycle of Christian celebrations provides a framework within which indigenous people accommodate their own ceremonies. Paralleling the opposition of the earth and the underworld are the cosmic forces that come to a climax at the time of the winter solstice, 21 June, and of the summer solstice, 21 December. Human ritual intervention at these times is necessary to ensure balance.

RITUALS OF REBELLION

Each of the ritually charged days has become identified with political events that are commemorated by the mining community. It is on these days that they express a heightened consciousness of their distinctive being as a class and as an indigenous race, alienated from their conquerors and exploiters.

The summer solstice was chosen as the day to stage a demonstration for higher wages in the mining encampment of Siglo XX-Catavi in 1942. The FSTMB had just been organized the year before. With rising food prices coinciding with the inflated price of tin during World War II, the miners were determined to improve their lot by united action. A walkout staged in the second week of December was nearly co-opted by the administration, until the workers retaliated. Ceferino, who started work as a child during the Chaco War in the Siglo XX-Catavi mines, told me about this event:

> Then came the strike of 1942. We had fifteen to twenty days of strike. The company announced, "The miners who do not want to work will be killed." They paid every man who went to work a bonus of two hundred pesos. With this tip, almost all of the workers reported to work: until 21 December, when six or seven thousand workers united at ten o'clock. We were going down to the administration, calmly, without any weapons. We were a mixed lot, women, children, men. María Barzola was a delegate for the *pallires* (concentrators of mineral). When she approached the soldiers, they shot her. We were about four hundred meters from the office, and they were firing on all of us. We were surprised by the attack on us.

The winter solstice is celebrated in conjunction with the fiesta of San Juan, 24 June. Some miners have heard the story of how San Juan entered into competition with Jesus Christ to split a rock by blowing a wind so cold it could cause frost. Campesinos celebrate the day by burning the stubble-grass over their fields; in this way, they help the Pachamama maintain the balance of heat and cold. Miners to this day celebrate the eve of San Juan by lighting fires, around which they gather to drink and dance. For the campesinos, lighting the fires signifies the maintenance of fertility for their land and their flocks, and each faggot that they burn stands for the renewal of the life of one animal for the year. The miners have generalized the theme of maintaining productivity to include minerals so that life itself can continue.

For the miners, 24 June has a particular significance. It was on the eve of San Juan in 1967 that General René Barrientos sent in his troops to massacre the inhabitants, betraying the very miners who—disillusioned with the MNR since the 1956 stabilization plan—had supported his 1964 coup d'état. Barrientos cut their wages, and when they resisted, he ordered the troops into the mines. The miners chafed under military occupation until 1967, when they called a meeting of the FSTMB, scheduled for 24 June at the largest mine encampment, Siglo XX—Catavi. The meeting was deliberately scheduled for 24 June, the day of San Juan. As the miners were gathering from all the nationalized mining centers to celebrate the fiesta and welcome the delegates, the army attacked the encampment. Simón Reyes, a union leader at Siglo XX who was later jailed, described the evening's festivities (Reyes 1967):

> The enthusiasm for the night of San Juan was linked with the welcome to the delegates, demonstrating in everything a sere spirit, confident for the outcome of the meeting. The enthusiasm was prolonged until 4:30 in the morning when some people returned to their homes to prepare to go to work while others continued dancing.

Just then, the military and the national guard, armed with machine guns, mortars, and hand grenades, entered the encampment and attacked people still dancing in the streets. They fired on them with machine guns and threw grenades into houses with sleeping occupants. In the streets everything that moved was fired upon, even dogs.

News of the atrocity seeped out slowly. La Patria, the daily newspaper of Oruro, reported on the following day that there were sixteen dead and one-hundred and seventy-one wounded, and that the operation had been carried out by the mining police, the Department of Criminal Investigation (DIC), and the United States Rangers, with airplanes circulating overhead. Colonel Prudencia, in charge of ground operations, announced that the army had occupied the mine centers of Siglo XX and Huanuni, another nationalized mine center, to capture sympathizers of the guerrilla movement led by Ché Guevara that was still operating in Santa Cruz, the eastern region of the country. Newspaper reports later revealed that at least eighty-seven were killed, including men, women, and children, and that many more were wounded; an eyewitness at the funeral, a shopkeeper in the mining town, assured me that even more were killed. He told me that the number of caskets he saw going by looked like a stream of ants, and that there were burials in common ditches of bodies so destroyed by bazookas that they were no longer intact.

The massacre of San Juan was more destructive than any previous terror let loose in the mines. It was not designed merely to eliminate guerrilla sympathizers, as the colonel in charge claimed, or to rid the community of labor agitators, but to attack a whole class indiscriminately in order to break its resistance to the military. The genocidal attack was designed to inspire fear in the mining community, where resentment against Barrientos was pervasive. When I visited the mining encampment of Catavi on the eve of San Juan in 1985, miners celebrated the fiesta with the same devotion as when I had seen it in 1970, with perhaps even more fires burning, in memory of the massacre as well as in devotion to the Pachamama.

Another date that commemorates a seasonal transition has also been the occasion for political protest. On 21 September, the day of the spring equinox, students and workers in 1970 took to the streets to protest against the government of General Ovando; in Bolivian tradition, the day commemorates youth and love. That year the demonstration commemorated the students who had joined the remaining guerrilla troops of Ché Guevara to stage an uprising in Teoponte, in the tropical zone of the Yungas, where there are plantations and a mining center. Just a few days before 21 September, Ovando had turned over the bodies of the youths, who had been brutally slain by the army when they were held in captivity; their bodies had been destroyed by bazookas and hand grenades. The FSTMB had not formally endorsed the guerrilla movement, but its leadership saw the rally as an opportunity to discredit Ovando's regime. Shortly after the procession, the government was ousted by a right-wing junta led by General Rogelio Miranda, who had been in charge of the San Juan massacre. Miranda proved so unpopular, even with the armed forces, that the way was paved for a coup led by the populist General Juan José Torres.

The meaning associated with many of the ritual observances is directly connected with class solidarity. In the enactment of these rites, fraternities of workers reinforce their common engagement in production. The dance groups and ceremonies relate them to a source of power independent of the religious and political institutions that shape their everyday existence. The political significance of the sacred festivities can be seen in Carnival and the Supay rituals.

CARNIVAL

Carnival in February involves all local union and fraternal groups in myths and rituals that combine Christian beliefs with indigenous ones. Coordination depends on a municipal organizing committee, but the real impulse comes from dance groups based on occupational syndicates.

Each act of Carnival follows historical precedents relating to preconquest or early conquest days. The traditions of the indigenous and Spanish populations are interwoven as distinctive strands. Each culture contributes to the dances and dramas to interpret the past and present. There are two main dramas: the first is the triumph over the monsters sent by Huari, the hill owner, which took place sometime before the conquest (over the centuries it has assimilated postconquest spirits and powers): the second is the conquest of the Indians by the Spaniards, and the consequent subjugation of the indigenous population in the fields and mines owned by the colonists.

Dances provide the major media through which cultural messages are transmitted and continuously revitalized (Buechler 1980). The first drama is played out in the Diablada dance and in the propitiation of all the mythical monsters and the second is enacted on the plaza during Carnival Sunday by the Children of the Sun, as well as by dancing the Diablada and Morenada.

Carnival dancing is both a propitiation of supernatural forces and an assumption of the powers they represent. The magic of identification is contained in the mask; as long as dancers wear the mask, they are the figure impersonated. On Sunday the dancers remove their masks and dance under arches constructed on the plaza in front of the Church of the Mineshaft. Laden with silver, they enter the church to pray. Although the magical element is not always assumed by dancers today, a sense of transformation remains in the dance as they perform improbable feats, leaping and cavorting like devils; weaving to and fro while bearing the heavy suit of the Morenada; pole-vaulting as Tobas, Indians of the Jungle. The procession advances for several miles from the north of the town to the plaza of the Church of the Mineshaft, where the Virgin is ensconced.

The dances of the Diablada and the Morenada are especially important to the consciousness of laborers in relation to their work. Both dances show a movement from representation of themselves as subordinated miners or slaves, accompanied by a single devil in each group, toward a configuration of power in the form of a devil or slavedriver. The devil mask worn by Diablada dancers combines the horns of Christian figures with three serpents sprouting from the forehead. The red coverall worn by the dancers is decked with a tunic emblazoned with cut-glass jewels and an apron of linked coins. Through the streets and up to the plaza, the devil dancers leap with their temptresses, men dressed as women in satin and jewels, who lure men to work for the devil.

The Morenadas represent black slaves, who once worked in the mines but were later transferred to the vineyards at low altitudes, where, it is said, they could better endure the climate. The mask they wear caricatures negroid features, with flaring nostrils, protruding lips, and bulging eyes. The lead dancer, representing the *cabecilla* (foreman), is the most elaborately dressed; he carries a pipe and cracks a whip as he leads the other dancers who carry jeweled flasks, from which they drink the wine they were forced to produce. Their costume is like a wine cask, a synecdoche for the transformation they undergo in the dance from enslavement to the embodiment of joy made possible by the liberating effect of liquor.

The devil dance captures the essence of Carnival in Oruro. According to legend, the dance began when a miner fell asleep after the *ch'alla* on the devil in the mine. When he woke up, he saw the devil himself dancing, and he followed him, dancing out of the mine. After that, the miners continued to dance in the streets following the *ch'alla* on the Friday of Carnival. The dance evolved from being a group of miners with a devil or two in their ranks to one in which devils predominate. At first, miners danced in homage to the devil, releasing their hopes, ambitions, fears, and joys. As the dance progressed, they transformed themselves into the attractive, alluring figure. The dance is an act of devotion to the Virgin of the Church of the Mineshaft, in which dancers complain to her of their troubles, and finally give themselves up to joy as they receive her blessing.

The Morenadas reveal the deep impression made upon the indigenous population by the black slaves who were imported to work in the mines. The choreography of the many Morenada dance groups tells the legend of a rebellion against a gang leader in the Marie Antoinette vineyards. A young black woman who was the delight of the old despot attracted the attention of the slaves. Burning with desire for her, they got the *caporal* (boss) drunk and then overthrew him in a rebellion. They forced the *caporal* to stamp on the grapes and move the winch, while they ridiculed him in satiric verses (Alessandri 1968: 10). It is an incomplete rebellion, one in which the agent of oppression, not the forces of repression, is attacked and forced to take on their humble role. Both dances assert the possibility of transformation from subordinate to superordinate positions by the enslaved proletariat. They are "primitive" forms of rebellion because they seek redemption in usurping the role of the dominant, not a collective identity in an alternative society.

Organization of dance groups provides an institutional base for important friendships and contacts, a theme that Hans Buechler highlights in his remarkable book *The Masked Media* (1980). In Oruro there are four major groups among eighteen dance societies, each representing a major occupational confederation. The railroad workers and the miners form the largest contingents; the dance groups both reinforce work-group solidarity and link them to the community.

Two separate Carnival acts, divided by time and place, but linked by common beliefs, are the *ch'alla* to the Pachamama and to Supay. The first takes place in most of the houses and yards of the townspeople at noon on the Tuesday of Carnival week. The second is performed inside the mines on Friday evening, beginning about sundown and lasting until midnight. The first brings together the members of a household and assures their health and welfare, and the productivity of whatever subsistence crops they grow in their gardens. The second reinforces the solidarity of the workgroup while ensuring the safety of men against accidents and their mineral yield. On the two occasions, offerings are made to gain the goodwill of the spirits of the earth and hills.

During Carnival, and on the 31st of July, the offering to Supay should include the sacrifice of a llama or sheep. The tin barons—Patiño, Hochschild, and Aramayo—used to purchase the sacrificial animal and attend the ceremonies before their mines were nationalized with the revolution of 1952. After the nationalization of the mines, some of the miners complained that these rituals were performed in excess of the Tío's needs. Juan, whose autobiography I elicited and edited (Rojas and Nash 1976), told me that going into the mine shortly after the revolution was like walking into a saloon. Such secular abuse of the ritual was curtailed in the latter part of the decade and, following military control in 1965, the rituals were entirely halted. The assault on the rituals intensified the hatred miners felt for the regime of Barrientos. The succeeding military president, Ovando, did not oppose the rituals. However, the State mining administration refused to subsidize the cost of the llama. The ritual that I observed during Carnival 1970 was limited to hot beef stew brought into the mines by workers' wives. Not until mine accidents occurred in July of that year was there a complete *k'araku*, or sacrifice of a llama in the mines.

The way that administrators respond to the rituals shapes workers' consciousness. When Patiño danced with the miners and offered each one a personal gift of a skirt or a shirt, he reduced—at least temporarily—worker alienation. The ambivalence of national mining engineers and supervisors after the revolution of 1952 toward these autochthonous rituals created more distance between them and the workers. Since an important part of the ritual is ensuring the continued productivity of the mines, the men felt that it indicated a lack of their concern for the future of the mines. Since the military did not comprehend this perspective, they opposed the rituals, and Barrientos's repression of the rituals succeeded in transforming them into an expression of class solidarity and opposition to the military.

The Friday before Carnival is devoted to a *ch'alla* of the serpent at the southern end of town, and on the following Wednesday and Friday respectively, people on the north side of town honor the toad and the image of the condor. The condor is not an autochthonous mythic figure, but he is offered a *ch'alla* during his celebration.

The special day for the serpent is the Day of the Cross, 3 May, and for the hoard of ants, 15 July. Each celebration combines a request for material goods—a house, a truck, good health, or good fortune—with an offering of liquor, incense, and a *mesa* (literally "table," an offering of sugar cakes, wool, and fat). In these active cults, people reveal the intensity of their desire for material improvement in their lives and their sense of the reciprocal balances in the universe. Most people I questioned said that they were successful in gaining the objects they requested of the enchanted images. On a deeper level, these rituals, superficially linked with "commodity fetishism" (Taussig 1980), link workers to the primordial past, rather than to capitalist institutions. Their sense of dependency on the mines or other sources of income is lessened as they reckon with these other powers.

In contrast with celebrations in other countries, Oruro Carnival processions are orderly, with precise dance steps and lavish costumes. It is not a wild excess of sex and drink, but a precise channeling of very deep passions and sentiments. It is both an expression of, and solace for, discontentment as well as a great source of pride, enabling them to rise above the grueling poverty and despair of their everyday lives.

Along the main street on Carnival Sunday, a drama group of miners, friends, and residents of the San José encampment—who call themselves Sons of the Sun—present a play depicting the Conquest. Protagonists include Pizarro; Diego Almagro and his cohort; the priest Vicario Hernando Luque; Ferdinand, the king of Spain; Atahualpa, the king of the Incas; Hualla Huisa as chief diviner; and fifteen *ñustas*, or Inca maidens. The conquistadores are heavily bearded; the Spanish king and his priest wear pink gauze masks with brightly rouged cheeks and widely staring blue eyes. This contrasts with the unmasked faces of actors playing their Inca forebears, who need no falsification.

In the enactment of the death of Atahualpa, players reenact their own Conquest and subjugation. The actors keep alive the spirit of rebellion by repeating Pizarro's outrageous betrayal of his promise to release Atahualpa after he had received the royal treasure. The dialogue in Quechua is an assertion of their own cultural survival in the face of Spanish domination and the effect of the drama is to reinforce resistance by enacting a moral triumph over unjust domination.

Why has Carnival not merely survived but also grown more elaborate over the years? Whenever people spoke about political repression and revolution, they concluded by asking me, "But have you ever been here during Carnival?" and proceeded to describe past processions and their role in them. I sensed that it was not a shift in the dialogue, but an extension of it. Carnival is an expression of a people's view of their history and an account of how they have transmuted their defeat into a triumphant statement of the value of survival and self-determination. Josermo Murillo Vacareza, an Oruro lawyer whose avocation was that of a folklorist, says (Murillo Vacareza 1969: 9):

The Diablada is a splendid transformation of the disenchantment that permeates the spirit of the pueblo, releasing the frustration from those forces that falsify its inner vitality. The daring and impetuous dance is the hidden impulse, equal to that of their ancestors, to demolish, fight, and subvert that which they oppose themselves to, whether to subjugation or inferiority; the epochal music is a stimulus to an insurgent movement, as a trumpet of continuity; its rich and beautiful clothing derives from a system of impoverishment, as if to say in the hyperbole of fired imagination, that we dare to believe that there is an end to it.

It would be simplistic to say that Carnival is a substitute for revolution. It is more accurate to say that it is a reminder to the people of the necessity for revolt when the historical conditions are appropriate, just as it is a denial of the misery and drabness of their everyday lives, and an expression of what they aspire to.

THE MONTH OF SUPAY

The month of August is the time for the preparation of the land for planting in September. It is a time to propitiate the power of the hills, which is identified with both Supay and Huari, sometimes called Supay's father (among the miners, the two beings are treated as one). It is simultaneously a time to recognize the Pachamama, since one must avoid the destructive potential of Huari at the same time as one wins the benefits of the earth's fertility. It is a time to ask for both fertility of the fields and mineral wealth from the mines.

The Barrientos government forbade Supay as well as Carnival-related activities. In early July of 1970, when I lived in the San José encampment, three young miners were killed inside the mines. The workers asserted that the deaths were due to the failure to keep up the ritual sacrifice of a llama to Supay. The ritual allegedly fed the spirit of the hills and satisfied his appetite so that he would not eat the workers. Consequently, a delegation of workers urged the superintendent of the San José mine to permit them to carry out the ritual on the customary night, 31 July, which was that very month. The superintendent agreed to this and offered to pay for the llamas when he saw that the men were reluctant to return to work. However, unlike Patiño, he refused to participate in the celebration. When I attended the festivity, a miner informed me: "the k'araku is held in order that there be some development in the mine, or so that we might discover a vein that would benefit the company. If they [the managers] had come, we workers would want to work with greater enthusiasm and will. Here we are waiting for some improvement to take place so that we all can benefit. But what benefit would it have? Only so that the administrators could take trips out of the country." He went on to explain the sense of reciprocity played out in the rituals: "We eat the mines and the mines eat us. For that reason, we have to give these rituals to the spirit of the hills so that he will continue to reveal the veins of metal to us so that we can live."

The multiplicity of understandings embodied in Supay are called into play in the mining community as they relate their present lives to his power. Through their lived relationship with Supay in the weekly *ch'allas* and the biannual *k'araku*, the miners overcome their own alienation in the mines. This enables them to generate an autonomous, liberating consciousness, though it does not ensure that this will be translated into an active movement. The force of this relationship can be co-opted by the owners if, as Patiño chose to do, they enter into the rituals and reciprocate gifts. The unfortunate translation by the Spaniards of Supay into the devil, in their own version of a dichotomized moral universe, transmogrified a pre-Hispanic vision of a power domain that contains good and evil in all the supernatural entities to which they relate. The recognition of Supay as the source of material abundance is only one aspect of his many powers. The miners feel that when they enter as a group to ask him to enrich the mines, they ensure the life of the community. It is only when they enter as individuals to seek his favor that they fall into a "pact with the devil." The wide range of attitudes and behaviors by which miners relate through Supay to their identification as an expropriated autochthonous group and as an exploited proletariat is far more complex than an interpretation that identifies the devil as a projection of commodity fetishism (Taussig 1980).

RITUAL, CLASS CONSCIOUSNESS, AND IDEOLOGY

Working-class consciousness among these Bolivian miners is founded in a strong identity as a common group, united by their collective work, in which they see themselves helped by these primordial sources of power. The rituals evoke this identity as workers discuss their problems and unite them against their oppressors. They are not so much a charter for behavior, as the early structural-functionalists in the field of anthropology surmised, as a generative base motivating political action that might take many forms. These could underwrite reaction and even support for the military (who have attacked them) as well as adherence to revolutionary movements.

In order to understand how these rituals relate to the politicized ideologies of national parties, we must respond to questions on at least three different levels: (1) What happens with the people relating to one another in the scene? (2) How does the ritual unite these participants to other significant reference groups? (3) How has the significance of the ritual changed over time?

A simple Malinowskian functionalism helps us to answer the first question. The *ch'alla* integrates men within the work site and thus promotes the solidarity of the primary group. This is best expressed in the words of Manuel, a carpenter in the mine:

> This tradition inside the mine must be continued because there is no communication more intimate, more sincere, or more beautiful than the moment of the *ch'alla*, the moment when the workers chew coca together and it is offered to the Tío. There we give voice to our problems, we talk about our work problems, and there is born a generation so revolutionary that the workers begin thinking of making structural change. This is our university. The experience we have in the *ch'alla* is the best experience we have.

Manuel, who was one of the top leaders in the union before the Barrientos coup, was perhaps unusual in equating primary group solidarity with the basis for revolutionary action. Although it is a basic Marxist proposition about the beginning of class consciousness, many union leaders seem to negate it and often criticize traditional rituals. This negation may stem from the fear, on the part of leaders who wish to impose their plan of action, to independent sources of consciousness and self-determination that are not controlled by the party or trade union.

The second issue of how the ritual relates workers to other significant reference groups requires an historical perspective. In the days of the tin barons before national-ization of the mines in 1952, when the owners, especially Patiño, would come to the celebration and dance with the *palliris* and the men, they overcame a great deal of the rebelliousness of the miners. The exchange of the *t'inka* (management's gift to the workers) and the *achura* (the workers' gift of prize ore to the owners) symbolized rec-iprocity in the labor relationship. Although this reciprocity was not equal, it reinforced a set of paternalistic ties that gave the workers greater spirit to work and sacrifice them-selves. It overcame, even if only momentarily, the rebelliousness of the work force. Furthermore, in the days of the tin barons, the workers within each work group were paid according to a contract figured on the basis of the mineral content of the ores they produced. Like piecework systems of payment in developed industrial countries, this promoted compliance with management and division among workers. There was a great deal of competition between work groups to secure the richest vein, and the hos-tility engendered was worked out in witchcraft. An old miner who had worked in most of the mines of Bolivia and a copper mine in Chile described these customs:

> The men in the mines who got high returns on their contracts were most often the targets of witchcraft. The miners used to go seek the shamans from among the campesinos who know more about this. These shamans have animal spirits. Here, and especially in Colquecharka, many miners use witchcraft to make their more fortunate companions lose the vein. They went into the mine with the shaman and they threw water with salt on the vein where their enemy was work-ing and this made it disappear. Sometimes the miners knew they were being bewitched and they called on the Pachamama.

In short, hostile competition was intense, and the solidarity built up in the *ch'alla* was limited to the immediate group of men working on the same contract. Following the nationalization of the mines, the base pay was raised and equalized for all the mines, and the negotiation for the contract was carried out by the union agents in open bargaining procedures. Workers felt that one of the most important gains they made was to have the contracts figured openly with the superintendent of the mine, foremen, and the head of the work group witnessing the contract statement.

Yet these bureaucratic controls introduced after the revolution had another conse-quence. The contract was paid to work teams of two men rather than to a work gang, and it was based on total output measured in cubic feet regardless of mineral content. Thus the solidarity of the work group was weakened at the primary group level, but a larger unity was maintained in the work force as a whole. The union welded together not only work units with the mine, but through the Federation of Mine Workers' Unions of Bolivia (FSTMB) created a massive political force of miners to other industrial work-ers and organized campesinos.

Militant political action, of which there was a great deal prior to the revolution, was separate from ritual relations, which were often rejected by the leaders both before and after the MNR entered power. The force of these rituals was in part co-opted by the private owners, although the currents of identity were not fully controlled by them. Only when the management forthrightly opposed them, as during the military occupation of the mines in Barrientos's presidency, did the reaction to domination become a subversive force realized in the rituals.

During the period of nationalist solidarity within the populist revolutionary government, the *ch'alla* in the mines served as a recreation more than as a point for mobilizing rebellion and focusing on dissatisfactions. This brief period of amicable labor-management relations came to an end in the early 1960s with the so-called Triangular Plan. This plan provided the Bolivian state with much-needed capital to modernize the mines, but the financiers made the loans conditional on the firing of hundreds of "excess" miners and the termination of workers' representation in the management of the mines. The foreign financiers in the process deprived miners of revolutionary gains. Labor-management relations deteriorated still further after the military occupation of the mines by Barrientos in 1965. The miners say that Barrientos suppressed the *ch'alla* because he was afraid of the solidarity promoted in these drinking sessions. The suppression of the *ch'alla* added to the resentment of the workers against both management and the government.

Along with the suppression of the *ch'alla* came a sharp drop in the production of high-quality ores. This was coincident with a falling off in exploration. Furthermore, the nationalized mining administration never succeeded in developing work incentives. The deterioration of wages, coupled with the rising salaries of administrators and army officers, resulted in both alienation of the workers and stagnation in production. A brief respite came with the populist Torres regime in 1970, when wages were reinstated to the pre-1965 levels, but his presidency came to an end after ten months with the military coup of Colonel Hugo Banzer Suárez. Management rejection of the *ch'alla* reveals the complete transformation of the ritual from one in which worker-management solidarity was reinforced to one in which the ritual becomes the basis for communication of rebellion.

The miners finally regained worker control, with the right of veto and participation in management, during Siles Zuazo's second term of office in 1984. Although Siles had undermined the labor movement during his first term of office with the stabilization plan and the Triangular Plan, he returned to power three decades later with labor's support. This time he remained loyal to his electoral ally. This meant that he could not, as a consequence, obtain needed foreign financial assistance. Because the state was bankrupt, labor's gains proved to be an empty shell and production reached a near standstill because tools and machinery were inadequate and mineral veins were depleted. As the director of labor relations in COMIBOL, the nationalized mining corporation, told me in 1985, the restoration of their earlier rights served to minimize worker hostility to management. Yet workers' rights had lost much of their historical significance as mine production, along with world prices, plunged.

We have partially answered our third question, how the ritual has evolved over time, in the course of analyzing the changing structure of relations. The ideology expressed through ritual has not been a one-way street from paternalism to revolution. When the conditions were ripe for revolt prior to 1952, especially in the early labor struggles of

1918 and during the Chaco War, the *ch'alla* became a point for mobilizing discontent. It did not come as a surprise when I learned that in 1918 the aggrieved workers of the San José mine chose the *ch'alla* on the night of 31 July to declare the first strike recorded for the mine. Again, when there was extreme discontent over the Chaco War, the shrine of the Sapo (toad) was chosen as an assembly point. Recognizing this, the general ordered that it be destroyed. These time-and-lace mementos of primordial supernatural power enhance the determination of those who still bear that culture to resist the oppression in which they live. After the general died of the stroke that paralyzed him following his sacrilegious act, the people of Oruro symbolized this by sculpting a new statue of the toad, resurrected on this same spot.

The 1952 revolution, in turn, did not result in long-term worker identification with the State. Even once miners won their ritual rights back after Barrientos had suspended them, workers felt alienated from the management of the state-run mines. The failure of the supervisors to attend the ceremonies accentuated their distance from the work force. As one worker said, on the occasion of the *k'araku*, "The Tío is the real owner here. The administrators just sit in their offices and don't help us in our work." The failure of the administration to make the traditional exchange of insufficient funds, minimized its impact. "The Tío is still hungry," another miner said on leaving the celebration, "and so are we."

Assumptions about traditional and modern systems of belief often fail to capture the complexity of selective changes in symbol systems. The Tío is more important now in reference to accidents than as a generator of mineral wealth. This is tied to a contract system, established after nationalization, in which the payoff depends on the total tonnage of output rather than the mineral content of the ore. The significance of rituals is directly related to this changing reality. The Tío is an explanation for the inexplicable, a rationale for the irrational destiny forced on the miner; their faith in him enriches a barren existence of unremitting toil. In the colonial period, when he appeared before the workers, he had the face and figure of the enemy, the devil, red-faced, horned, and dressed in the royal robes of a medieval underworld denizen. In the period of private large-scale exploitation, he appeared as a gringo, wearing a cowboy hat, boots, red-faced, and larger than life. When one makes a contract with him, one is assured of riches even at the price of one's life, but he pays off with a greater certitude than government bureaucrats or officials. Supay transcends the medieval conception of the devil imported by the Spaniards; he is the source of wealth and power as well as the agent of evil. He is not only a projection of the fetishism of commodity production in capitalism whereby all social relations are transformed into those of the cash nexus, as one very imaginative anthropologist has claimed (Taussig 1980), but a means to satisfy communal goals when approached collectively. When a lone miner works with the devil in solitude, it is believed that he will die within ninety days and that his heirs will never enjoy the wealth he accumulates. In contrast, when the devil is given an offering by the miners as a group in the *k'araku*, he reveals to them veins that all can work to make it possible for the mine to remain productive and sustain the people who live on it.

Supay is a multifaceted power, neither all good nor all bad. As the central figure in Carnival, Supay is both an expression of the frustrations and anxieties in the lives of these people and a projection of their desire to overcome them.

RELIGIOUS BELIEF AND POLITICAL BEHAVIOR

The power of these pre-conquest beliefs, reinforced by ritual observances, lies in their stimulus to collective identity and the sense of when that has been violated. The ritual calendar becomes a schedule for acts of protest that have frequently upset governments and disturbed a given covenant in industry. These events and the political repercussions that followed became part of the collective memory of a people as they drew, and continue to draw, upon their indigenous traditions to resist exploitation.

Resistance may take many forms, but it is always strengthened by the self-determination of a people who have not yet lost their self-identity. Rituals and belief combine to reinforce the myths that encompass their history, and the celebrations of Carnival, the *ch'alla*, and the earth-warming ceremonials prepare that people for a time when they can shape their own destiny. Sectarian political leaders and orthodox religious leaders usually reject ritual protest as deviance. However, if one thinks of it as a rehearsal that keeps alive the sentiment of rebellion until an historically appropriate moment, it may reinforce political movements.

REFERENCES

Alessandri, A. Z. 1968. "Facetas de 'la morenada': Un ensayo" in *Ensayo de interpretación del Carnaval Orureno: Leyendas, tradiciones, costumbres*. Oruro: Instituto de Filosofía Indígena Oruro.

Beltrán, H. B. Augusto. 1962. *Carnaval de Oruro y proceso ideológico e historia de los grupos folklóricos*. Oruro: Edición del Comité Departmental de Folklore.

Buechler, H. C. 1980. *The Masked Media: Aymara Fiestas and Social Interaction in the Bolivian Highlands*. Hawthorne, N.Y.: Mouton.

Murillo Vacareza, J. 1969. "El diablo de Oruro y la supervivencia de un anhelo." *Fraternidad Revista Cultural* [Oruro]: 7–9.

Nash, J. 1979. *We Eat the Mines and the Mines Eat Us: Dependency and Exploitation in Bolivian Tin Mines*. New York: Columbia University Press.

Reyes, S. 1967. *La masacre de San Juan*. Oruro: n.p.

Rojas, J., and J. Nash. 1976. *He agotado mi vida en la mina*. Buenos Aires: Nueva Visión.

Taussig, M. 1980. *The Devil and Commodity Fetishism in South America*. Chapel Hill: University of North Carolina Press.

PART THREE

MOBILIZATION AND REPRESSION

5

Popular Religion, Protest, and Revolt: The Emergence of Political Insurgency in the Nicaraguan and Salvadoran Churches of the 1960s—80s

Sharon Erickson Nepstad

A North American journalist once asked Father Ernesto Cardenal—poet, Catholic priest, and former Minister of Culture in the Sandinista government—why he had participated in the Nicaraguan revolution. He replied, "It was my religious faith that led me to revolution, not my politics.... I think Nicaraguans who separate Christianity from Revolution are mistaken. Here they are the same thing" (Barbé 1987: 38; Simon 1981: 8). Such statements have piqued renewed interest in the oppositional capacity of religion. Long considered merely a preserver of the status quo, religion is now being recognized for its potential to help instigate protest, resistance, and even revolution. This potential has been recognized by even the most powerful military nations in the world. The 1980 "Santa Fe Document," that profoundly shaped President Ronald Reagan's Latin American policy, stated that the emergence of liberation theology and formation of grass-roots Christian base communities in the region pose a threat to U.S. national security (Zwerling & Martin 1985: 31).

Revolutionary movements in Latin America cannot develop or sustain political and military insurgency without a strong base in the poor masses. These masses are often profoundly influenced by Catholicism, which is deeply rooted in Latin American culture. In fact, religion and culture are so inextricably connected that José Carlos Mariategui, a Peruvian scholar, claims we can only understand the people's longing for liberation when we take into consideration "the religious factor" (Candelaria 1990). However, the religion of the poor masses does not mirror the Catholicism of the Vatican or elite classes. Rather, this religion, known as "popular religion," is shaped by the political and social realities that the poor face. As Chilean theologian Segundo Galilea put it: "The poor and the oppressed are the subjects of their own form of religion; hence, folk piety is of singular importance in mobilizing the masses for the struggle of liberation" (Galilea in Candelaria 1990: xii).

The goal of this chapter is twofold. First, I seek to build a theory that explains the mobilization of political protest within the popular church. Synthesizing Antonio Gramsci's insights with James Scott's theory of the great and little traditions, I explicate the factors that may lead the popular church from oppositional ideas and acts of "everyday resistance" to overt revolt against the State. Second, I examine the response of state and Church leaders to political resistance from the popular church, analyzing the latter in Nicaragua and El Salvador as historical examples from which theory can be inductively developed.

THEORETICAL BACKGROUND

Within the sociology of religion, both structural-functionalists and Marxists share the perspective that religion serves to support the status quo, legitimate the authority of the elites, and encourage submission to the existing order. Many in the Functionalist tradition hold that religion is necessary for establishing a consensus about moral values and societal obligations, while also granting a constraining power which helps reinforce customs and morals (Durkheim 1947; Parsons 1964; Wilson 1982). In short, religion is the moral glue that holds society together.

Marxists, on the other hand, view religion as a form of social control used by the ruling classes to preserve their power. Marx argued that the religious faith of the proletariat was a manifestation of false consciousness, a search for compensation by people in their misery. This longing for compensation, however, leads them to live in an illusory happiness and to not revolt against the conditions that cause their suffering. Marx stated that "religion is the sigh of the oppressed creature," and believed that it functions primarily to dull the pain of their situation. In Marx's view, it is necessary to "pluck the imaginary flowers from the chain not so that man will wear the chain without fantasy of consolation but so that he will shake off the chain and cull the living flower" (Marx and Engels 1957: 41–42). Marx maintained that a just social order could not be established without the abolition of religion.

More realistically, however, we must acknowledge that religion actually can move in two directions. It can serve as an apology and legitimation of an unjust status quo, on the one hand, yet also as a source of resistance and protest, on the other hand. Empirical research shows no clear, unidirectional relationship between religion and conservative politics. Religion often serves to support the ruling elites. At other times, it foments opposition and revolt (Billings 1990; Schoenfeld 1992; Smith 1991; Westhues 1976; Wuthnow 1973).

Italian neo-Marxist Antonio Gramsci offers insight into this dual nature of religion. Gramsci noted that "Every religion is in reality a multiplicity of distinct and often contradictory religions" which differ according to social class (1971: 218). He disagreed with Marx, who asserted that religion and culture are merely byproducts of the material infrastructure and the bourgeoisie's control of the mental means of production. Rather, Gramsci held that the material base and the cultural superstructure mutually influence each other. Therefore, cultural expressions such as religion are semiautonomous and the ideas of the dominant group are never completely exclusive.

Noting the differences between popular and orthodox religion, Gramsci argued that the beliefs of popular religion are influenced by the particular life experiences of the peasantry, which vastly differ from those of the elites. Thus, popular religious ideas often conflict with "official"—i.e. orthodox—teachings. According to Gramsci, these

unorthodox ideas can potentially develop into an oppositional force under two conditions. First, the working class and peasantry need to produce their own leaders—whom
he called "organic intellectuals"—who can develop worldviews that challenge the status quo. These new worldviews can foster a critical perspective, leading to an insurgent
consciousness that would eventually undermine the hegemony of the ruling class
(Fulton 1987; Gramsci 1971). Second, this new awareness of the poor needs to be reinforced through "structures of social support" that sustain and reaffirm this resistance
among participants in popular religion (Billings 1992).

The concept that popular religion can hold an oppositional perspective which challenges the established order has been elaborated by political scientist James Scott
(1977). Scott builds on the work of anthropologist Robert Redfield (1961), who
acknowledged that the religion of the peasantry does in fact differ from that of the
upper classes. Redfield coined the terms "little tradition" to refer to the religious beliefs
and practices of the folk stratum, and "great tradition" to refer to the orthodox teachings of religious leaders and their elite constituency. Redfield argued that the little tradition—popular religion—develops when missionaries take their message to the coun-
tryside. There they encounter a preexisting set of beliefs, practices, and symbols. If the
peasantry accepts the message of the great tradition at all, it is assimilated into their
own cultural practice.

Scott argues that this phenomenon occurs uniformly throughout the world, despite
the large variations in peasant cultures and religions, precisely because this "slippage"
between the great and little traditions is intentional and based on social structure. The
two religious traditions reflect sociologically distinct groups: the affluent and the poor.
Thus, religious symbolism and rituals are appropriated according to class interests, and
can become a channel through which resistance to the class structure is expressed.
Therefore, changes in the religious beliefs and practices of the great tradition are not
mere misunderstandings of orthodox teachings, as religious leaders often assumed.
They are, Scott argues, intentional profanations which serve as a form of everyday
resistance against the authority of the great tradition, and the class structure it
represents.

Scott furthermore contends that these profanations of religious practices may also be
forms of resistance against the State, if the dominant religious order is closely aligned
with the political system. Since official church and State are often mutually reinforcing,
particularly in agrarian societies, expressions of religious resistance can be tantamount
to protest against the government. Religious profanations can serve as a political
weapon for the poor, just as the religious teachings of the elites often serve to legitimate
and maintain the socio-political status quo.

According to Scott, popular religious resistance may be embodied in a variety of
forms. One central manifestation of protest is the rejection or reversal of elite culture,
values, and beliefs. This reversal may be present in folklore and myth, popular enter-
tainment, music, folk art, and language. Secondly, peasants may oppose the inequality
maintained by elites by structuring their local institutions in a very egalitarian manner.
This is a symbolic reversal of the existing social order, and is almost universally manifested in their religious practices. Third, peasants may profane sacred rituals as a
protest against the great tradition. Christian rituals such as mass, baptism, and

communion, for example, are likely to acquire new meanings more congruent with indigenous beliefs or political views. Finally, profanations may entail open mockery of the religious hierarchy and suspension of deference to the great tradition (Scott 1977).

Scott's theory of little-tradition profanation is a great advance toward understanding the oppositional capacity of popular religion. However, it needs to be developed further. Scott fails to specify adequately the conditions which encourage the little tradition to shift from everyday resistance toward overt revolt. Little traditions exist in a myriad of societies, yet relatively few popular religions move beyond the mere "small heresies" of resistance to attempts to overthrow the State. Scott briefly mentions a few conditions that may facilitate insurrection (Scott 1977: 232):

> The situation in which [little tradition] themes are likely to become mobilizing social myths involve not only material distress but also a loss of everyday social meaning as well. Wars, plagues, earthquakes…may appear to destroy the normal categories in which reality is apprehended and organized and thereby provide the social soil for latent millennial beliefs to become manifest. At such times the prophets and champions of popular themes of religious liberation are apt to attract an enthusiastic following.

While Scott claims that "material distress" and "loss of everyday social meaning" can instigate peasant revolt, this clearly not does sufficiently explain the mobilization process, since these conditions are rather constant across peasant cultures. Disease and natural disasters have occurred throughout the world and history, but not always have they been an impetus to revolution. Other factors must play a role. An examination of specific cases in which the little tradition did move successfully from everyday profanations of resistance to full-scale revolution may help identify the factors which instigate revolt against the State. The next section will employ Scott's theory to analyze the popular church in Nicaragua, which played an important role in the 1979 Sandinista Revolution, and in El Salvador, whose members struggled for social and political change and, in some cases, participated in the national revolt headed by the Farabundo Marti National Liberation Front (FMLN).

THE IRRUPTING POPULAR CHURCH IN CENTRAL AMERICA

Central America's little tradition formed during the era of colonization by Spain. But the popular church did not become a visible and potent force in Central America until the 1960s. Prior to this, the masses were virtually excluded from church life, since the clergy devoted most of their efforts to serving the upper classes through private schools and ceremonies. Then, realizing that they had lost the peasantry and the working class, some church leaders decided to win them back. To gain an understanding of the experiences and needs of the poor, many pastoral workers in the 1960s broke from their traditional pursuits and went to live and work among the people (Berryman 1984; Smith 1991: 140–43).

Although their original intention was often simply to evangelize the poor, many pastoral workers became acutely aware of the injustices and oppression suffered by the

Central American masses. Most visible was the extreme poverty of the majority and the tremendous wealth of the few. During the 1960s–1970s, approximately sixty percent of Nicaraguans suffered from malnutrition, thirty-six percent were unemployed, seventy-three percent lived in substandard housing, and eighty percent of the children did not have access to school. Illiteracy was greater than fifty percent nationally, and as high as ninety percent in some rural areas. Health care existed only for the wealthy, and Nicaragua had one of the highest infant mortality rates in Latin America (del Rio 1982; Randall 1983). El Salvador suffered similar conditions. Approximately eighty percent of Salvadoran children in the 1970s were malnourished. These problems were generated by the fact that 90 percent of the peasants in Salvador have no land while two percent of the population owns fifty-eight percent of the arable land. In the 1970s, rural unemployment was estimated at fifty-four and four-tenths percent; the average rural worker could only get one-hundred forty-one days of work per year (Berryman 1984: 103; Golden 1991: 106; Lernoux 1980: 62).

The harshness of the socio-economic conditions and the brutal repression exercised by the Somoza dictatorship in Nicaragua and the elite-backed military government in El Salvador caused many priests and nuns to identify themselves with the interests of the poor. Rather than converting the masses to the great tradition, the pastoral workers were being converted to the popular church. They began working with peasants and the urban poor, who were questioning the way they had been socialized to interpret the world and its structures as the will of God. Together they began reinterpreting the Bible in light of their political and economic experience, which led them to different biblical interpretations of society than they had always been taught to believe. In other words, they were developing Gramsci's alternative worldview (Berryman 1984; Boff 1984; Kirk 1992). This new worldview and the religious perspectives of the poor were affirmed by the great tradition leaders who were pleased with the renewed church life among the peasantry and the working class.

Simultaneously, the religious hierarchy was opening doors of political opportunity for the growth of the popular church by articulating several important ideas in the Second Vatican Council of 1962–65 and the Latin American Bishops Conference in Medellín, Colombia in 1968 (Smith 1991). Pope John XXIII set the great tradition on a new course by emphasizing that all had the right to a decent standard of living, education, and political participation. He also questioned the absolute right to private property and the "Church's unswerving allegiance to capitalist individualism in the Cold War against socialist collectivism" (Lernoux 1980: 31). Moreover, the Vatican II documents stated that the church is and should be involved in *this world*, and should not focus exclusively on other-worldly, spiritual matters. The leaders also stated the church is a community of equals. Whether one is a bishop, priest, or lay person, each has ability to offer and a responsibility to share (Berryman 1984; Lernoux 1980; Smith 1991).

Three years after Vatican II, the Latin American bishops met in Medellín to discuss how the ideas articulated at the Vatican Council could be applied to the situation in Latin America. The bishops, influenced by a number of theologians who had been working with the poor, stated that the people should not be objects but agents of their own history. The resulting Medellín documents emphasized the right of the masses to participate in the process of social change and to assume their responsibilities in civic and public life. Additionally, the Medellín conference declared that justice would be achieved through organization and action by the popular sectors of society (Levine 1980; Smith 1991). In Nicaragua and El Salvador, these documents were embraced as a validation of the poor's right to establish justice and challenge unjust military regimes. It affirmed their alternative worldview and further encouraged their resistance. Vatican II and the Medellín conference were incendiary in Central America (Millman 1988).

These developments in Latin America's great tradition indicate that Scott's model may be oversimplified. Religious authorities may not always oppose popular religion; on the contrary, they can foster and support its growth. Scott does acknowledge that the great tradition may tolerate the small heresies of popular religion, as long as their interests are not diametrically opposed. The Central American popular church illustrates how it can provide the necessary organizational structure that enables the expression of people's revolutionary aspirations. In both Nicaragua and El Salvador, at least part of the pastoral workers of the great tradition committed themselves to accompanying the poor, and the interface of the two traditions was particularly powerful. The religious profanations of the little tradition may not always be aimed at the entire great tradition but rather at those members who continue to support the interests of the elite and the State. A closer examination of the forms of profanation and resistance in the Nicaraguan and Salvadoran churches will allow us to understand this phenomenon more fully.

REVERSAL OF GREAT TRADITION BELIEFS

LIBERATION THEOLOGY

The alternative worldview takes a number of forms consistent with Scott's theory. First, the popular church began articulating religious beliefs that reversed great-tradition teachings. These biblical beliefs of the poor were expressed within what has become known as liberation theology. This theology went far beyond Vatican II and Medellín as a radical theological system that challenged the great tradition by assigning different meanings or reversing orthodox Christian teachings (Smith 1991: 25–50). A brief review of liberation theology's key tenets will illustrate how these changes facilitated popular-church revolt. First, a central premise is that *theology must be contextual.* There is no timelessly-true or culturally-neutral theology. Rather, theology must be culturally relevant and cannot be separated from its socio-economic and political contexts (Gutierrez 1973; Segundo 1976). Imported European theology did not fit the political experiences of Latin America in the mid-1960s and so was recreated to correspond to its circumstances—this exemplifies the "slippage" Scott discusses. One popular church participant put it this way (quoted in Golden 1991: 64):

> For many the teachings of the church are immutable dogmas. They are self-evident truths, set in stone, that no one can change. We don't believe in unchangeable absolute truths. World history—the history of nations, of human development—is always in flux, and it is that unfolding history itself that helps clear up things little by little. The church of the poor is a church that is always creating. It's not satisfied to remain stuck in the past.

A second premise of liberation theology is that God makes a *"preferential option for the poor."* While the popular church does believe that God loves both the rich and the poor, it also sees that the rich have created oppressive structural sin. Through capitalism, the rich have exploited the poor and caused their suffering. In response, God chooses the side of the poor in their struggle for liberation (Boff and Boff 1987; Gutierrez 1983). Hence the concept of sin takes on a new meaning in popular religion. In the great tradition, "sin" is usually understood as personal, individual wrongdoing—liberation theology indicted structural oppression as sin. This comports with Scott's position that "the major transformations which have done violence to peasant life—the imposition of law or custom, the incursions of the market and agrarian capitalism—also reappear as part of the definition of present evil" (1977: 227). Capitalism, according to liberation theology, is the element that has most threatened peasant life in Latin America, and is therefore labeled "sin."

Third, liberation theology maintains that *salvation is an historical and social project of God*. In striking contrast to the great-tradition teaching that salvation is a personal reward given to a Christian in the afterlife, the little tradition holds that there is only one reality and one history and that salvation comes in *this world*. The kingdom of God is an ambition for a just society in this lifetime, not a reward to be obtained after death. Such utopian visions, according to Scott, consist of reversals of the social inequities and injustices of this world. God's kingdom is a place where there are no classes, private property, or ruling elite. The salvation message is changed to mean a human liberation in the present, instigated by popular church adherents. This transformed understanding of salvation means that the Christian mission no longer consists only of proselytizing souls, but also of establishing social justice. Salvation work consists of eliminating oppressive social, economic, and political conditions through protest, raising awareness, and subversion (Boff and Boff 1984; Bonino 1975; Gutierrez 1973; Levine 1986). Two Salvadoran women, who are members of the popular church, articulated these ideas forcefully (quoted in Golden 1991: 43, 98):

> This book of God is subversive because it turns the tortilla over, because it throws down the order of kings and empires and puts the poor on top.... This book taught us that we, the poor, are the preferred ones of God, that God wants the poor to stop being poor and that God calls us to work to change things.

> I believe that we have a responsibility as the church of the poor and as Christians to be immersed in the revolution; this is a way of getting closer to what all Christians desire, the Reign of God. I think that a Christian who is not part of this revolutionary process is also not part of the search for the Reign of God.

FOLK ART

Scott argues that symbolic opposition to the State will often find expression through folk life and peasant culture. The ideas of liberation theology and religious resistance to Central American military regimes were indeed evident in folk art. Perhaps the best known political artwork was produced in the 1960s–70s in Solentiname, an archipelago of thirty-eight islands in Lake Nicaragua where a base Christian community of ninety families began. The community members, almost all peasants, painted and crafted woodcarvings that depicted scenes from the life of Christ embedded in a distinctly Nicaraguan context, with clear messages against the dictator Somoza. For example, those who crucified Christ are portrayed in Solentiname artwork as National Guard soldiers and Somoza supporters. Other paintings portray the resurrection of Christ in which, after conquering death, Christ reappears in a black and red cape—Sandinista colors—which bears the letters FSLN, the Sandinista National Liberation Front. The resurrection is symbolically and literally connected to the political and economic victory the FSLN was struggling to obtain (Scharper and Scharper 1984).

MUSIC
The Nicaraguan little tradition also expressed opposition to Somoza through its religious music. For example, Carlos Mejia Godoy, a FSLN supporter, wrote a mass that was sung throughout the popular church. Known as the "Misa Campesina Nicaraguense" (Nicaraguan peasant mass), it clearly articulated the resistance of the popular church and the alternative worldview of the poor (Kirk 1992; Sölle 1990: 114–15):

> You are the God of the poor,
> The human and simple God,
> The God who sweats in the street,
> The God with a tanned (dirty) face....
> You are the laborer God, the worker Christ.
>
> You go hand in hand with my people,
> Struggle in the countryside and city,
> Get in line in the camp,
> So that they pay you your day's wage.
> You eat snowcones there in the street
> With Eusebio, Pancho, and Juan Jose
> And even protest about the syrup
> When they don't add much honey.
>
> I've seen you in the general store,
> Installed in a shack,
> I've seen you in the gas stations,
> Checking the tires of a truck
> And even patrolling highways
> With leather gloves and overalls.
>
> Christ, Christ Jesus, identify with us.
> Be in solidarity with us,
> Not the oppressor class
> That squeezes and devours but with the oppressed one,
> With my people, who thirst for peace.

The worker class
That from its beginning
Looks for its labor
From the plowed land
Sings to you,
From each scaffold
And even from the tractor,
Masons, carpenters,
Tailors, day laborers,
All equally,
Blacksmiths and longshore workers,
And the shoe shiners of Central Park....

I believe in you, comrade
Human Christ, worker Christ,
You are resurrecting in each arm that rises up
In order to defend the people
Against the exploitation of the rulers.
You are alive and present in the hut,
In the factory, in the school.
I believe in your ceaseless struggle,
I believe in your resurrection.

In El Salvador's popular church, music also was a means of expressing resistance against both the conservative clergy and the government. Hymns also helped emphasize self-worth and the necessity of organizing. The following was sung frequently in base Christian community meetings in El Salvador (Galdamez 1986: 36):

When the poor believe in the poor,
That's when we'll be free to sing....
When the poor seek out the poor,
And we're all for organization,
Then will come our liberation.

PROFANATIONS OF SACRED RITUALS AND THEMES

As Scott suggests, the little tradition may also intentionally profane or alter religious rituals to protest the established order. Numerous examples of such profanations can be found in the practice of the Central American popular church. Baptism, for example, frequently acquired a different meaning. Randall (1983: 32) described one such baptism in Nicaragua:

[The priest] explained the meaning of the ceremony, applying the reinterpretation of liberation theology. "We know that original sin consists of society's division into classes.... Let all selfishness, capitalism, Somozism, go out of this little girl," as he touched the girl's forehead with water.

An additional form of profanation can be seen in the widespread application of sainthood in ordinary life. Sainthood was at times stretched beyond the church's formal canon of those who show preeminent holiness and godliness. For example, cars, buses, and homes often had decals of the Virgin Mary and Catholic saints next to portraits of Augusto Sandino, Che Guevara, and Camilo Torres—a Colombian priest killed in combat after joining the guerrillas (Levine 1990).

EGALITARIAN STRUCTURES AS A REVERSAL OF ELITE AND CHURCH STRATIFICATION

Another tactic of little-tradition protest is to contrast the structure and values of orthodox religion with opposite structures in local peasant institutions. The Central American popular churches in the 1960s and 70s were, in many respects, a negation of the Roman Catholic hierarchy. They were not concerned, in Lernoux's words (1987), about the Vatican's "institutional clutter of ecclesiastical pomp and rank. Everyone was equal." The great tradition had historically remained at a distance from the peasants. Their dress, speech, and lifestyle emphasized distance, and the poor regarded the clergy and bishops as semi-mystical figures who could only be approached with great deference. In contrast, the priests involved in the popular church were called by their first names. They lived among the people, dressed in a similar manner, and shopped at the same stores (Levine 1990).

In addition, the format of popular church worship services was radically restructured. Priests had previously been the only ones allowed to interpret scripture and administer the sacraments. Within the popular church, the priests' homilies were replaced by group dialogue. The Bible was read and the poor would discuss its meaning for their lives (Cardenal 1984; Levine 1990). Furthermore, lay people were commissioned and trained to lead worship and prayers when priests were not able to attend. Due to the great shortage of priests, pastoral centers were opened to train thousands of catechists and lay "Delegates of the Word" during the 1970s. These lay leaders took on increasing responsibility for tasks previously performed by ordained priests. In some cases, they have even performed baptisms and marriages (Boff 1984; Lernoux 1980).

The little tradition also brought equity to the popular church by allowing lay and religious women to take on leadership roles in the church, which official Catholicism resisted. In El Salvador, for example, women formed their own alternative religious orders. These orders were treated by the Vatican as illegitimate since they pronounced their vows to the base Christian communities—referred to as CEBs from the Spanish term, *comunidades eclesiales de base*—rather than to the ecclesial authorities of the Vatican. Progressive Archbishop Oscar Romero, however, endorsed and blessed these independent orders of nuns. These vowed women also took on tasks that previously had been the exclusive domain of priests. One Salvadoran Sister (quoted in Golden 1991: 55) stated:

> We have offered sacraments in those areas where the people have no priests. Why not? I want to be very honest with you. Yes, I celebrate Mass. We have brought a tortilla, blessed it and shared it with the people. I want to be honest but if our local bishop finds out we'll be excommunicated at once.

REFUSAL TO GRANT DEFERENCE TO THE CHURCH HIERARCHY

While the popular church in both Nicaragua and El Salvador since the 1960s was supported by a significant portion of parish priests and nuns, most of the Church hierarchy viewed popular-church activism as a threat. With the notable exception of Archbishop Romero of El Salvador and his successor, Arturo Rivera y Damas, most bishops tried to suppress these religious acts of political protest. Nicaragua's hierarchy, under the leadership of Archbishop Obando y Bravo, did not support the movement to oust Somoza until the final weeks of the insurrection, when even the elite and business sectors had turned against Somoza. After the revolution, the hierarchy became one of the most outspoken critics of the Sandinista government. Thus, popular church resistance occasionally took the form of refusing to grant deference to church leaders who were seen as supporting the military regime of El Salvador or who did not support the Nicaraguan revolution.

When Salvadoran Archbishop Oscar Romero, who was considered the "voice of the voiceless" and an outspoken advocate of the poor, was assassinated in March 1980 while conducting Mass, many in the popular church refused at his funeral to grant the deference that was normally accorded church leaders. They considered the other members of the hierarchy to be allies of the oligarchy by not choosing the "option for the poor." At Romero's funeral, a group of priests, nuns, and lay workers in the popular church began a fast to protest the killing, and they hung a large banner on the cathedral of San Salvador announcing that the four conservative bishops, the papal nuncio, and the U.S. ambassador were not welcome. The only one of Salvador's six bishops who was welcomed was Rivera y Damas, who supported the popular church (Libby 1983).

The same refusal to grant deference was apparent in Nicaragua during the Pope's 1983 visit. The Vatican had expressed concern that the popular church was getting out of hand and was too closely aligned with the revolutionary Sandinista party. The Pope's visit was intended to reassert the power of the church hierarchy and support the bishops who opposed the Sandinistas. Members of the popular church were deeply disappointed with his approach and refused to show the respect normally given the head of the Catholic faith. Randall described the encounter between the great and little tradition (1983: 33–34):

> We knew that the Pope was coming to give the Nicaraguan bishops a shot in the arm, to criticize "priests in [the revolutionary] government" and to bolster the counter-revolution. But we had no idea it would be as bad as it was. Everything was compounded by the fact that the day before the Pope's visit there was a mass burial of seventeen young Sandinistas.... The next day, beginning with the Pope's initial address to the government and the people at the airport, it was clear that he had come to lecture and not to listen.... Father Ernesto Cardenal, poet and Minister of Culture, was on the reception line with his cabinet colleagues. When John Paul came to where he stood, a short exchange took place.... Ernesto fell to his knees and tried to kiss the Pope's hand. What the head of the Catholic faith had said was, "You'd better put your relationship with the church in order...." The day culminated in Managua with an outdoor mass in the July 19 Plaza, an event attended by an estimated 800,000 people (one-fifth of the

country's population). The day before 10,000 had gathered in the same square to pay tribute to the young Sandinistas who had died. Friends wanted the Pope to understand what was happening in Nicaragua, to feel their pain, to sympathize with their desire for a principled peace. But he refused. The mothers of the most recent victims [of the Contra War], standing up front, held photos of their sons for the Pope to see. But all they received was his angry cry "Silence".... His inappropriate sermon was then increasingly interrupted by the people shouting "People Power, People Power, People Power."

REPRESSION AGAINST THE POPULAR CHURCH

As the popular church's resistance became increasingly overt, church and governmental authorities understood this little tradition's potential for disruption, and responded with repression and reassertion of authority. Pope John Paul II, for example, spoke out strongly against the church of the poor, calling it an "internal enemy" and accusing it of being "highly dangerous precisely for being internal to the Church, responsible for the main conflicts within the Church and for diverse acts of aggressions against orthodoxy and ecclesial unity" (quoted in Melendez 1992: 556). The Pope also adamantly emphasized the importance of "ecclesial identity as an attachment to both orthodoxy and hierarchical ecclesiastical power" (quoted in Melendez 1992: 555).

In Nicaragua in the 1970s and El Salvador in the 1970s–80s, the military dictatorships also severely repressed the popular church for being the instigators of popular mobilization and new political awareness among the poor. The Nicaraguan dictator, Somoza, often targeted church-trained leaders and clergy in his attacks against the population. In particular, an organization known as CEPAD (Center for Rural Education and Development) had been established by Jesuits, who trained "Delegates" to lead worship in their Christian communities and teach basic agricultural skills. These individuals eventually constituted a nation-wide network of Delegates who could coordinate and support local peasant actions. During 1975, Somoza declared martial law and instigated a wave of repression that targeted CEPAD, among other groups. By mid-1977, the repression had become so severe that it had to operate semi-clandestinely (Berryman 1984: 71). By that point many CEPAD-trained leaders had joined the FSLN.

In the Zelaya province of Nicaragua, Capuchin priests had also trained nine-hundred Delegates. The training included discovering respect for the dignity of the poor and learning to organize and work together to change their conditions. As Berryman (1984: 70–1) put it, "This process was not aimed at moving the peasants to take up arms against the dictatorship but to develop a critical judgement, getting beyond fatalism." The Capuchins collected data on the repression suffered by the people in this region. One documented case was the village of Sofano, which was attacked by the National Guard in February 1976. The Guard came with a list of names, and moved from one home to the next, taking out the men, beating and torturing them in front of their families, and demanding that they give names of guerrilla supporters in the area. The men were then taken into the fields and executed. Many women and children were also killed, including an 8-year-old boy who was hanged and decapitated. Within two years, the Capuchins documented three-hundred and fifty people who had been killed or disappeared

(Berryman 1984). Many of these were Delegates of the Word and CEB participants.

In El Salvador, repression was aimed more directly at the church. One of the first attacks against a priest was in April 1970, when Father José Alas was kidnapped and beaten hours after he presented the official position of the archdiocese in support of agrarian reform. Two years later, Father Nicolas Rodriguez was killed by the Salvadoran National Guard, and in 1975 Father Rafael Barahona was captured and tortured (Montgomery 1982). A more severe wave of repression against the church began in 1977. Father Rutilio Grande, a priest who had been central in the development of base Christian communities in his parish of Aguilares, was gunned down in March 1977 by the military on his way to say evening Mass. That same month the army undertook a military sweep of Aguilares, attacking the parish house, beating priests, and violently dragging people out of their homes. Some were assaulted simply for possessing pictures of Father Grande. In fact, the security forces named the attack "Operation Rutilio." Troops then occupied the church, turning it into barracks (Berryman 1986). One month later, Father Alfonso Navarro was murdered in his parish. Between February 21 and May 14 of that year, ten priests were exiled, eight expelled, and two arrested and tortured (Montgomery 1982: 218–19).

Shortly after the attack on Aguilares and Father Grande, a paramilitary death squad known as the White Warriors announced that the remaining Jesuits had thirty days to leave the country or they would be murdered. Anonymous pamphlets were circulated urging people to "Be a patriot! Kill a priest!" The Jesuit University in San Salvador was bombed six times and the Church's weekly newspaper, *Orientación*, was also bombed several times. The repression against the popular church and its leaders continued in the succeeding years with the assassination of Archbishop Romero in March of 1980, the rape and murder of four North American church women in December 1980, and later the brutal murder of six Jesuit priests and their housekeepers at the Central American University in November 1989. In addition, thousands of church workers and Delegates had disappeared, been arrested and tortured, or killed (Berryman 1986, Lernoux 1980, Melendez 1992; Montgomery 1982; Prendes 1983).

FROM BASE CHRISTIAN COMMUNITIES TO MILITARY MOBILIZATION

The popular church paid dearly for its progressive stance and empowerment of the masses. Yet the military regimes of Nicaragua and El Salvador were unable to crush the church. On the contrary, the repression appears to have further strengthened and radicalized members of the popular church. Levine (1990: 335) notes that repression worsens life conditions, thereby pushing more people into opposition, determined to change these conditions. Many may join the popular church as a means of expressing resistance if they do not perceive other outlets available to them within the political structure. Thus repression can spur growth of the little tradition, but only, he cautions, if the church has already made efforts to empower the poor and support their actions. A closer examination of two base communities, one in Nicaragua and one in El Salvador, will elucidate the process whereby the communities became radicalized and eventually joined the insurrection against the dictatorships.

SOLENTINAME, NICARAGUA

Perhaps the best known base Christian community experience in Nicaragua occurred in Solentiname. Founded by Father Ernesto Cardenal in 1965, the community, located in the southern part of Lake Nicaragua, was quite poor and isolated. In his masses, Cardenal would invite the congregation to bring their wisdom and insights into the discussion of the Scripture reading. Over several years, these conversations grew more radical as the political and social climate in Nicaragua worsened and as repression increased. Many young members of the community concluded that conditions would not change until Somoza left and Nicaragua's entire political and economic system was restructured. Their experience in the base communities had convinced them that their oppression was not God's will, and that the Gospel, interpreted through a perspective of liberation, justified their decision to join the FSLN.

In October 1977, a group of young people from the Solentiname joined the Sandinistas and participated in an attack on the National Guard barracks in San Carlos, on the southeastern coast of the lake. They had intended to persuade the soldiers to desert, but when the Sandinistas surrounded the barracks, the Guard began firing at them. When the shooting ceased, a Solentiname member named Alejandro Guevara was ordered to burn the barracks. When he entered, however, he found several soldiers who had been wounded and was unable to burn them alive; so they withdrew. But the following day the National Guard retaliated by burning the Solentiname community, forcing the people into exile or to flee into the mountains (Montgomery 1983: 84).

Solentiname is only one example, yet many Christian base community members also joined popular organizations and, eventually, militant groups. The FSLN did not have a Party structure through which they could work, and these CEBs often served as an organizational base and a place to meet and talk with young people. Many of the youth worked in the parishes and communities, networking for resistance against the Somoza regime. As one priest stated, "In a sense, the parish replaced Lenin's idea of a cell" (Marchetti 1982: 45). This alliance between base community members and the FSLN solidified further during the insurrection, as Christians continued to work for the revolution in a variety of capacities. Members of CEBs sheltered FSLN combatants in their homes. A Capuchin priest transferred a Sandinista commander to Managua as well as Bluefields, a city on the east coast, disguised as a seminary student from Costa Rica. The Sisters of Christ in Siuna received ammunition and medical aid by air and transferred them to the Sandinistas (Berryman 1984: 88). The participation of popular-church members in the revolution was so significant that the Sandinistas published a Communique on Religion shortly after their triumph in which they acknowledge the role of Christians in the revolution, who "preached and practiced their faith in conjunction with the needs for liberating our people" (FSLN 1979: 1–2).

SUCHITOTO, EL SALVADOR

The process of radicalization of Christians followed a similar process in El Salvador. The promotion of CEBs was more systematic and organized, however, and the first half of the 1970s was called "the flourishing of the Christian communities" (Prendes 1983: 275). In Suchitoto, Father José Inocencio Alas began to form CEBs in 1968, and within a few months, thirty-two communities were functioning. Alas held courses on Biblical and socio-political themes in these CEBs. By 1969, the communities became socially active when two wealthy landowners bought local land and announced that they would sell small parcels of it for private-enterprise initiatives. The price they asked for the land, however, was a three-hundred to seven-hundred percent increase over the initial purchase price. Peasants were outraged, since they had been promised a reasonable price and they organized a demonstration of three-thousand in front of the farm. The landowners did not change their position so four-hundred peasants demonstrated at the National Assembly in San Salvador. As a result of their action, the Assembly passed a law requiring landowners not to sell the land for more than one-hundred percent profit. This action was conducted by the CEBs in Suchitoto, not the popular organizations or unions (Montgomery 1983: 85).

The work of Suchitoto's CEBs continued, and in April, 1974, Father Alas and a group of lay leaders met with representatives of student groups, teacher organizations, and labor unions to form the first mass popular organization: the United Popular Action Front (FAPU). The formation of FAPU was the first explicit case in Latin American history in which a mass, revolutionary organization was directly formed out of the experience of the church (Montgomery 1982: 213).

In addition, the growth of other popular organizations in El Salvador was a direct result of the leadership training of Delegates and consciousness-raising of the poor. Seven training centers had been created throughout the country within a decade, and approximately fifteen thousand catechists and Delegates received instruction on leading Bible studies and liturgy, public speaking, and agriculture and health care. Montgomery (1982: 220) claims that "dozens, if not hundreds, of revolutionary leaders acquired their organizational skills through training as Delegates and catechists." Perhaps the best known is Juan Chacón, a catechist who was the Secretary General of the Popular Revolutionary Bloc (BPR). This is not surprising, since three-hundred pastoral agents had met in January, 1976 for the Pastoral Week of the Archdiocese and had committed themselves to work for human rights, as well as to create more CEBs that would promote an awareness of how the poor could bring about social change. Therefore, as Bishop Rivera stated, it was natural that "as repression increased the social and political consciousness, a good percentage of the best among the Delegates of the Word joined the rank and file of the peasant organizations FECCAS [Christian Federation of Peasants] and UTC [Union of Rural Workers]" (quoted in Prendes 1983: 278).

In both countries, the popular church served as an organizational structure which combined the vocabulary and culture of resistance with a framework for developing skills, raising a critical awareness, and training lay leaders. The CEBs helped empower people at the local level, which was transmitted to social action at the national level, eventually resulting in participation in revolutionary movements.

FACTORS FACILITATING POPULAR CHURCH REVOLT

Reflecting on the elements of little-tradition protest present in the Nicaraguan and Salvadoran popular churches, we see several factors that appear essential in mobilizing the little tradition into an effective force for social change. First, the little tradition moved from small heresies to revolt once they gained the loyalty and allegiance of a number of great-tradition members. The clergy who were "converted" by the poor facilitated the protest, encouraging peasants actively to change their society as an expression of their religious faith. They also articulated these ideas in formal theological language, granting legitimacy to the little tradition and helping to further disseminate the ideas through church conferences, pastoral institutes, and documents (Smith 1991). Priests and nuns were the critical interface between the popular church and the hierarchy. Hence, their conversion to the worldviews of the little tradition began the undermining of the great tradition's hegemony and the strengthening of the alternative worldview.

Second, the egalitarian structure of the people's church was essential for empowering a sector of the population that did not otherwise have opportunities to develop leadership skills for organizing a political movement. Participation in the popular church was widespread, and many experienced democracy for the first time within these local structures. Skills gained through leadership roles led to the emergence of peasant leaders—what Gramsci called "organic intellectuals." Evidence indicates that many popular organizations and labor unions came into being through the influence of popular church members and Delegates of the Word (Adriance 1991; Eckstein 1989; Millman 1988; Ruchwarger 1987).

Third, the development of egalitarian structures in the popular church was furthered by a shortage of clergy. Scott argues that the little tradition is egalitarian because it desires to be the opposite of the stratified society it opposes; the lack of great tradition leaders may additionally propel the poor into leadership out of necessity. Latin America has had a severe shortage of priests; in some regions there are ten-thousand parishioners per priest, and they simply were not able to keep pace with the flourishing popular church (Barbé 1987; Smith 1991). This encouraged lay people to take on ecclesiastic responsibilities.

A fourth important influence was the developing "structure of support" for popular church perspectives. Gramsci argued that while peasants might not understand all of the intellectual justifications of a new worldview, they would become convinced that justifications do exist, since "so many like-thinking people can't be wrong" (Gramsci 1971: 339). Popular-church rituals and liturgy, such as the Nicaraguan peasant mass, helped to affirm this alternative view and eradicate the sense of isolation. Archbishop Romero's weekly mass quickly became the single most listened-to radio program in El Salvador; it also helped affirm the popular church's struggle and legitimated their militancy (Berryman 1986; Montgomery 1982). Perhaps the most fundamental aspect of support was the encouragement, largely unintentional, given by the church hierarchy through Vatican II and the Medellín conference. The documents that emerged from these meetings supported the interests of the poor as well as their right to be agents of change and to protest injustice.

Finally, the presence of established opposition movements which had viable chances of overthrowing the State was crucial in drawing popular church adherents into overt revolt. The popular church in Nicaragua often lacked protection from the hierarchical church and was persecuted by Somoza's National Guard; consequentially, its members forged strong links with the FSLN. Their new religious identity emerged somewhat simultaneously with their revolutionary political consciousness. Thus, religious resistance was able to merge with the broader political movement (Dodson 1984). A similar situation developed in El Salvador's popular church and the central revolutionary group, the Farabundo Martí National Liberation Front (FMLN). Popular church clergy in Salvador took the lead when they stated that the FMLN constituted, for political purposes, the "authentic representatives" of the Salvadoran people. As many as seven priests joined the FMLN guerrillas, and at least one was a commander. This facilitated the merging of the popular church and the political opposition (Montgomery 1982).

In view of these five conditions, the Nicaraguan and Salvadoran cases suggest that the popular church mobilized revolt when it combined elements of both the great and little traditions. The little tradition's symbolic opposition to dominant values provided the cultural basis and worldview which encouraged resistance among the poor. The great tradition's involvement helped establish political opportunities and a "structure of support" through which skills could be developed and "organic intellectuals" could emerge. The opposition of the popular church and members of the clergy fostered a blending of the two church traditions from which a distinct hybrid tradition developed. This hybrid tradition was more powerful, since it provided an interaction between the classes, empowered the poor, and granted legitimacy to alternative religious views. This hybrid tradition gave the poor a structure through which their collective strength could be organized, leadership skills could be developed, and their ideas could be affirmed.

CONCLUSION

The examination of religious opposition to the State in Nicaragua and El Salvador offers some important contributions to sociological understanding of religion and disruptive politics. First, these cases confirm Gramsci's assertion—contrary to orthodox Marxism—that cultural expressions do not merely reflect the material base; they are semi-autonomous and therefore can affect the base as well. Hence, religion can be either a force for social change or a legitimation of the status quo.

Furthermore, these cases show that, while James Scott makes an important contribution to understanding the role of the little tradition in political resistance, his theory is incomplete. He discusses the various forms of everyday resistance and states that it can become the basis of revolt, but he fails to identify the factors that move the little tradition beyond "small heresies." We have seen in Nicaragua and El Salvador that the blending of the little tradition's culture of resistance with the great tradition's structure of support can lead to a hybrid popular church that enables acts of everyday resistance to develop into organized revolt. While the popular churches in Nicaragua and El Salvador are similar to the little traditions that have emerged throughout Latin America, there clearly remains the need to assess these theoretical propositions, to test their validity in other contexts.

Popular religion is often a neglected, but extremely important factor in understanding the oppositional capacity of religion, particularly in societies experiencing civil and class conflicts. Religion is an important part of peasant and working-class culture, especially in Latin America. These religious-cultural expressions of resistance ought not to be neglected when examining factors that instigate revolt among subordinated classes.

REFERENCES

Adriance, M. 1991. "Agents of Change: The Roles of Priests, Sisters, and Lay Workers in the Grassroots Catholic Church in Brazil." *Journal for the Scientific Study of Religion.* 30:3 (September): 292–305.

Barbé, D. 1987. *Grace and Power: Base Communities and Nonviolence in Brazil.* Maryknoll, NY: Orbis Books.

Berryman, P. 1986. "El Salvador: From Evangelization to Insurrection" in *Religion and Political Conflict in Latin America,* ed. D. Levine. Chapel Hill, NC: University of North Carolina Press.

_____. 1984. "Basismo and the Horizon of Change: A View from Central America."*Journal of Interamerican Studies and World Affairs* 26 (1): 125–129.

_____. 1984. *The Religious Roots of Rebellion: Christians in the Central American Revolutions.* Maryknoll, NY: Orbis Books.

_____. 1984. "Basic Christian Communities and the Future of Latin America." *Monthly Review* 36 (3): 27–40.

Billings, D. 1990. "Religion as Opposition: A Gramscian Analysis." *American Journal of Sociology* 96: 1–31.

Boff, C. 1984. *Feet-on-the-Ground Theology.* Maryknoll, NY: Orbis Books.

Boff, L. and C. Boff. 1984. *Salvation and Liberation: In Search of a Balance Between Faith and Politics.* Maryknoll, NY: Orbis Books.

_____. 1987. *Introducing Liberation Theology.* Maryknoll, NY: Orbis Books.

Bonino, J. 1975. *Doing Theology in a Revolutionary Situation.* Maryknoll, NY: Orbis Books.

Candelaria, M. 1990. *Popular Religion and Liberation: The Dilemma of Liberation Theology.* Albany: State University of New York Press.

del Rio, E. 1982. *Nicaragua for Beginners.* New York: Writers and Readers Publishing Cooperative.

Dodson, M. 1984. "Comparing the Popular Church in Nicaragua and Brazil." *Journal of Interamerican Studies and World Affairs* 26 (1): 131–136.

Durkheim, E. 1947, *Elementary Forms of Religious Life.* Glencoe, IL: Free Press.

Eckstein, S. 1989. *Power and Popular Protest: Latin American Social Movements.* Berkeley: University of California Press.

FSLN (Sandinista National Liberation Front). 1979. "Communique on Religion." Managua, Nicaragua.

Fulton, J. 1987. "Religion and Politics in Gramsci: An Introduction." *Sociological Analysis* 48: 197–216.

Golden, R. 1991. *The Hour of the Poor, The Hour of Women: Salvadoran Women Speak.* New York: Crossroad.

Gramsci, A. 1971. *Selections from Prison Notebooks.* Q. Hoare and G.N. Smith (eds.). New York: International.

Gutierrez, G. 1983. *The Power of the Poor in History.* Maryknoll, NY: Orbis Books.

_____. 1973. *A Theology of Liberation.* Maryknoll, NY: Orbis Books.

Kirk, J. 1992. *Politics and the Catholic Church in Nicaragua.* Gainesville, FL: University of Florida Press.

Lernoux, P. 1987. "In Common Suffering and Hope." *Sojourners* 12: 22–28.

_____. 1980. *Cry of the People.* New York: Penguin Books.

Levine, D. 1990. "From Church and State to Religion and Politics and Back Again." *Social Compass* 37 (3): 331–351.

_____. 1990. "Popular Groups, Popular Culture, and Popular Religion. *Comparative*

_____. 1986. *Religion and Political Conflict in Latin America.* Chapel Hill, NC: University of North Carolina Press.

Libby, R. 1983. "Listen to the Bishops." *Foreign Policy* 52: 78–95.

Marchetti, P. 1982. "Church and Revolution in Nicaragua." *Monthly Review* July–August: 43–55.

Marx, K. and F. Engels. 1957. "Contribution to the Critique of Hegel's Philosophy of the Right." In *On Religion.* London: Lawrence & Wishart Ltd.

Melendez, G. 1992. "The Catholic Church in Central America: Into the 1990s." *Social Compass* 39 (4): 553–570.

Millman, J. 1988. "Nicaragua's Revolution Rests Largely on Scripture and Christian Base Communities." *In These Times* February–March: 79–83.

Montgomery, T. S. 1983. "Liberation and Revolution: Christianity as a Subversive Activity in Central America." In *Trouble in Our Backyard*, ed. M. Diskin. New York: Pantheon Books.

_____. 1982. "Cross and Rifle: Revolution and the Church in El Salvador and Nicaragua." *Journal of Interamerican Affairs* 36 (2): 209–221.

Parsons, T. 1964. "Christianity and Modern Industrial Society." In *Religion, Culture, and Society*, ed. L. Schneider. New York: Wiley.

Prendes, J. C. 1983. "Revolutionary Struggle and Church Commitment: The Case of El Salvador." *Social Compass* 2: 261–298.

Randall, M. 1983. *Christians in the Nicaraguan Revolution.* Vancouver: New Star Books.

Redfield, R. 1961. *Peasant Society and Culture.* Chicago: University of Chicago Press.

Ruchwarger, G. 1987. *People in Power: Forging a Grassroots Democracy in Nicaragua.* South Hadley, MA: Bergin and Garvey.

Scharper, P. and S. Scharper. 1984. *The Gospel in Art By the Peasants of Solentiname.* Maryknoll, NY: Orbis Books.

Schoenfeld, E. 1992. "Militant and Submissive Religions: Class, Religion, and Ideology." *British Journal of Sociology* 43: 111–140.

Scott, J. 1977. "Protest and Profanation: Agrarian Revolt and the Little Tradition." (Parts I & II). *Theory and Society* 4: 1–38 and 211–246.

Segundo, J. L. 1976. *The Liberation of Theology.* Maryknoll, NY: Orbis Books.

Simon, J. L. 1981. "Tensions in Nicaraguan Church Over Revolutionary Process." *Latinamerican Press.* December 10: 78.

Smith, C. 1991. *The Emergence of Liberation Theology: Radical Religion and Social Movement Theory.* Chicago: University of Chicago Press.

Sölle, D. 1990. *Thinking About God.* Maryknoll, NY: Orbis Books.

Westhues, K. 1976. "The Church in Opposition." *Sociological Analysis* 37: 299–314.

Wilson, B. 1982. *Religion in Sociological Perspective.* New York: Oxford University Press.

Wuthnow, R. 1973. "Religious Commitment and Conservatism." In *Religion in Sociological Perspective*, ed. Glock. Belmont, CA: Wadsworth.

Zwerling, P. and C. Martin. 1985. *Nicaragua—A New Kind of Revolution.* Westport, CT: Lawrence Hill & Co.

6

Church Leadership, State Repression, and the "Spiral Of Involvement" in the South African Anti-apartheid Movement, 1983–1990

Tristan Anne Borer

On April 27, 1994, millions of South Africans, of all racial and class backgrounds, voted in that country's first democratic election, ending forty-five years of apartheid rule and more than three hundred years of segregated rule. The 1994 election swept to power by an overwhelming majority the African National Congress (ANC), the African continent's oldest liberation movement. The apartheid system, established in 1948, was a highly institutionalized system of segregation, accompanied by massive human rights abuses. Under this system, black South Africans, who comprise eighty-seven percent of the population, were forced to live on only thirteen percent of the land. At the time of birth, each individual was classified according to one of four racial groups—whites, coloreds, Indians, and Africans. This racial categorization determined all aspects of a person's life from the time of birth until death—including residency, education, occupation, health benefits, even where one could be buried. In the 1970s, the South African government spent fourteen times as much on the education of a white child as on that of an African child. Through the creation of ethnically separate "homelands," black South Africans were stripped of their citizenship, and forced to travel long distances to "white" South Africa, where they often worked. There they were deprived of all civil and human rights, and were subject to massive harassment by the South African government. Until 1994, no black had the right to vote or to be represented in the government. Those who dared to protest these human rights abuses were subject to repression, torture, and, often, death.

This system spawned a highly organized and well-funded transnational social movement that worked to brand the South African State an international pariah, and to establish international sanctions to end this regime. In addition, South Africa's domestic liberation movement gained strength in the 1970s and 80s, despite repression, forcing the apartheid regime to abandon its policies and enter into negotiations with the opposition. In order to understand the collapse of apartheid in 1990, one must take into account not only the success of the pro-sanctions movement, but also the growing strength of the domestic liberation movement. In particular, one must understand the role that church organizations played in this movement. Over seventy percent of South Africans are Christians, many of whom, through resistance and defiance, joined in the struggle against apartheid's racial and economic oppression.

This chapter examines how two church organizations—the South African Council of Churches (SACC) and the Southern African Catholic Bishops Conference (SACBC)—became increasingly politicized, through a process of spiraling involvement in civil society and increasing church-State conflict, to become two of the most important actors in the domestic anti-apartheid movement. As organizations, they intensified their overt political involvement, became active in the struggle to ensure the collapse of apartheid and the emergence of a democratic South Africa, and viewed this commitment as an integral part of their Christian mission. What began as relatively mild statements denouncing the government's human rights abuses evolved into a consistent pattern of overt political activity to bring the apartheid regime to an end. By the decade's close, mobilized Christians were in the forefront of the Anti-apartheid struggle, leading protest marches, boycotting elections, and meeting in solidarity with banned organizations at home and in exile. The process by which this evolution—from mildly protesting the government to challenging the State's right to exist—took place in these two organizations is the subject of this chapter.

Two characteristics of the South African political situation in the 1980s distinguish it from that of any preceding time and it was precisely these characteristics that contributed to the increasing activism of both SACC and the SACBC. The first was the *intensity of the opposition* to the government, predominantly through the United Democratic Front (UDF), with the diffusion of protest throughout all aspects of everyday life. As Price indicates, the uprisings of the 1980s were "more radical, more violent, more widespread, and more sustained than anything witnessed in modern South African history" (Price 1991: 152). This was not true for previous periods of protest. This intensity of protest in the 1980s was accompanied by an organizational sophistication that was unprecedented. The explosion of grass-roots organizations and their embrace of "alliance politics" laid the foundation for a nationwide liberation movement of such strength that the government was never able to fully control or extinguish it. Again, this characteristic was absent from every preceding period in South African political history. The second distinguishing characteristic of the 1980s was the *intensity of the South African State repression* in its attempts to quell the rising protest. The government's "systematic campaign of repression combined a number of elements that in both their intensity and combination were new to the South African scene" (Price 1991: 257).

It was to these two distinguishing characteristics that the SACC and SACBC responded, becoming increasingly politicized by being drawn into a "spiral of involvement." In the context of increasing repression, political expression by civil society became much more difficult. Churches and church leaders became vehicles for this expression, which engendered harassment or worse for church members. This, and the new levels of military and police brutality, led to the church denouncing the government which, in turn, set off a deeper spiral of even greater repression directed against the church by the State. In a reactive process, this reinforced even greater church involvement in politics, as the church increasingly came to see its responsibility as representing the interests of the majority of the people. Thus, while in the early 1980s, the SACC and SACBC were politically involved primarily at the level of denouncing repressive legislation and human rights abuses, by the late 1980s they had become actively politicized. This story begins in 1983, the year a new constitution was introduced to the country.

1983–1985

The promulgation of a new South African constitution jarred the SACC and SACBC into adopting a more overtly political level of involvement in the anti-apartheid struggle. For example, when, despite exhorting their constituents not to support the new constitution, sixty-six percent of voters in a whites-only referendum supported it, SACBC President, Archbishop Hurley (1984) attacked:

> We cannot accept the new constitution because, far from recognizing the right to participation of all in the economy, in politics, education and culture, it continues to enshrine the apartheid principle of separation...separate, unequal and powerless. Until the principle of genuine participation is recognised it is not possible to accept a constitution, nor is it right to expect those adversely affected to pay to an apartheid constitution the tribute of a vote that would appear to legitimate it.

The seeds of religious politicization were sown in speeches such as this, with their implicit support for acts of civil disobedience and passive resistance. In successive years, such moral support turned into active support as church leaders joined, and finally led campaigns of civil disobedience.

The move towards greater political engagement was also evident in the conference resolutions of both organizations. In 1983, the SACC began slowly moving beyond the making of mere statements to the passing of resolutions that actually required action by its members. It undertook, for example, a much more serious investigation of the feasibility and desirability of economic sanctions than it had previously, although at this stage it stopped short of calling for economic sanctions outright. The Council also increasingly supported such political acts as boycotting institutions, by calling on its member churches to, "encourage their membership to evaluate their participation in bodies, agencies, organizations and institutions that constantly undergird the unjust political apartheid system, and to refrain from such participation wherever practical" (SACC 1983a: Resolution 22).

Such statements by church leaders, as well as conference resolutions, were enough in and of themselves to incur the anger of the State against the SACC and the SACBC. The church-State conflict further escalated, however, when both organizations joined the UDF. Included among the original thirty organizations attending the Johannesburg launching of the UDF, which pledged to "fight together side by side against the Government's constitutional and reform proposals" (Harbor 1983), were the Witwatersrand branch of the SACC and the Johannesburg Justice and Peace Commission of the SACBC. In response, the State threatened Catholic Archbishop

Hurley with a warning to churches not to meddle in politics. Hurley was then charged and prosecuted for statements he made regarding alleged atrocities carried out by South African-trained security forces in Namibia, which further escalated the growing church-State conflict. The government also harassed other church workers, For example, Father Smangaliso Mkhatshwa, SACBC General Secretary, was forcibly detained barely four months after a banning order against him had been lifted.

Thus, by the end of 1983, several interrelated processes were at work that served to draw both the SACC and the SACBC into the social and political struggle in a deeper way. First, certain church leaders became increasingly aware of their own responsibility in speaking out against human rights abuses. Second, by acting upon these new convictions, these leaders provoked the anger of the State, which reacted by banning church reports and harassing church workers. Third, by 1983, as the State relied increasingly on the rule of force, leaders of the resurgent liberation movement were increasingly being detained, jailed, exiled, or killed. Consequently, the churches, though not eager to enter the political fray, steadily drifted into serving as the main vehicle for the expression of black political aspirations. They were increasingly called upon to provide leadership and articulation for black South Africans, the vast majority of whom were Christians. A final source of politicization was that several church leaders themselves became directly involved in the rekindled liberation movement. For example, Smangaliso Mkhatshwa, while General Secretary of the SACBC, was elected a UDF patron, and Frank Chikane, then General Secretary of the Institute for Contextual Theology and later General Secretary of the SACC, became vice-chairman of the Transvaal Branch of the UDF. Altogether, this changing political scene of the early 1980s led to spiraling involvement of the SACC and SACBC in confrontational politics.

The State responded to this increased politicization by investigating the SACC's finances, which evolved into a four-year-long, major harassment campaign against the Council. Known as the Eloff Commission of Inquiry into the South African Council of Churches, the investigation drew worldwide attention. That the government itself viewed the Inquiry as a response to the increasing politicization of the SACC and the need to silence it, was evident in this South African Police [SAP] statement (quoted in SACC 1984: 1–2):

> It is the task of the SAP to be on the alert against people or organisations which intend to bring about fundamental change in the South African political and economic system by unconstitutional means. The SACC is alleged to be an organisation of this nature.... Furthermore, the SACC covers up its work of "destabilising" South African society and the South African State by religious arguments and activities and by a particular type of theology.

In his oral testimony, the Chief of the Security Police, the State's key witness, alleged that the SACC was cooperating closely with and supporting the ANC, and accused especially Bishop Tutu of helping to improve the ANC's credibility. State charges that the SACC only spent a small percentage of its funding for theological purposes, and the money it did spend was not motivated by Christian compassion, but by political considerations. These charges only deepened the antagonism between the SACC and the government. During his testimony before the Commission, Bishop Desmond Tutu, then General Secretary of the SACC, responded (SACC 1983b: 5):

> If we have contravened any laws of the country, then you don't need a Commission to determine that. There is an array of draconian laws at the disposal of the Government, and the Courts of Law are the proper place to determine our guilt or innocence. This Commission, with respect, is totally superfluous.

Moreover, Tutu informed the Commission that he fully intended to defy the State, should it come to that: "I want to declare here as forthrightly as I can, that we will continue to do this work come hell or high water" (SACC 1983b: 29).

Through the Commission, the government attempted, by administrative means rather than through overtly political methods such as a trial, to curtail those activities of the SACC which it considered political. The government could have cracked down much more harshly against the SACC. However, in addition to the sensitive issue of religious freedom, the State did not want to further tarnish its global reputation, as worldwide attention during the Commission's hearings was focused on its repressive activities. Nevertheless, world sentiment regarding both the South African government and the SACC became clear when the Nobel Peace Prize was subsequently awarded to Bishop Tutu. This accolade and international approval of the SACC's activities served as a further impetus to politicization. This was clearly indicated in the SACC's response to the award, which it saw as "a call to all churchmen who were in doubt about Bishop Tutu and the SACC to confidently join hands and intensify the fight against apartheid and its evils, even if it means becoming so-called 'political priests'" (*ICT News* 1984: 5).

The second major "politicizing" event of 1984 was the publication of the joint SACBC/SACC report on forced removals in South Africa, entitled *Relocations*, which detailed the number of people forcibly removed by the apartheid regime, the repressive methods used by the government to achieve removal, and the deleterious effects on those forced to be internal refugees. The report pushed both organizations into greater confrontation with the State, because it specifically challenged the churches to act against this abuse of human rights, and encouraged them to accept their "responsibilities of working for radical social change of this socio-economic system." (SACC and SACBC 1984: 57). Both the SACC and SACBC pledged to resist further forced removals without specifying exactly how. The report drew tremendous attention, sold over twenty thousand copies within South Africa, and was translated into twelve languages, including nine African languages, as well as Swedish, Dutch, and German. Additionally, a joint SACC/SACBC delegation traveled to several countries, the United Nations, and the Vatican, briefing government and church officials and giving conferences on the report. The South African government was extremely displeased with the international attention generated by these actions.

Another issue that gained prominence in 1984, which eventually drew churches into the spiral of involvement, was the End Conscription Campaign (ECC). The Campaign was formed to protest the 1983 Defence Further Amendment Act, which recognized the principle of conscientious objection only for religious pacifists, while all other objectors were liable to a six-year prison term, substantially longer than the length of required military service. The State's narrow definition of conscientious objection, combined with the increasing use of the South African Defense Force to quell unrest within South Africa, especially after the imposition of the 1985 State of Emergency, sparked the October 1984 nationwide movement to abolish conscription.

As both the SACC and SACBC had strong histories of supporting conscientious objection, they naturally supported the ECC. Archbishop Hurley recognized that this support would anger the State (*Crisis News* 1988: 1):

> In the South African situation, conscientious objection should be adopted as a principle by the churches. I believe that the churches should adopt this view, even at the risk of open confrontation with the government. Confrontation has to occur some time.

Support for the ECC had a strong politicizing effect on the Catholic Bishop's Conference, because it led them to debate whether to declare the war in Namibia unjust—since many Catholic conscientious objectors used a just war argument at their hearing before the Board of Religious Objectors. This came to a head in the 1986 hearing of conscientious objector Philip Wilkinson, at which Archbishop Hurley testified. When asked point-blank whether he considered the activities of the South African Defense Force, both inside and outside South Africa, as constituting an unjust war, Hurley replied (CIIR 1988: 19), "Yes, personally I think that we are in a situation of an unjust war, promoted by the SADF as the armed-force of the South African Government against the oppressed people of South Africa."

By the end of 1984, both the SACC and SACBC were reevaluating their identities, and increasingly integrating a political dimension in their self-understandings. However, at this time, both organizations were still cautious, not yet willing to State publicly that they should play a role in the political transformation of South Africa. For example, in its response to the Eloff Commission Report, the SACC's Presidium, while denouncing the State's conceptualization of the role and mission of the SACC, nevertheless went to great lengths to deny that it was slowly becoming more politicized. Within a few years, however, as the political situation in South Africa deteriorated and the church-State conflict continued to grow, such caution—especially on the part of the SACC—was thrown to the wind. Soon, many church leaders and SACC office-holders were publicly calling for economic sanctions, actively supporting, and eventually participating in, acts of civil disobedience, and meeting with and declaring support for the exiled liberation movements.

1985–1988

In 1985, the political situation took another turn for the worse with the July imposition of a partial State of Emergency, which was renewed and widened in June 1986, and yet again in 1987. Once again, the SACC and SACBC's response to the changing political context spiraled those organizations into further political involvement. In the year following July 1985, almost twelve hundred political deaths were recorded and more than thirty thousand people had been detained. In November 1985, the UDF was declared an "affected" organization, meaning it was no longer eligible to receive foreign funding, thus bringing it more under State control. In this political context, the SACC and SACBC adopted a much more overtly political level of action.

Beyers Naudé, who had by this time taken over as General Secretary of the SACC, responded to the new political situation by urging member churches to take visible actions of resistance to the government, including well-planned acts of civil disobedience. He warned that the church would lose its credibility if its verbal criticism was not accompanied by non-violent actions to "break the power of an oppressive and unjust system and thereby bring it to its knees" (Nash 1985: 57). The Council responded to this call by issuing a resolution that for the first time officially called for "disinvestment and similar economic pressures," (still stopping short of using the term "economic sanctions"). Not only was this a much more overtly political stance on disinvestment than the SACC took during the Eloff Commission investigation, but this SACC resolution actually broke the law, in that, by this time, it had been declared illegal to even discuss economic sanctions. Any organization or individual who publicly supported sanctions was liable for a ten-year prison sentence, a R20,000 fine, or both. Nonetheless, Naudé reiterated his stance, stating that, "even if in advocating [disinvestment and economic sanctions], I have to go to jail, I plead for them, and I'll take the consequences for the sake of the future of our land" (Naudé 1985). Before the end of the SACC's 1985 Conference, Naudé received a message from the Minister of Law and Order, stating, "The present campaign which you are conducting to encourage civil disobedience can lead to illegality, licentiousness, confrontation with the authorities and eventually violence.... There is no lack of clarity regarding the implications contained in civil disobedience" (Nash 1985: 5).

Two other events in 1985 drew church organizations, especially the SACC, still further into the country's now tumultuous political struggle. The first was the September publication of *The Kairos Document*, and the second was the December consultation of church and political leaders held under the auspices of the World Council of Churches. The *Kairos Document* was the product of a group of some one hundred fifty-two South African theologians who came together to assess the way that churches were and should be involved in the political crisis. The document clearly challenged all church organizations to adopt an overtly political level of action, stating it was insufficient for churches to merely pray for a change of government. Rather, it stated, churches "should also mobilise their members in every parish to begin to think and work and plan for a change of government in South Africa." Churches were challenged actually to participate in acts of civil disobedience, in the full realization that if they took their responsibilities seriously in the present circumstances they would have to confront and disobey the State in order to obey God. The document criticized the SACC and SACBC for carrying out "mere ambulance ministry," not the "ministry of involvement and participation." The only way to rectify this was to wholeheartedly join in the struggle for liberation (Kairos 1985: 28–30).

South African church leaders took *The Kairos Document's* challenge to heart. In a dramatic show of civil disobedience, church leaders from all over the country participated in illegal protest marches. In a march in Cape Town led by Beyers Naudé and

Allan Boesak, for example, three hundred church leaders descended on Parliament to deliver a petition demanding that police be kept out of black townships and that the government speak to leaders chosen by the people. When the police arrived to break up the march, the procession knelt on the pavement and began singing hymns. Naudé, Boesak, and two hundred seventy others were arrested, although no charges were filed. Similarly, in Durban, Archbishop Hurley led a three hundred person-strong dawn procession, carrying a six-foot cross on his back, to a prison where UDF members accused of treason were being held (*Ecunews* 1985: 2–4).

Shortly thereafter, in December 1985, church leaders from South Africa and other countries, under the aegis of the World Council of Churches and the South African Council of Churches, held a consultation in Harare, Zimbabwe on the South African crisis. During this conference, representatives of political organizations and trade unions were invited to present to the churches their analyses of the root causes of the current crisis and their judgments about how to affect fundamental change. In the final session, the churches stated that they could no longer make a distinction between prayer and political action. While just a few years earlier, church leaders called on the government to reform its policies, the Harare Declaration now rejected this option as nonviable: "apartheid can in no way be reformed; we therefore reject categorically all proposals for modification of apartheid.... A radical break has to be made with the present." In order to accomplish this, the Declaration called for the churches inside and outside South Africa to support movements working for the liberation of their country, for an end to the State of Emergency, the release of Nelson Mandela and other political prisoners, and the repeal of the ban on all political movements. Most importantly, it also called on the international community to impose immediate and comprehensive economic sanctions and to refuse to refinance South Africa's foreign debt (*ICT News* 1986: 3).

The SACC responded to the challenge by adopting the Harare Declaration at its 1986 National Conference. With this, the SACC's stance on sanctions had shifted decisively, illustrating its increasing political commitment in the face of an intransigent apartheid regime. While it had refused to call for sanctions in 1984, with the partial State of emergency in 1985 it began calling for "disinvestment and economic pressure." By the time of the imposition of the nation-wide State of Emergency of 1986, it was ready to call for comprehensive sanctions as the only remaining non-violent method for ending apartheid and forcing the regime to negotiate.

Although the SACBC also became increasingly politicized on the sanctions issue, it always remained more cautious than the SACC. In their "Pastoral Letter on Economic Pressure for Justice," the bishops pronounced that, in their view, "economic pressure" was a morally justifiable means of bringing about an end to injustice which, when applied, should be qualified and selective and should be implemented in such a way as to not destroy the economy (SACBC 1986: 14). In the Letter's introduction, the bishops admitted that in the context of "the enormity of the present suffering of the oppressed people of South Africa and the horrifying specter of escalating violence," the time had come to be overtly political, and that a "prophetic calling requires us...to make a direct intervention in the affairs of our country" (SACBC *Bishops Speak* IV: 16).

Consequently, the church-State conflict escalated to a new level of intensity. In the face of mounting church pressure, the State hardened its attitude towards church activists. Whereas in early marches headed by clergy, while every effort was made to process and quickly release arrested religious participants—for example, the Cape Town march ended in the release of all two hundred sixty-seven arrested without bail—by the end of 1985, at another mass march, clergy were badly beaten, nuns were stripped and searched on arrival at prison, bail was denied, and clergy who arrived at court singing in the back of a police van were teargassed while still locked inside (Leatt 1987: 9). It became clear that a deliberate decision had been made at the cabinet level to crackdown and counter the increase in Christian resistance to apartheid. Church leaders from around the country were now monitored, harassed, detained, interrogated, and sometimes—as in the case of Frank Chikane, who succeeded Naudé as SACC General Secretary, and Smangaliso Mkhatshwa, General Secretary of the SACBC—severely tortured. At one point in 1986, the Catholic Church was represented among political detainees by twelve priests, three deacons, four religious sisters, twenty seminarians, and seven lay persons active in church work (IMBISA 1987: 5). In May 1986, the Catholic bishops published a pastoral letter in which they declared, "Let there be no mistake—we are not neutral in the current conflict in South Africa. We support fully the demands of the majority of people for justice" (SACBC Bishops Speak IV: 8). That Church members were now being carefully targeted for State repression had a clear politicizing effect on the Bishops and on many Catholic believers throughout the country. As one church worker stated, "One priest in prison did more to conscientize Catholics than a thousand sermons or statements" (Kelly 1991).

The more hardline attitude towards the churches was also evident when the State finally brought Archbishop Hurley to trial in February 1985 for accusing South African trained security forces of perpetrating atrocities in Namibia. This was the first time in thirty years that a Catholic Archbishop had been tried anywhere in the world, and the Vatican sent representatives to South Africa to attend the trial. After three years of preparing for the trial, the State withdrew its charges thirty minutes into the trial, because of insufficient evidence. Clearly, the primary reason for charging Hurley was merely to intimidate him. In that case, the State was sorely mistaken, for the charges and trial only served to further entrench within the SACBC a commitment to fighting apartheid.

By 1985, many clergy and lay leadership had become directly involved in resistance politics, establishing close ties between church members and civil society groups. When UDF and other political protest leaders were arrested and held for trials, activist church leaders were positioned to move from exercising spiritual leadership to political leadership, and filled the ensuing political vacuum. Thus, when the State increased its repression against what was by that time called the Mass Democratic Movement, clergy and lay religious leaders often found it virtually impossible to delineate whether action by church activists was primarily "church action" or "political action." Either way, the result was the same: it fueled the spiral of SACC and SACBC involvement in confronting the apartheid regime. As more and more priests, sisters, and lay Christians were arrested for their activities in the liberation movement, these actions came to be seen as attacks on the church itself. By this time, State actions against the church were becoming indistinct from the general repression taking place in society as a whole. Thus, in May 1985, Frank Chikane, General Secretary of the Institute for Contextual

Theology, was arrested and charged with high treason, not because of his activities as a minister, but on account of his role in the UDF's anti-election campaign.

In 1987, a conference was held in May in Lusaka, Zambia, again under the auspices of the World Council of Churches. The theme of what came to be known as the Lusaka Conference, was "The Church's Search for Justice and Peace in Southern Africa." Its purpose was to promote dialogue with the liberation movements, in an attempt to clarify the role of the church in the ever-increasingly violent Southern Africa. Almost two hundred representatives from the international churches, the exiled liberation movements, the United Nations, and other foreign political dignitaries attended. Once again, this overtly political act of meeting with the ANC and PAC was spurred by the deteriorating political scene. Specifically, in the eighteen months following the Harare Conference, continuing political confrontation in South Africa had produced an ongoing State of Emergency and the detention of some twenty thousand apartheid opponents. In the face of these worsening conditions, the SACC felt it had no choice but to become more deeply involved in the political struggle. The Lusaka Conference, however, was also a response to the escalating church-State conflict. In his address to the gathering, Beyers Naudé, who had succeeded Tutu as General Secretary of the SACC, asked the participants to take into account several major sources of tension which characterized the background to the conference. One of these was the increasing threat by South African State President Botha to prevent any further funding from overseas of "political programmes and projects which did not enjoy the support of the government." In the final "Lusaka Statement," the institutional church for the first time took the momentous step of declaring the South African State illegitimate, stating (WCC 1987):

> It is our belief that civil authority is instituted of God to do good, and that under the biblical imperative all people are obliged to do justice and show special care for the oppressed and the poor. It is this understanding that leaves us with no alternative but to conclude that the South African regime and its colonial domination of Namibia is illegitimate.

Once the legitimacy of the State was questioned, it followed that its police and defense forces were also illegitimate. It was through this recognition that the SACC could consider the use of counter-force by the liberation movements to be legitimate. Hence the statement declared that, "while remaining committed to peaceful change we recognize that the nature of the South African regime which wages war on its own inhabitants and neighbors compels the movements to the use of force along with other means to end oppression" (WCC 1987: 28–9). While up to this point the SACC had been somewhat hesitant to work openly with the ANC, as this might imply that it was supporting violence, the Lusaka Statement allowed the SACC, in Frank Chikane's words, to "move beyond the debate." While it did not have to agree with the use of violence, nor did it have to advocate violence itself, by recognizing the ANC's need for counter-violence, the SACC had finally opened itself to fulsome support for the goals, if not the means, of the armed liberation struggle. As both the SACC and the ANC had a long history of working against apartheid, this new understanding of the use of force allowed for a growing cooperation between and, indeed, a united front of the two. The

SACC could now move from the support of church action *in theory*, to carrying out that action in practice.

Adopting the Lusaka Statement also allowed the SACC to question more seriously the legitimacy of the government. Although the Lusaka Statement addressed only the theological illegitimacy of the State, the SACC took it a step further and considered the issue of legal legitimacy. In his speech to the 1987 National Conference, outgoing General Secretary Naudé stated that (quoted in Jacob and Mtshali 1987: 58):

> If from the point of view of the gospel, this [illegitimacy] is conceded, another question immediately arises i.e. to what degree this government can any longer be seen to be constitutionally legal?.... Where a State of emergency has become such an almost permanent feature as a pre-requisite for effective government rule, the legality of such a rule is decidedly at stake.

The Conference recommended to its member churches that they question the assumed moral obligation to obey a number of unjust laws, including the Population Registration Act and the Group Areas Act. In addition, the National Conference called on its members to support the "structures which are recognised by the people as their authentic legitimate authority." Declaring the State illegitimate and calling for disobedience had profound implications for the politicization of the SACC. It opened the door for an unprecedented level of determined political activity in the wake of the worsening political situation in 1988.

Alarmed by the open questioning of its legitimacy and mounting church-based political action, the government cracked down even harder on Christian resistance. In April 1987, the Commissioner of Police announced a State of emergency regulation prohibiting campaigns for the release of political detainees, including prayer services. When several prominent church leaders objected to this direct interference in religion, the government backtracked and stated that it was permitted to pray for detainees in a "bona fide church service," but any action that might "incite" the public to "participate in a campaign" aimed at the release of detainees would remain illegal. Tutu, by then Archbishop of Cape Town, reacted by saying he could no longer keep religion and politics separate. "I will continue," he declared, "to call both within and outside services for the release of detainees, despite the regulations" (*Crisis News* 1987: 1). Church leaders began increasingly to use the only free space at their disposal for legally opposing the government—the pulpit. Catholic Archbishop Wilfred Napier, who had taken over the SACBC presidency from Hurley, in his reaction to the regulation, underscored the fact that not only was the State trying to silence the liberation movement, it was also trying to silence churches (*Internos* 1987: 9):

> These latest restrictions are draconian by any standards. But now they affect the work of the Church directly, in that they presume to determine what the Church can or cannot do in its care for those in need.... This we cannot and will not tolerate.... We must obey God rather than men.

State harassment of church workers also intensified in the post-Lusaka Conference period. By May, 1987, at least fourteen SACC national and regional office workers were in detention.

In sum, by the end of 1987, both the SACC and SACBC had adopted a highly politicized self-identity. As a result of this more politicized identity, the SACC and SACBC were well-positioned to take major initiatives in the next wave of the liberation struggle—the defiance campaign of 1988–1989.

1988–1990

On February 24th, 1988, the South African political situation took a further, dramatic turn for the worse when the Minister of Law and Order banned seventeen anti-apartheid organizations, including the UDF, and eighteen individuals, including both the president and the vice-president the UDF. These measures represented the largest clampdown on legal protests and civic rights movements in the history of South Africa. With this final attempt to crush the opposition, virtually all mass, non-violent, legal means of opposing apartheid were eliminated, leaving the churches as the only viable organizations able to mount further resistance. Many leaders and lay Christians embraced the challenge to move to the forefront of the fight against apartheid.

An emergency meeting of church leaders, including the leadership of the SACC and SACBC, was held the day after the bannings. They produced a strong statement, declaring "the ban on the activities of the seventeen organisations is a blow directed at the heart of the Church's mission in South Africa, because the banned organisations are organisations of and for our people, the majority of which belong to our churches." Since the prohibited activities of banned organizations were declared "central to the proclamation of the Gospel," church leaders now felt compelled, irrespective of the consequences, to take over their activities. Church leaders were now explicitly involved in the politics of liberation. They dismissed the suggestion of meeting with the State President because of his past intransigence towards negotiating for peaceful change. This refusal in itself represented a new approach for these leaders, who had been more than ready in the past to talk to government officials in the face of crisis. Instead, the church leaders agreed to march to parliament as a public witness against the bannings. They also organized a petition to the State President, urging him to take several immediate actions including lifting the recent bannings, ending the State of Emergency, legalizing the ANC and other illegal political organizations, releasing political leaders, and commencing negotiations (Chikane 1988: 7–8).

On February 29, 1988, twenty-five church leaders, accompanied by more than a hundred clergy and several hundred lay Christians, held a short service in the Anglican Cathedral, which adjoins parliament. There they read the contents of the petition, gave instructions on the principles of non-violent action, and informed the congregation of the possible consequences of the march on which they were about to embark—which subsequently became known internationally as "The Clerics March." When they left the Cathedral, before reaching the end of the surrounding wall, the police intervened. Confronted in this way, all three hundred or so marchers knelt on the ground, whereupon the leaders were arrested, and forcibly removed to a police station where they were released within several hours. The remaining clerics and other marchers, still kneeling, were bombarded by a water cannon and arrested as well. This police action shocked the country and the international community. In a press conference held within hours after their release, the clerics acknowledged that the church was now truly the "voice of the voiceless." Reverend Frank Chikane, General Secretary of the SACC, stated that it was the churches' responsibility to speak out on behalf of banned organizations. "We will continue doing it," he declared, "irrespective of the consequences" (SACC 1988a: 9–10).

February 1988, therefore, marked a watershed for these organizations. Not only were they protesting the collapse of the rule of law, underscored once again by the 1988 bannings; they were also recognizing their responsibility for those who were being denied any legal opportunity to voice their opposition. Finally, because of the bannings and the march, they were also drawn into direct and sustained confrontation with the State.

The march was followed by a dramatic and public exchange of hostile letters between the State President and various church leaders, which accelerated the dizzying spiral of church-State conflict. President Botha dismissed the "so-called march on Parliament" and the petition as mere "ANC propaganda," stating, "the question must be posed whether you are acting on behalf of the kingdom of God, or the kingdom promised by the ANC and the SACP [South African Communist Party]? If it is the latter, say so, but do not then hide behind the structures and the cloth of the Christian church." Frank Chikane responded by charging that the majority of church members in South Africa had never experienced brutal repression under Marxists, the ANC, or the SACP, but "under your government" (SACC 1988b). In his response, Botha called Chikane irresponsible and a liar, and repeated his charge that the SACC was merely a communist front. Moreover, he stated that he found it alarming that (quoted in JTSA 1988: 73):

individual members of the clergy who claim to be messengers of God, are in reality messengers of enmity and hatred while parading in the cloth, and hiding behind the structures of the Church; and instead of pursuing reformation, they are engaged in the deformation of religion, through the proclamation of false so-called 'liberation theology'...through its acceptance of the Kairos Document, Harare Declaration, and Lusaka Statement.

The conflict continued with Tutu's written response to the President to this attack on the SACC's theology, in which he stated that (quoted in JTSA 1988: 73):

the Bible and the Church predate Marxism and the ANC by several centuries.... We are law abiding. Good laws make human society possible. When laws are unjust then Christian tradition teaches that they do not oblige obedience.

Tutu ended his letter to the President with the question: "I work for God's Kingdom. For whose Kingdom with your apartheid policy do you work?" (JTSA 1988: 87).

This exchange of letters was one of the most dramatic and direct confrontations between the church and State in the 1980s. As the SACC and SACBC moved to fill the vacuum created by State repression and the restriction of democratic organizations, the

State attempted to denigrate and thwart their initiatives by attacking their actions as communist-inspired, insisting that the regime itself upheld the values of Christianity. To these ends, State-run television programs on "liberation theology" maligned Tutu, Hurley, Boesak, and Chikane, questioning their integrity as Christians.

The State repressed the SACC and SACBC in other ways as well. One week after the February bannings, the Promotion of Orderly Internal Politics Bill was introduced in Parliament. Its intent was to restrict foreign funding to any anti-apartheid organization, as well as funding for humanitarian aid carried out by churches to victims of apartheid. The Bill authorized the Minister of Justice to declare both individuals and organizations "affected"—thus requiring them to obtain permission to raise foreign funds (*Ecunews*, July 1988: 20). Although the SACC had narrowly escaped being declared an affected organization in the aftermath of the Eloff Commission report—thus continuing its ability to raise money both inside and outside South Africa—it was again being threatened. By the late 1980s, the SACC had become so politicized that its activities were clearly considered "political" under the legislation. Even if the SACC were granted the authority to raise funds, it could still be prosecuted if the money was used for purposes which the State regarded as political. In effect, the Bill applied sanctions against the SACC, to which the 1988 National Conference responded by resolving not to abide by the legislation, because it was "designed to prevent legitimate, orderly, organized, disciplined, and constructive work for peaceful changes by cutting off funding from secular organizations as well as from the Church." The Conference further declared that it "would not be bound by the government's desire to maintain its own power at any cost" (SACC 1988c: 179).

Next, in May 1988, the SACC and SACBC launched the Standing for the Truth Campaign (SFT). This Campaign was the product of a Convocation of Churches attended by two hundred thirty participants from twenty-six churches, twenty-one regional councils, and fourteen other church organizations. It was convened to commit a broad coalition of churches and religious organizations to develop effective non-violent actions in the face of the deepening crisis. With the Campaign, church leaders asserted that they were not obliged to obey unjust laws which militated against the truth, but, in their obedience to God, would be forced to disobey the emergency regulations and apartheid laws. The mandate of the campaign's national committee was to "plan, coordinate and promote the campaign; set up regional structures, mobilize churches and create grassroots networks for mass action; to set up training programs, and to generate the necessary resources for the campaign" (SACC 1988d). Areas of possible non-violent actions included acts of non-collaboration and non-cooperation with apartheid in social, economic, and political fields such as supporting rent and tax boycotts, defying group-area restrictions, and withdrawing chaplains from the SADF. They also included nonviolent interventions, for example by having church leaders present at possible violent situations. The Campaign's "Theological Rationale" recognized that in the political context of the late 1980s, churches no longer had an option but to become the voice of those silenced and thereby to take on a political role: "Many organisations attempting to bring to light and to redress wrongs have been banned or restricted, leaving the Church to guard and struggle to restore essential civil liberties, such as the rights of freedom of assembly and access to information" (SACC 1988d).

In 1988, the Campaign's most defiant and far-reaching nonviolent action was to call for a boycott of the October municipal elections. Anticipating this move, the State had simply declared any such call illegal and punishable. Nevertheless, for the first time ever, a broad coalition of church leaders stood together and, in defiance of the law, called for a boycott. The SFT Campaign opposed Christians, either as candidates or voters, taking part in the elections, because it felt that they would be neither free nor fair. The State responded by seizing thirty thousand copies of the Western Province Council of Churchs' (WPCC) newsletter, *Crisis News*, which had published this "Statement of Faith" in defiance of emergency regulations, while the Minister of Law and Order threatened to "clip the wings of certain church and community organizations." In response, Archbishop Tutu gave a sermon in which he described the elections as "ludicrous" and "unjust," and urged black people not to vote. Faced with this serious challenge, the State responded with a police raid on Archbishop Tutu's home and the offices of the SACBC. Having removed the opposition leadership of civil society, the State now went after the church, which by this time had taken over that leadership in many cases.

The SACC and SACBC hardly had mobilized this campaign when their headquarters were bombed and burned; Christians were stunned. Non-violent acts of civil disobedience—statements, marches, and boycotts—had been countered by State-backed violence. In August, Khotso ("Peace") House, the headquarters of the SACC, was bombed, which some press reports referred to as "one of the most powerful if not the most powerful blast yet in South Africa" (*Ecunews*, August 1988: 1). No arrests were ever made in connection with the blast but the Minister of Law and Order did State that the building had probably been blown up in error by "ANC terrorists," asserting that Khotso House had long been used by guerrillas for the storing and manufacturing of explosives. Rejecting this charge, the SACC issued a statement that placed blame for the attack squarely on the State, asserting that, "We are...shocked, but not surprised by this act of violence against the Church.... While we are under no illusions that this has been the last such attack upon us, we reaffirm the commitment to see apartheid destroyed today" (HAP 1989: C27).

Then, in October, Khanya House in Pretoria, SACBC headquarters, was set alight. Again, no one was arrested for the attack, which caused extensive damage. Afterwards, Archbishop Napier, SACBC President, noted that increasing conflict with the State only served further to politicize the SACBC and SACC. He said, "The attack on Khanya House and the subsequent pathetic attempt to discredit the SACBC, far from succeeding in intimidating into silence those committed to justice, will lead to the resurgence of an even more vigorous engagement in the promotion of peace through justice" (SACBC 1989: 1).

The SFT both encouraged and was, in turn, given a strong sense of purpose and direction by the launching of the Mass Democratic Movement's Defiance Campaign on August 2, 1989, a struggle directed against the upcoming September elections for the tricameral parliament. Both the SACC and SACBC were prepared to step into a leadership position, declaring the Campaign's program of action as compatible with their commitment to peaceful non-violent actions to bring about change (*Crisis News* 1989: 2). The Campaign had multiple goals, from direct non-violent action to force desegregation of social services such as hospitals, schools, and transportation, to setting up "a process through which people and organisations will gradually un-ban themselves" (ICT 1989: 10).

The State responded harshly to the Defiance Campaign, and increased its repression further. Church leaders were arrested, teargassed, and sprayed with purple dye. In September, Tutu and his wife were each arrested twice in the span of one week, once for trying to enter a police-barricaded church. On another occasion, the Security Police entered the Archbishop's Cathedral carrying firearms, and attempted to remove everyone from the building and prohibit entrance. Additionally, in May 1989, Frank Chikane was poisoned, and an independent Board of Inquiry into attacks on anti-apartheid groups and activists later provided evidence implicating an SADF hit-squad in the poisoning. Furthermore, the Commission of Inquiry into Certain Alleged Murders uncovered an SADF-affiliated hit list of sixteen people, including Boesak, Chikane, and Tutu (SAIRR 1989/1990: 290). In 1989, the church-State conflict was spiraling out of control.

The days leading up to the election saw the SFT Campaign in Cape Town at the forefront of protest and resistance. The campaign was active in pickets, marches, meetings, and other acts of defiance, during which Christians and others were beaten and detained. The State responded by banning all rallies. The newly constituted Church Leaders Group responded in turn by organizing a worship and protest service in a Methodist Church, to which the police reacted by claiming that the ban covered church services as well as rallies. Nailing the banning order to the church door, they surrounded the church and used teargas to keep people from entering. The Central Methodist Mission took the Commissioner of Police to the Supreme Court to have the banning order set aside. While the police argued that church services were consistently being used to promote illegal political goals, a judge ruled, "I am not prepared to ban a church service." The service proceeded at 11 p.m. (Villa-Vicencio 1990: xi).

Clearly, the church-State conflict was further heightened by the decision of the SFT to join the Defiance Campaign. The churches had won this particular battle. The most determined attempt to that date by the State to eliminate the space opened up in the churches for resistance under the State of emergency was at least temporarily defeated. However, in response to levels of police brutality increasing dramatically in the days following the service, on September 13 church leaders led a "Peace March," the largest march since that led by the Pan Africanist Congress which precipitated the banning of the ANC and PAC in 1960. In the following weeks, similar protests were held in all the major cities and several rural areas, with ANC flags flying openly and bishops, clergy, women religious, and lay Christians leading and supporting marches. In the three weeks following the first Peace March, more than three hundred fifty thousand people participated in these marches (*Crisis News* 1989: 1). Organizations had simply "un-banned" themselves. Less than a month later, eight top ANC leaders were released from prison, followed by the release of Nelson Mandela—all less than five months after the Cape Town Peace March. Finally, in September 1989, the SACC and SACBC-sponsored "Conference on the Legitimacy of the South African State" in Harare declared the moral, theological, *and* legal illegitimacy of the State. The apartheid regime was finally beginning to unravel.

CONCLUSION

For a brief time in the late 1980s, the institutional church and the prophetic church came close to being one and the same. The political context of South Africa in the 1980s forced the SACC and SACBC to reevaluate their mission and their proper role in society. Worsening political conditions shook the SACC and SACBC, and eventually galvanized them into action. No longer, they believed, could they simply stand on the sidelines as spectators, making pronouncements against the increasingly brutal regime. As the regime became increasingly repressive, a growing number of church leaders came to realize that in order to legitimately represent their constituency, they had to become actively involved in fighting apartheid. Being jarred into action then produced the unintended consequence of further politicizing the SACC and SACBC through an escalating spiral of State reactions against church leaders and counter-reactions by these church organizations. As church leaders and workers became targets of the State's repression, their level of politicization increased dramatically. Finally, South Africa in the 1980s saw both the increasing rule of force and decreasing consent or obedience by the majority of the people, resulting in a huge increase in arrests and detentions without trial. As the opposition leadership of civil society was removed and silenced, the churches became the only arena left for internal, legal opposition. As church leaders moved to fill civil society's vacuum, they were increasingly forced to assume political leadership. Accepting this responsibility fostered a new, more political self-identity. The interaction of these processes resulted in what I have termed a "spiral of involvement" that produced a highly politicized SACC and SACBC, both of which were crucial in ending the apartheid regime in South Africa.

REFERENCES

CIIR (Catholic Institute for International Relations). 1988. "Testimony of Archbishop Denis Hurley" in *Country and Conscience: South African Conscientious Objectors*. London: CIIR/Pax Christi.

Chikane, F. 1988. "The Church's Prophetic Witness Against the Apartheid System in South Africa (25th February—8th April, 1988)."Johannesburg: SACC.

Crisis News 15 (April/May). "Clergy Defy the Detainees Proclamations." 1987.

Crisis News 21 (April/May). "What Others Say on Violence and non-Violence" 1988.

Crisis News (September). "Nation-Wide Defiance Campaign Activities." 1989.

de Gruchy, J. 1979. *The Church Struggle in South Africa*. Grand Rapids: Eerdmans.

Ecunews. 1984. (February).

_____. 1985. (March/April).

_____. 1988. (April).

_____. 1988. (July).

_____. 1988. (August).

HAP (Human Awareness Program). 1989. *Info. '89*. Johannesburg: Human Awareness Program.

Harbor, A. 1983. "United—In the Politics of Refusal." *Rand Daily Mail*, June 8.

Hurley, D. 1984. Address given on August 22. Quoted in *South Africa Information Pack*. Dublin: Trocaire.

IMBISA (Inter-territorial Meeting of Bishops of Southern Africa). 1987. "Plenary Assembly Report on the Situation in South Africa." (Personal Archive).

ICT (Institute for Contextual Theology). 1989. "Negotiations, Defiance and the Church." Johannesburg: ICT (on behalf of the Standing for the Truth Campaign) pamphlet.

_____. 1984. 2 (December).

_____. 1986. 4 (March).

Internos. 1987. 2 (April).

Jacob, S. and O. Mtshali (eds.). 1987. *Refugees and Exiles: Challenge to the Churches*. SACC National Conference Report.

JTSA. 1988. "Documentation: The Church—State Confrontation, Correspondence and Statements February—April 1988." *Journal of Theology for Southern Africa*. 63 (June).

Kairos. 1985. *The Kairos Document: Challenge to the Church: A Theological Comment on the Political Crisis in South Africa*, Revised Second Edition. Grand Rapids: Eerdmans.

Kelly, Sr. M. 1991. "The Catholic Church and Resistance to Apartheid." (Personal Archives).

Leatt, J. 1987. "The Church in Resistance Post 1976." Revised Research Paper for a Conference on *South Africa Beyond Apartheid*. January. Boston, Massachusetts.

Nash, M., ed. 1985. Women—*A Power for Change*. SACC National Conference Report.

Naudé, B. 1985. Address given in November 1985 to the British Council of Churches. (Personal Archive).

Price, R. M. 1991. *The Apartheid State in Crisis*. New York: Oxford University Press.

SACBC. 1986. "Report on Extraordinary Plenary Session of the Southern African Catholic Bishops' Conference." 29 April–1 May.

_____. 1986–1987. *The Bishops Speak: IV*.

_____. 1989. *After the Fire: The Attack on Khanya House*. Pretoria: SACBC.

SACBC and SACC. 1984. Relocations: The Churches' Report on Forced Removals.

SACC. 1983a. National Conference Resolutions.

_____. 1983b. The *Divine Intention*. Presentation by Bishop D. Tutu, General Secretary of the South African Council of Churches to the Eloff Commission of Inquiry. Johannesburg: SACC.

_____. 1984. "Response to the Evaluation of the Activities of the SACC Division of

Justice and Reconciliation in the Memorandum of the South African Police, Submitted to the Eloff Commission."

_____. 1988a. "Senzenina [What have we done?]: The Day 300 Church Leaders, Clergy and Laity marched on the South African Parliament." Johannesburg: SACC.

_____. 1988b. "Letter from Rev. Chikane to P.W. Botha, March 18, 1988," in "Emergency Convocation of Churches in South Africa." Johannesburg: SACC.

_____. 1988c. Church *Action in the South African Crisis.* The South African Council of Churches National Conference Report.

_____. 1988d. "The Standing for the Truth Campaign," (pamphlet).

SAIRR (South African Institute for Race Relations). 1988/1989. *Race Relations Survey.* Johannesburg: SAIRR.

Villa-Vicencio, C. 1990. *Civil Disobedience and Beyond: Law, Resistance, and Religion in South Africa.* Grand Rapids: Eerdmans.

World Council of Churches (WCC). 1987. *The Churches' Search for Justice and Peace in Southern Africa: Report on Meeting in Lusaka, Zambia, 4–8 May, 1987.* WCC: Program to Combat Racism.

PART FOUR

SYMBOLIC WORLDS AND
ACTIVIST IDENTITY

7

For God and the Fatherland: Protestant Symbolic Worlds and the Rise of German National Socialism

David Sikkink and Mark Regnerus

On March 21st, 1933, church bells rang throughout Potsdam, Germany for the commencement of the German Reichstag, the governing body of the country, which for the first time had more Nazi party representatives than any other. An organ and choir chimed in as the Nazi leadership, riding the crest of a five-year blitzkrieg at the ballot box, strode into the Protestant Garrison Church. Joseph Goebbels, the future Nazi Minister of Propaganda, ushered in Protestant church leaders, while Adolf Hitler led an entourage of the Roman Catholic hierarchy. From the pulpit, Hitler delivered a message which proclaimed the Reich government protector of Christianity's ethical and moral foundations (Scholder 1987: 225–226). The National Socialist party, according to Hitler, "regards Christianity as the unshakable foundation of our national life and morality" (quoted in Matheson 1981: 9).

The message was not surprising, since National Socialists went to great lengths to define who they were and what they were about by using biblical images, symbols, and categories, such as sacrifice, redemption, heart and soul, and Providence. One Nazi writer claimed that "the blood and wounds of Christ, the blood and wounds of the patriot bring victory and salvation; as the dying Christ was for Christianity, the dying patriot is the savior of his fatherland" (quoted in Dahm 1968: 39). The use of biblical imagery did not make the Nazis a Christian social movement. Many of the Nazi leaders were more inspired by neo-paganism than Christianity. In fact, after coming to power, Hitler expected to take care of the "problem" of the Christian church after he dealt with the Jews, and expected that faith in National Socialism would supersede the Christian faith (Pois 1986). Yet the language used to articulate Nazi identity testifies to the persistence of Protestant symbolic worlds in early twentieth-century German society (Rhodes 1980; Bergen 1991). Many Protestants clearly linked who they were as Christians with support for the Nazis. According to these Protestants, support for Hitler was simply "loyal evangelical witness in the secular sphere," and they claimed, "We want to serve: through our church to serve God, and thereby our fatherland" (Matheson 1981: 23). According to a favorite hymn of many German Protestants, "This is the man, he who can die for God and fatherland" (Bergen 1991: 540).

As the language and ritual show, there was extensive collaboration between the Nazi party and important segments of Protestantism, especially during the later years of the

Nazi rise to power, and the Protestant vote was critical to Nazi electoral success. Why was the National Socialist Party (NSDAP) attractive to many Protestants? What was it about Protestant identities, as constructed in the rapidly changing social context of 1920s and early 30s Germany, which translated into support for Hitler? How can we explain the motives of the Protestant voter?

Several schools of thought have emerged to answer the question of who supported the Nazis and why. One of the earliest and best-known is the lower-middle-class thesis, which was popularized by Lipset (1960). According to this theory, the ideal Nazi supporter was "a middle-class self-employed Protestant who lived either on a farm or in a small community, and who had previously voted for a centrist or regionalist political party strongly opposed to the power of big business and big labor" (Lipset 1960:.149).

Mass society theories provide a second explanation. Kornhauser (1959; also see Bendix 1952; Kuechler 1992: 26) popularized mass-society explanations, which emphasized social psychological estrangement. The "mass society" is the social condition in which a large number of people become "self-estranged" and separated from previously-established ties, such as relationships in church and community.

In contrast, contemporary theorists in Germany and America have shifted toward the theory that the NSDAP was a people's party, or *Volkspartei* (Falter 1991). The Nazi appeal transcended social class and occupational boundaries to reach a broad electorate, which even included the upper-middle class (Childers 1983; Hamilton 1982). Hamilton (1982), for example, after arguing that the complex nature of city neighborhoods makes it impossible to find evidence to support the lower-middle-class thesis, develops a "group bases" explanation that focuses on interpersonal influences, including family political outlooks, values, religious commitments, and ethnicity, which may explain NSDAP voting patterns. Thus the *Volkspartei* theorists not only provide evidence that questions the middle-class thesis, since Hitler's appeal crossed social boundaries, but also move toward a more systematic exploration of the cultural mechanisms that link structural positions and the action of voting for Hitler.

As the *Volkspartei* theorists have pointed out, it is difficult to uncover definitive evidence for understanding why nearly fourteen million Germans actively supported Hitler (Rhodes 1980; Maier 1986). Most studies of electoral support for Hitler, however, agree that rural Protestants, which in Germany were primarily Lutheran, were much more likely to support Hitler than other groups. And while the most widely respected social and political explanations of the rise of the Nazis have strong, if implicit, assumptions about the motives and interests of supporters of National Socialism, the precise connection between Protestant religion and voting for the Nazi Party, the motive and orientation of Protestant voters, has received less systematic attention. What can be surmised from the available evidence about the thought-world, the cultural system of meaning, which made sense of support for Hitler for so many rural Protestants?

This paper argues that Protestant traditions provided cultural tools to construct a vision of reality which pointed to Hitler as the logical choice to deal with the ills of social and institutional change. Within Protestant systems of meaning, support for Hitler was constructed as the revitalization of German religion and nation through the pursuit of spiritual purity. In the conditions of perceived spiritual decline in all areas of German life, the re-infusing of spirit was called for within church, State, and Nation.

PROTESTANT VOTING PATTERNS

After pouring over the available data from electoral results and census surveys, researchers have shown that the strongest Nazi support was rural and Protestant. Since the culture of these small communities often took on the tenor of the dominant church in the region, individual voting patterns can be compared across regions to get some handle on the relationship between broad religious identities and voting for Hitler.

Strong Protestant and Catholic identities marked many cities and virtually all rural areas and communities in pre-war Germany (Lohmöller & Falter 1986: 121). Of the 36.9 million votes cast in the July 1932 Reichstag election, where the NSDAP garnered 37.3 percent of the total vote, 21.4 million (fifty-eight percent) of these were cast in communities with populations which did not exceed twenty-five thousand. This shows the importance of rural and smaller community voters in these elections. In addition, NSDAP support was greatest (41.3 percent) in these communities, while support declined with increasing community size (Hamilton 1982: 38). Since the cultural tenor of a region was shaped by the dominant church, voting data from communities and regions can reveal a great deal about the relationship between religious persuasion and party support.

An early study of Lower Saxony found that, in the July 1932 Reichstag election, the NSDAP received fifty-five percent of the vote in Leer county, which was primarily Protestant, but won a mere 8.3 percent in Aschendorf-Hümmling, a neighboring Catholic county in which the Catholic *Zentrum* party claimed 79.5 percent (Noakes 1971: 219). In analyzing the 1930 Reichstag election in which the NSDAP gained eighteen percent of the total vote, Falter (1981: 422) found a large contingent of Protestants, who were primarily middle class and rural, among the NSDAP following. The Protestant-NSDAP connection only strengthened between 1930 and 1933, while Catholics remained hesitant. In the two years between the 1930 and July 1932 Reichstag elections, the NSDAP expanded its constituency in rural Protestant regions by 23.2 percent (Falter 1986: 209). With this evidence, Hamilton (1982: 38) concludes that in July 1932, "the vote for the National Socialists was very disproportionately Protestant."

Studies of smaller districts reinforce these claims. In the largely rural and Protestant sections of Pomerania, Frankfurt an der Oder, and East Prussia (all in northern Germany), support for the Nazis reached 48.0, 48.1, and 47.1 percent, respectively (Hamilton 1982: 38). Time-series data on votes cast in the largely Protestant regions of Schleswig-Holstein and Hannover and the Catholic region of Bavaria show that, in the decisive 1932 election, 51 percent of Schleswig-Holstein's voters and 45 percent of Hannover's supported the NSDAP, as compared to 33 percent in Catholic Bavaria (Loomis & Beegle 1946: 728). Similar statistics for the Catholic *Zentrum* and Bavarian People's parties reveal dismal 1.2 and 8.4 percent support in Protestant Schleswig-Holstein and Hannover, respectively, but a brighter 32.3 percent in Catholic Bavaria, Hitler's region of origin. Lohmöller and Falter (1986: 117) observe that the *Zentrum* and Bavarian People's parties "gathered...practically no votes outside of the Catholic voting sector."

While the NSDAP made impressive gains across the board between 1928 and 1932, clearly its greatest gains were concentrated in the rural, Protestant north, which was dominated primarily by the Lutheran Church. The more Catholic southern regions, as well as urban areas, lagged behind. The consistent pattern and magnitude of these differences indicate the importance of religious affiliation for interpreting elections during the Weimar years. But how can this relationship be explained?

THE HISTORICAL SETTING: INTERPRETING SOCIAL CHANGE AND CHURCH STRUGGLE

The familiar world of the Protestant rank-and-file appeared to be coming apart in the early 1900s, and especially after the post-World War I downfall of the monarchy. The increasing movement to the cities, the especially rapid industrialization of Germany, the apparent loss of the longstanding alliance of throne and altar, the divisions and stalemate in the new Parliamentary system—all these problems were pressing in the 1920s. To make matters worse, relative economic prosperity was broken in the late 20s by the international depression and massive unemployment. How did Protestants perceive these changes?

Protestants were particularly likely to see the growth of the cities as a threat to *Gemeinschaft* society, and associate it with the loss of an idyllic rural village. From a Protestant perspective, the rise of cities and "city life" meant the loss of the spiritual essence, morality, and organic unity of the *Gemeinschaft* society. One man explained that he became a pastor because, after working for a "Jewish bank," he became disgusted by "mammonism" and "materialism" and disillusioned by the "spiritual-moral confusion of the big city psyche" (Bergen 1991: 124). For many Protestants, the city represented a spiritual wasteland of moral degradation and "materialism."

The rapid industrialization of Germany concerned many Protestants, who saw in it a basic struggle between a good *Gemeinschaft* society and the world of large-scale, bureaucratic organization. Shopkeepers, independent artisans, and small businessmen—the old middle class—were pinched by big business and bureaucracy, on the one hand, and organized labor on the other (Merkl 1980: 149). The cultural tools of Protestant traditions were particularly important in interpreting these trends in terms of the "little man" up against the daunting world of lifeless and sterile bureaucratic institutions, which destroy the direct, personal relations of local community life.

In the context of rapid social change, Protestants supported the burgeoning Youth Movement in Germany in the 20s, which grew rapidly in response to the perceived impact of industrialization and urbanization. Many groups that were a part of the Youth Movement were all-male and emphasized hiking, camping, and guitar-playing, and included pledges to get back to nature and maintain the inner purity of heart and mind (Barnett 1992: 22). As a German pastor said, approvingly, of the Youth movement, "A whole new lifestyle grew out of this sense of life...a simple and natural way of life" (quoted in Merkl 1980: 17). The Youth Movement was a "protest against the sterile urban and industrial world of their middle class elders" (Merkl 1980: 204). Protestants were especially likely to identify with the Movement, since it called for purifying the spirit against the "soulless, secular trends" of modernity.

Protestants also viewed the "experiment" with parliamentary democracy after World War I as a failure, partly because of the character of the "system," which created divisions, factional fighting, and stalemate. As some Protestants put it, "The Parliamentary period is out of date for church as well the nation," and in its place should be a national, dynamic, spiritual force that unites the nation (Matheson 1981: 5). Parliamentary democracy was part of a "system" that paralyzed the *Volk*, the mystical German peoplehood, and created disunity (Rhodes 1980: 47).

Finally, the rise of Bolshevism and Communism, and the secularization of German society, including the decreasing legitimacy of religion, were understood by many Protestants in terms of the struggle for the soul of modernity.

In the minds of many Protestants, German society had become more secular following the Great War (Helmreich 1979: 81). And there were ample reasons for drawing that conclusion. Though Church membership increased when the National Socialists came to power (Douglass 1935: 278; Zabel 1976: 4), withdrawals were exceeding additions before the war. And while the total number of defectors was not large, the fact that they were often inspired by campaigns of atheist or some socialist leaders only made a worse impression on those in the Church (Helmreich 1979: 37). Though membership increased during the war, most studies suggest that the churches in Germany lost some members during the Weimar years. Two sources claim that 2.4 million people withdrew their membership from the Protestant Church during the Weimar years, confirming the Protestant concern for an increasingly secular *zeitgeist* pervading the country (Douglass 1935: 278; Zabel 1976: 4). A more accurate estimate suggests that withdrawals, though numerous, were much more modest than these rates (Helmreich 1979: 81). Yet, certainly, German Protestantism did not see the Weimar era as their golden years, and most Protestants defined the situation during the 1920s as one of decline and loss for the legitimacy of the church.

Besides the perception of membership decline, the rise of secular movements, such as the Free-Thinking Movement and atheist organizations, in culture and politics shaped the Protestant view of the world (Dahm 1968: 10). If the Communists weren't enough to ring Protestant alarm bells, the Social Democrats were advocating abolishing the church tax and eliminating support for parochial schools. One Protestant minister's son told how the Social Democrats held a demonstration in front of the town statue of Luther and called workers to leave the church—which turned his father to the political right from then on (Barnett 1992: 14–5). Many Protestants of the early 1920s called the positions of the SPD, which were seen as disrupting the relation of Protestantism and German culture, "anti-Christian" (Dahm 1968: 34). Within Protestant frameworks, Communists, social democrats, and other emerging secular groups were viewed as "godless and revolutionary," and the Church felt it had to respond to these secular trends (Dahm 1968: 33).

For many Protestants the struggle between modernity and spiritual purity was given meaning through the concept of the *Volk*, the mystical, spiritual unity of the German "people" based on blood and soil. They saw a spiritual struggle of the *Volk* against the threats of system. In 1926, one pastor framed the *Volk* explicitly within Protestant language: "And then the miracle occurred, in the midst of all our darkness, God made a light glow, he gave a command, he bestowed an idea: the *volkisch* idea. The flash of this idea was a salvation...the *volkisch* idea is a command, a challenge, a gift, a duty" (quoted in Bergen 1991: 303). The *Volk* embodied a spiritual essence that could rejuvenate the secular trends of modernity. The German Church League connected the rebirth of *Volk* and Christ: "We look at Jesus as the Son of God, Savior and Lord—and also as our Redeemer, who frees us from the bands of sin and who clears the path to our personal freedom, to true worth, and thereby also to the rebirth of our *Volk*" (quoted in Bergen 1991: 305). Other Protestants "maintain[ed] the conviction that it is impossible for the Germans to become the *Volk* without the power of Christianity" (Bergen 1991: 332).

A CONTESTED CHURCH

At the same time that Protestants were struggling to interpret political, economic, and cultural change, the Protestant Church was going through an internal struggle for its own soul. Within Protestantism, conflicts emerged over what was going to count as legitimate religion. Three groups in particular struggled over the direction of the church. Confessional groups defended the autonomy of the Church, but were not necessarily opposed to being "national," that is, to espousing "Christian patriotism" which was nationalistic and often allied with the political right (Barnett 1992; Feige 1990). By far the largest group, the conservative mainstream, especially within the Lutheran churches, generally was protective of the autonomy of the church, which translated into an "apolitical" stance (Barnes 1991; Barnett 1992), but was also concerned to continue or restore the cultural hegemony of the Church. Finally, the radicals sought a restructuring of the Protestant Church in line with the national "rebirth" in Germany (Feige 1990: 144). One radical group, the German Christians, self-styled "stormtroopers of Christ," sought a revitalization of the faith against the deadness of the old Protestant structures, but was challenged by Confessionals and, to some extent, the conservative mainstream, who were unwilling to abandon historical theological positions. The sectarian challenge of the German Christians increased in significance through alliances with the Nazi Party (Dahm 1968: 43; Mzimela 1980: 29).

In the midst of growing secularization and religious indifference (Diephouse 1987; Ziegler 1989: 90), many nominal and active laity as well as some Church leaders viewed the church as a rigid and antiquated institution, which lacked life and vitality, and was out of touch with the people (Micklem 1939: 21; Helmreich 1979: 122). According to Karl Barth, "it was again and again asserted" that the Church was "petrified" (Frey 1938: 44). The Church was supposedly beholden to an upper- and middle-class social background and culture, and unable to establish contact with the people (Noakes 1971: 208).

Many within the formal Church and without called for the renewal of a stodgy institution. The 1920s saw a revival of the Pietist movement, which emphasized the place of a passionate inner faith and piety (Diephouse 1987: 48; Pierard 1970; Barnett 1992: 25). Shaped by the language of Pietism, but despising its "unmanliness," religious radicals called for a revolution of Protestant institutions through a reawakening of a vital and "life-affirming" religion of the heart. One leader of the radicals blamed the stuffy, orthodox theologians of the conservative mainstream for the "fact" that "almost eighty percent" of Germans were alienated from the church. In contrast to the dead institutions of Protestantism, the radicals' stated aim was the "heart of the people" (quoted in

Bergen 1991: 109, 110).

The heavyweight of the Protestant church was the traditional conservative main-stream: it is estimated that between 70 and 80 percent of Protestant clergy were both conservative and nationalist in political perspective (Helmreich 1979: 77). Thus, much of the conservative mainstream was sympathetic with the German Christians' approach to national life, but were skeptical of the direct mixing of religion and politics in the Church, and despised the strong-arm and disruptive tactics of the German Christians. National restoration was welcomed, but, in the church at least, German Christians were not. The conservative mainstream labelled the German Christians "political," and charged that their faith was not of the Bible (Barnett 1992: 27–28).

The German Christians, by contrast, were committed to opposing the dead weight of the religious Establishment with a life-affirming religion of the heart. The German Christians sought a "positive Christianity that is truly affirmative...a truly national faith in the spirit of Luther and heroic piety" (quoted in Matheson 1981: 5). A German Christian flyer identified the Establishment Church with old women, and claimed a religion of life is necessary for the new age (quoted in Bergen 1991: 554):

> We want a kind of Christianity—with which one can do something in life, a Christianity of which our youth will say: that is alive, there is heroism there. That is not "only" for old women, but for the life-affirming men of the Third Reich.

The German Christian manifesto proclaimed that the "church needs to be restruc-tured...we are not challenging the confessional basis of church, but offering a confes-sion of life" (Matheson 1981: 5).

Against rigid hierarchy and the gulf between leaders and laity, the German Christians' aim was a more egalitarian church in which the laity was empowered through the spiritual awakening of every believer. The guiding principles of the German Christians stated, "We pledge ourselves to service in our parishes—and expect the pledge of all Protestant men and women, not just of those in the professional work of the church" (Matheson 1981: 23). The German Christians opposed the professional clergy with the "simple truth of the gospel." A German Christian Youth pastor stated, "Faith in Christ has always had only one opponent: the clericalism within us and around us. True faith awakens a childlike quality in us, a simple, joyful, reliance that even the most manly man cannot do without" (Bergen 1991: 106).

As part of their contempt of the religious Establishment, German Christians wore their rough-and-readiness as a badge of honor. The formality and concern with reli-gious propriety of the conservative mainstream was seen as part of the problem with the institutional church. The German Christians reveled in the charges from the con-servative mainstream of "inappropriate" behavior in church services, crude speech, and loose lifestyles of some German Christian clergy (Bergen 1991: 156). They went out of their way to violate the rules and regulations of the established Church as a statement about what real Christianity should be about. Codes of church-like behavior were con-sidered too confining (Bergen 1991: 139, 160).

The German Christians were bent on unifying the regional churches into one national church. Their motto was "One Reich, One Faith, One Church." The German

Christians claimed that they were not a "narrow political group, but appeal to all Protestant Churches of German descent.... We want a dynamic, *national* church, which expresses the living faith of our people" (quoted in Matheson 1981: 6). Opposed to a religious "system," the German Christians sought a "dynamic," living faith that would create a spiritual unity to challenge the petty divisions of the institutional church. As one widely-read leader put it, "the restoration of the pure teaching of the Savior" meant creating a German National Church which overcame confessional divisions and proclaimed "an appropriate faith" to the German people (Scholder 1977: 94).

Unity, according to the German Christians, must be based on a religious revolution in the depths of one's inner being, and that regeneration enabled the creation of the *Volk*. What was important, in their words, was that the "entire soul resonates in its very depths," creating a "passionate love [of] church and fatherland" (quoted in Bergen 1991: 269, 639). Inner regeneration naturally led to mystical unity of hearts, which was the creation of the *Volk*. According to one pastor, "the power of Christ...is where heart finds heart in forgiving love, there where the Holy Spirit comes into people's hearts, to bind together what had been separate...[but] belongs together: humanity and God, as well as brothers and sisters of the same blood and *Volk*" (Bergen 1991: 77).

The concern for inner renewal and mystical oneness did not mean the German Christians insisted on the historical dogma of the Church. Protestant traditions became quite a different thing in their hands. In fact, the German Christians, reconstructing traditions from German Pietism, argued that a religion of the head would get in the way of the purity of heart and mystical unity of the faithful. Thus religious orthodoxy was second to the main goal of creating an "inclusive people" church (Bergen 1991: 106). Luther was the man with a "courageous spirit of faith," they said, and stood in sharp contrast to the spiritual hollowness of the "pharisees and scribes" who were overly-concerned with orthodoxy and scriptural texts (Bergen 1991: 109). "Certainly no inner renewal of our church will come from...the cast of scribes [i.e., the professors and theologians]," according to the German Christians (Bergen 1991: 112).

Spiritual renewal and unity should not only rejuvenate the soul but also the nation. Thus, the German Christians argued that the Church had to be on the forefront of the "awakening" that was taking place through the dynamism of the National Socialist Movement. Thus, the German Christians wanted a spiritual revitalization of the faith, parallel with the National Socialist revival in politics, in which the Church would provide a spiritual homeland, a spiritual foundation, for the nation-state (Bergen 1991). They sought to (Matheson 1981: 5),

> recover...the German sense for life...and to give [the] church real vitality.... In the fateful struggle for the freedom and future of Germany, the leadership of the church has proved to be too weak in the fateful struggle...against Marxism, the enemy of God, and against the unspiritual Center party...[The church] must not stand aside or distance itself from the fighters of freedom.

The synthesis of NSDAP and Christianity offered the only hope for Church survival, according to many German Christians (Bergen 1991: 560).

A third group in Protestant religion grew rapidly in direct response to the perceived

sacrilege of the German Christians. The Confessional positions and some of the conservative mainstream opposed the German Christians on grounds of what a Church organization should be as well as what constituted a Church (Mzimela 1980: 32).
Confessional positions, while far from directly opposing National Socialism, sought to
defend the autonomy and integrity of religious institutions against the German
Christian's sectarian challenge. The point of contention for groups like the Confessing
Church was the principles of the independence of the church and the sovereignty of the
gospel (Wright 1977: 416). For example, the Young Reformers' "Gospel and Church"
group challenged the German Christians, but also saw a bureaucratic Church in need
of spiritual renewal (Matheson 1981: 29):

> Our aim is a new form of church in which the power of repentance, faith and
> brotherly love is not choked to death by an inflated bureaucracy on the one
> hand, or by mass movements on the other. We fight for a *free church*...It can
> only serve the German people as it should if it *declares the Word of God in com-*
> *plete freedom*. The Church of the Gospel is in danger...Church must remain
> church!

The Confessing Church sought to "protect the inner being of the Church by being
separate from politics and specific [political] programs in the church.... We must not
accept the divinization of the state" (Matheson 1981: 8). One Protestant leader argued
that race and blood had nothing to do with the biblical Christ. In order to preserve the
"individuality of the church," defenders of the autonomy of the religious enterprise
sought to centralize church organization to defend better the religious sphere against
the German Christians (Wright 1977: 413, 415).

THE NAZI MOVEMENT AND PROTESTANT SYMBOLIC WORLDS

The Protestant Church's reception of Hitler varied. In the Nazi movement's early years,
the conservative mainstream leadership generally held the Nazis in contempt. The
Nazis were seen as unsophisticated at best. More often they were considered fanatics
and bar-room brawlers (Wright 1977: 397). But that shifted over time; many radical
religious groups, such as the German Christians, were obviously enthusiastic while
other religious positions were indifferent. The overwhelming majority of church members, however, found themselves straddling these poles, while their denominations and
local churches often resisted declaring an official position on NSDAP.

Hitler, however, was able to tap into the *weltenschauung* of ordinary rural
Protestants. While imprisoned in 1924, Hitler wrote, "I believe today that I am acting
in the sense of the Almighty Creator: *By warding off the Jews, I am fighting for the*
Lord's work" (1941: 60). *Mein Kampf* contains many similar religious references, which
combined with the Nazis' language which juxtaposed "system" and "heart," their opposition to the "enemies" of religion, and their incessant God-talk to convince many
Protestants that the Nazis were the political expression of faithful Christianity.
"Thousands of Germans" believed "that the program of Adolf Hitler is Christianity
applied with courage to life" (Douglass 1935: 306).

GOD-TALK

The Nazi's early face showed a healthy respect for the religious basis of Germany—at least one could conclude that, given the ubiquitous God-talk which developed as the movement progressed. Besides the references in *Mein Kampf*, the God-talk was carried to extremes by a central figure in the movement, Joseph Goebbels, who later became Reich minister of Propaganda, and editor of the Nazi-sympathetic daily newspaper *Der Angriff*. A one-time Christian believer, he was aware of the power of the church in the lives of its members (Reuth 1993: 223). Goebbels, in one of his frequent lectures to Berlin crowds in 1926, captured the connection between Protestants and National Socialism that made sense to many Protestants. He assured them that Nazism "could move mountains," and was a "gospel" which could "create a new Reich in which true Christianity would be at home" (Reuth 1993: 82). During an official meeting of the Protestant and NSDAP leadership, Franz Stöhr, a member of the executive branch of the Nazi Reichstag Party, assured church leaders that the Party was "a secular, political movement but that it was led by Christians who intended to put Christian ethics into practice by legislation" (Wright 1974: 81). According to Stöhr, the Party was "far from hostile to the church," and, despite several Catholics in leadership positions, was "Protestant in direction" (Wright 1974: 81).

What made the "Protestant direction" claim credible was the pervasive religious imagery and allusions that surrounded the Nazis. The Nazi faithful argued that National Socialism "is in essence a religious movement" and "the German without religion is unthinkable" (Childers 1983: 115). Nazi leaders rejected the "atheist" label, despite their paganism, and instead called themselves "God-believing" (Diephouse 1977: 55). Hitler in the late 1920s cultivated an image as a believer of Christianity in general, and a broad, nondenominational, Protestant theology (Douglass 1935: 306).

Further, the Nazi Party was on record in support of "Positive Christianity." If the Nazi platform had been free of any identification with Christianity, it would have been very difficult to overcome anxieties among Protestants and Catholics about the anti-Semitism and cultic nationalism of the Nazi vision. But the official 25-point party program, which Hitler called "the dogma of our faith," declared that religious groups and denominations (except Jewish groups) would be free to practice their faith, and that National Socialism supported "positive Christianity" (Waite 1977: 29). Support of "Positive Christianity" placed the Nazis squarely in favor of revitalizing the Church along with the nation. Hitler advocated "a new spiritual ideal which would meet the desires of modern humanity" in an age when the "vital and progressive forces" of Christianity had "run dry" (Rhodes 1980: 101).

ANTI-MARXIST

Besides a general Christian tenor, the National Socialists opposed the most vivid symbol of all the forces of secularization: the "godless atheism" of the Communists and the Bolshevik Revolution. One of the key elements of Nazi ideology was the destruction of "Marxism" (Allen 1986: 15; Noakes 1971: 209). As Hitler put it in 1924, "The future of Germany means the annihilation of Marxism" (quoted in Rhodes 1980: 32). Typical was one Nazi who labeled the Communists "the anti-religious Marxist parties," and, when murdered National Socialists were not allowed the consolations of the Church, the same Nazi could not understand why the church did not believe "Our repeated avowals of the proximity of National Socialism to Christianity" (quoted in Abel 1986: 97).

Nazi anti-Marxism was particularly attractive to Protestants (Noakes 1971: 208). Protestant women, for example, expected that Hitler would deal with the threat of atheism and Communism (Koonz 1986). The 1917 Bolshevist Revolution in Russia and the rising influence of the Communist Party in Germany made Protestants fear that Germany was on the verge of a Marxist revolution. Confessionals joined the chorus that, "We were just barely rescued from Bolshevist chaos by Hitler" (quoted Barnett 1992: 33). An influential church memorandum stated the widespread assumption that the rise of National Socialism was chiefly necessary in order to combat Marxism, which was "an immediate threat to the state and the churches." Even the persecution of the Jews was considered a necessary byproduct of the need to purge Germany of the Marxist elements that supposedly infiltrated Germany after the fall of the monarchy in 1918 (quoted in Matheson 1981: 12, 13). In this climate, it was not surprising that on the eve of church elections of April 1932, the Nazi newspaper, *Der Angriff*, which Goebbels edited, published a full-page notice to "Protestant Christianity" which warned readers of the godless atheism of Marxism and Bolshevism and proclaimed that National Socialism was a vanguard against these threats (Wright 1974: 85).

MORALITY AND DECENCY

The Nazis also positioned themselves as defenders of good morals and decency in the face of an increasingly decadent modern world. Hitler claimed to have been concerned early on with the "filth" in the press, art, and literature, which he linked to the Jews. According to Hitler, an evil "system" reached its tentacles into Germany through the media, schools, and theater (Rhodes 1980: 47). The Nazis, promised to "fight all enemies of the Christen faiths as well as all things in the press, in literature, in the cinema, and on the stage" that were against culture and religion (Childers 1983: 114). Though not against modern "progress," the Nazis gave the impression that they would reorient modernity toward Christian decency and morality.

Many rank-and-file Nazis said they supported Hitler because they "experienced a shocking spiritual catastrophe, namely the sudden perversion of German morals" (quoted in Rhodes 1980: 92). Other Hitler followers were most enraged about the "moral ruin" after the War (Rhodes 1980: 93). According to the Nazi faithful, "Houses of prostitution shot up out of the earth. All the sewers of vulgarity seemed to have opened. The...upright part of the population carried on an almost hopeless struggle against this filth" (Rhodes 1980: 94). One Nazi connected moral degradation with religious blasphemy (quoted in Rhodes 1980: 93):

> Promiscuity, shamelessness, fraud, and cheating were elevated to the throne. The German women seemed to have cast off German essentiality. The German man appeared to have forgotten the German sense of honor and German honorability. Jewish writers and the Jewish press could blather with impunity and drag everything in the mud. They did not even stop before our holiest feelings and they even dared to mock our Lord on the Cross in public exhibitions.

Besides the loss of "basic morality," the Brownshirts viewed modern art in Germany as the "morbid excrescences of insane and degenerate men" (quoted in Rhodes 1980: 94). Against the excesses of "modern" culture, the Nazis were positioned as the defenders of morality and decency.

To deal with the moral and spiritual degradation, the Nazis demanded "public education on a Christian and *volkisch* basis." The Nazis claimed in 1930 that they would champion the cause of religion over atheistic socialism. In practice that meant being against the secularization of the schools, and maintaining, against the SPD, the influence of religion in education (Noakes 1971: 207). According to Hitler, "The national government will guarantee the Christian confessions their due influence in school and educational matters" (quoted in Matheson 1981: 9).

Further, National Socialism claimed to provide an antidote to the breakdown of family life, and advocated the "healing of the *Volk*, the establishment of a new fatherland, and the creation of a greater *Volksgemeinschaft* based on the German Christian family" (Childers 1983: 114). National Socialism claimed that modernity had destroyed traditional roles in the family. One of the most popular Nazi slogans, "Kinder, Kirche, Küche," called for the return of women to children, church, and the kitchen. National Socialism would restore the male role in economic and political life (Koonz 1986).

PROTESTANT NARRATIVES AND SYMBOLS

The Nazi Party made extensive and judicious use of biblical concepts and images to identify who they were and where they stood. The Nazi vision was set strongly within the images of rebirth, regeneration, and renewal. In words echoing a Protestant conversion, Hitler described his personal journey to National Socialism as a "regeneration" which followed the "the greatest inner soul struggles" (Rhodes 1980: 52). Early on, Hitler used the Christian themes of death and regeneration in his understanding of the *Volk*. The *Volk* is invincible, according to Hitler, and even its destruction "assures the rebirth of the *Volk* and is the seed of life from which a new tree some day will strike secure roots" (Rhodes 1980: 58). Hitler claimed that his government had taken on the "work of national and moral renewal of our nation" (quoted in Matheson 1981: 9).

Several of the Nazi followers used the terms, "renewed," "reborn," and "awakened" to describe their National Socialist experience. Others claimed to glow with "the spirit" and "inner power" (quoted in Rhodes 1980: 60). Becoming the new man was "a great change...one of the most completely reforming inner renewals" (Rhodes 1980: 79). Nazi actions were understood in terms of the spiritual renewal of society. One Brownshirt exclaimed that a thundercloud had been lifted from his "black" city by the Nazis, who brought "purifying and cleaning...and again a healthful wind blows through our fatherland" (Rhodes 1980: 70).

The National Socialists set their movement within Protestant traditions by cultivating an image in which Hitler was the savior of Germany, parallel to Christ. Even as early as 1925 Hitler saw himself as a messiah (Rhodes 1980: 68). He declared in 1932, "We are the chosen," and "whoever claims allegiance to me is one of the chosen" (Rhodes 1980: 60). In 1933, Hitler, using the language of the Lord's Prayer, promised that under him a new kingdom would come to earth. Setting himself within the narrative of Christ, Hitler suggested that if he did not fulfill this mission, "you should then crucify me" (Waite 1977: 27). The messianic imagery placed Hitler in the grand scheme of salvation history, according to one Nazi: "I was not about to give up my Nazi membership since I believed Hitler to be Germany's salvation" (Merkl 1980: 94). An artist depicted Hitler preaching to early supporters in a painting entitled "In the beginning was the word," a phrase which refers to Christ in Protestant tradition (Lutzer 1995: 63). For the rank-and-file, the messiah imagery gave meaning to the entire movement: "Some day the world will recognize that the Reich we established with blood and sacrifice is destined to bring peace and blessing to the world" (Abel 1986: 218).

Hitler fit himself and his movement into the Protestant traditions through the doctrine of Providence (Dahm 1968: 44). According to this doctrine, God has not withdrawn from the created world, but continuously sustains and rules his creation, taking an active role in determining the events of history. The Nazi Party reconstructed the doctrine of Providence to place their movement within Protestant narratives. According to the Party, the increasing popularity of the party in the early 1930's was in the divine will. Hitler saturated his speeches with images that placed the Nazi movement within God's Providence, and insisted that National Socialism alone recognized the virtuous gifts God had given to Germans, including pure blood and light complexion. Because the Nazis' thanked God for these gifts and were committed to racial purity and abolishing Jewish influence, the Almighty was blessing National Socialism, according to Hitler (Prange 1944: 87). Similarly, Goebbels wrote in his diary that both he and Hitler were "instruments of divine will" (Reuth 1993: 75). In 1934, after the death of former President Paul Hindenburg, Rudolf Hess insisted that "Providence has worked in the life of Adolf Hitler," giving him the abilities and strengths to overcome continually difficult circumstances in order to fulfill his goal, the "salvation of Germany" (Hess 1990: 15).

The Nazi symbol, the swastika, also drew on Protestant traditions. For the symbol of the movement, Hitler chose a type of cross, personally altering the design to form the swastika (Waite 1977: 29). Though critics charged that the bent Christian cross was blasphemous, Hitler argued that the swastika was "the political manifestation of what the Christian Cross intends" (Prange 1944: 88).

In speeches between 1927 and 1932 published in the NSDAP official newspaper, *Voelkischer Beobachter*, Hitler also connected National Socialism with the Christian concept of "covenant." He proclaimed that, "the Lord gave us [Germany] His blessing because we deserved it; the Lord revoked His blessing because we were not worthy of it" (Prange 1944: 87). A similar example of placing the movement within the Protestant framework was the use of the phrase "Thousand Year Reich," which was a variant of the apocalyptic period over which Christ rules, described in the book of Revelation.

Even the relation of the Party to other groups was articulated within Protestant images and allusions. During the electoral campaign of July 1932, Hitler's challenge to the DDP and *Zentrum* parties came directly out of Revelation: Just as Christ warned against the lukewarm apathy of the church at Laodicea (in Revelation 3:15-16), these lukewarm parties will be spat out since they are neither hot nor cold. He declared, "In that [God] permits the destruction of the lukewarm, He wishes thereby to give us victory" (Prange 1944: 89). In challenging religious powers, the Nazis clothed themselves in biblical language. The Nazi reason for opposing the "meddling" of Catholic and institutional Protestantism in politics was that the Nazis had to "maintain the purity of religion by following the example of the Lord, who drove the usurers and charlatans out of the temple" (Childers 1983: 115).

Many Protestants enthusiastically embraced the wrapping of the Nazi movement in Protestant images and symbols. The German Christians saturated their journal with "Nazified" Christian symbolism and themes promoting the intertwining of the *Volk* with Christianity. Many overlaid a Christian cross on the swastika to show that Christianity was completely reconciled with allegiance to National Socialism. Melding Christian and Nazi symbols became commonplace in religious ceremonies. Photographs of "Nazi baptism" show the baby lying by a table draped with Nazi flags. Photos of a mass wedding show a couple kneeling before an altar draped in the Nazi flag. The dean of the Magdeburg Cathedral, standing amidst swastika-emblazoned flags in 1933, declared that "whoever reviles this symbol of ours is reviling our Germany," and that the flags surrounding the altar "radiate hope" (Bethge 1970: 191).

SPEAKING THE PROTESTANT LANGUAGE

Besides the legitimacy of placing the movement within the grand sweep of Protestant history and myth, the National Socialist movement spoke a language of system versus heart, and used these categories to interpret the social change in the 1920s. The Nazis were obsessed with an "uncanny system that exerted arcane powers over the whole of existence," and argued that achieving German salvation depended on destroying the "system" (Rhodes 1980: 50, 181). As early as 1922 Hitler used the term, "system," and Goebbels popularized the symbol in his newspaper, *Der Angriff*. By 1933, the "system" was the number-one expressed fear of the movement. The vast majority of the Nazi rank-and-file believed that the "system" was crushing them (Rhodes 1980: 212–213). The Nazi faithful saw their experience as National Socialists as a search for "deeper causes," which often meant uncovering the "wirepullers" and the machinations of the "system" (Rhodes 1980: 54). Their answer was the purity of spiritual renewal, which was tied up with the revival of the *Volk*.

Often the opposition of heart and system was expressed by the Nazis in terms of "*Volk*" versus "Jew." Reviving the pure spiritual essence, the *Volk*, and destroying the Jewish face behind the "system" represented the redemption of the decadent, materialistic, modern world (Noakes 1971: 210). Hitler saw the Jews as creating a "system" through a network of institutions to destroy the German people (Rhodes 1980: 46), in particular, international Jewish capital cast a "golden net" which entangled the German *Volk* (Rhodes 1980: 179). In 1928, Hitler summed up the struggle of *Volk* with Jews and the system-world of modernity: "Before us the eternal enemy of the *Volk*, the Jew, democracy, capitalism—all only expressions of the same spirit which always negates" the existence of the *Volk*. "Either we will succeed in bringing the *Volk* to consciousness and to attack against the supranational powers," he declared, "or it is the end" (Rhodes 1980: 66). The Nazi rank-and-file juxtaposed purity of heart and the Jewish "threat." One recruit related "the struggle for the German soul [and peeling] off the alien layers from the German soul" with creating "a certain people," which meant purifying the *Volk* of Jewish influence (Merkl 1980: 226).

The spiritual purity of the heart was challenged by modernity. The cities, according to the Nazis, were lifeless and void, and required inner spiritual renewal. Hitler derided the possibility that "some day people might admire the department stores of a few Jews as the mightiest works of our era, and the hotels of a few corporations as the characteristic expression of the culture of our times." Since "in them there is no dominant higher idea...our cities...lack the outstanding symbol of national community" (Rhodes 1980: 120). In addition to the lack of spiritual meaning, conditions in the cities stimulated burlesque and pornography, according to Hitler, who claimed that as a result "our whole public life today is like a hothouse for sexual ideas and stimulations" (Rhodes 1980: 94).

National Socialists believed industrialization contributed to the rise of crass materialism, and sought to reinfuse industrial development with the life-affirming impulse of spirit and *Volk*. Goebbels, using biblical language, saw the cultural changes as an "obscene dance round the golden calf.... I can see no peace either in this world or in my own soul" (Rhodes 1980: 94). Industrialization was associated with "mammonism" and was destroying the inner purity of the soul. Meaning was lost in the expanding system as, in Hitler's words, "Quality lost its value and was supplanted by quantity" (Rhodes 1980: 93).

Modernity must be infused with a spiritual essence and meaning. Rapid technological change was not in itself a threat, but required a spiritual infusion to make it whole. Goebbels declared that (quoted in Herf 1986: 39):

> technology will make men soulless. National Socialism [has as] one of its main tasks...to fill it inwardly with soul, to discipline it and to place it in service of our people and their cultural level.... National Socialism understood how to take the soulless framework of technology and fill it with the rhythm and hot impulses of our time.

Hitler agreed that art, science, and technology are good since they are the creative product of the Aryan, but they are given meaning only through the spiritual purity of sacrifice and community (Rhodes 1980: 109). The material world needed spiritual direction. According to Hitler, the stifling system of modern industrial production needed the infusion of the heroic action of the "new man," which would do away with "the spirit of materialism" (Rhodes 1980: 79).

The Nazis constructed a similar meaning of economic threats. One Nazi writer contrasted the moral decay of the Depression with the spiritual purity of the Nazi movement: "the soul eating, character-murdering unemployment" and blamed unemployment, on "the system," as did many Nazis (Merkl 1980: 190). Nazis constructed their understanding of parliamentary democracy as the loss of *Gemeinschaft* and spiritual unity. The factionalism of parliamentary democracy was opposed to the spiritual unity of *Gemeinschaft* society, according to one party member (quoted in Merkl 1980: 251), while the Nazis embodied a

> sincere commitment to the German people as a whole whose greatest misfortune was being divided into so many parties and classes. Finally a practical proposal for the renewal of the people! Destroy the parties! Do away with the classes!

True *Volksgemeinschaft!* [The Nazis] alone gave hope of saving the German fatherland.

The Nazis sought an "organic structuring," in which each member of the Volk would be a spiritually living being, united as one "organism" (Rhodes 1980: 112–113).

The secularization process was lamented by the National Socialists as well. Hitler stated (Rhodes 1980: 93):

> For fourteen years Germany suffered under a process of decay which is unparalleled in history. All values were overturned. "Evil be thou my good" was the password. What was healthy was no longer the aim of human striving, and decadents and monstrosities became the heroes of a so-called new culture.

Rank-and-file Nazis were morally incensed by the perceived secularizing trends: "[T]he moral disintegration at home and...the human meanness, cowardice, and cravenness" of the changeover from the old society to the new caused him to "still feel the nausea rising in me today when I think of it" (Merkl 1980: 115). But the "new man of community" would bring spiritual vitality to "an extravagant, spiritually hollow age...[with] obsolete and rotten liberal social orders and forms" (quoted in Rhodes 1980: 59). The rank-and-file opposed the secular *zeitgeist* with the spiritual purity of the new man.

If the growth of a meaningless and spiritually bankrupt system-world was the problem for the Nazis, the solution was cast in terms of inner spiritual revival. Hitler traced the German downfall to an inner spiritual essence: the events of the 20s, he claimed, were "the greatest outward symptom of decay amid a whole series of inner symptoms" (Rhodes 1980: 60).

According to Nazi rank-and-file, inner renewal was crucial to the National Socialist movement. One exclaimed, "The philosophy of National Socialism must take roots in one's very heart!" (Abel 1986: 70) Another saw the central place of inner renewal (quoted in Rhodes 1980: 59):

> We young German men are beginning to understand only gradually that, not only in the *Volk* seen as a whole but in us men ourselves the process of a great change has been taking place, one of the most completely reforming inner renewals...Scarcely any generation living before us has had to fight for such a thorough renewal which upsets all the depths of man.

Early Nazi Party "discussion evenings" had the air of a revival meeting as members strove for spiritual purity and commitment through the mutual strengthening of their faith (Merkl 1980: 254).

The external material world stood opposed to the purity of inner spirit, and, as explained by a Nazi recruit, the spiritual aspect must be brought into focus to revitalize the outer, societal world (quoted in Merkl 1980: 241):

> A non-Nazi who has not experienced the enormous elementary power of the idea of our Fuhrer will never understand any of this.... When I say so little in this

vita about my external life, my job, etc., this is only because my real life, the real content of my life is my work for and commitment to Hitler and toward a national socialist Germany.... Hitler is the purest embodiment of the German character.

All of these ways of constructing reality resonated with the life experience of German Protestants.

THEORETICAL CONCLUSIONS

Explaining support for National Socialism requires a systematic analysis of the identities of rural Protestants. What about the German social and cultural context made voting for Hitler a moral stance for so many Protestants?

Identity, the answer to the question, "who are you?" is constructed through the taking of moral stands (Taylor 1989). It is often multiple and conflicting (Calhoun 1994), but is socially constructed within the structure of alternate identities of a particular institutional sphere, or differentiated social space (i.e., a "field"). Thus, understanding the dynamics of a differentiated social space (Bourdieu 1992), in the Protestant religious field, is essential for explaining how support for Hitler became a moral stance which was part and parcel of identity construction for rural Protestants. The processes of defining legitimate religious capital and negotiating the boundaries between the religious and political fields (Bourdieu 1991) shaped the construction of Protestant identities that expressed fundamental moral commitments in voting for National Socialism.

The emergence of the Nazi movement depended on the structure of relations between actors in religious social space, in which identities were constructed with the categories of system and heart. The salience of system/heart was rooted in interpretations of experience *within* the Protestant church. The Church's cultural role in small towns, and thus in the life-experiences of ordinary Protestants, ensured that the symbolic world of grass-roots Protestants was strongly influenced by the struggles within the religious field.

Reconstructing Pietistic traditions, actors within the field mapped the religious landscape in terms of an increasingly rigid system-world which had obfuscated the vital, inner, spiritual essence. The salience of these categories increased as dominated religious positions, such as the German Christians, challenged the principles which organized the field by championing a nascent faith (Warner 1988) marked by a vital spiritual purity. According to the religious radicals, the formality, hierarchy, and concern with orthodoxy—all of the commitments that made sense to dominant religious producers—threatened the spiritual re-awakening of Germany.

This spiritual renewal was not to be limited to the religious sphere, since, for religious radicals, all of life was in the throes of decay to the lifeless and "neutral" spirit of modernity. Dominated producers sought the spiritual unity of the *Volk* which reinfused all spheres of life with a dynamic, life-giving spiritual essence. Nascent religious radicals, with less stake in the autonomy and principles of the religious field, were more open to bringing political capital into play within the religious field.

But why the alliance with National Socialists? Because the Nazis occupied a dominated position in the political field, analogous to the radicals in the religious field, and thus spoke the Protestant language. The Nazi position used the categories of system and heart to challenge Marxism and other evils of modernity, including cultural change in education and family. The radicals' strategy was to purify the religious field through heartfelt faith, while the Nazis pursued the same for the German nation. The answer was not a longing for a "golden age," but a radical movement to reinfuse the mundane, material world with the vitality of pure spirit and hearts.

In sum, identity construction for dominated actors in the religious field was analogous to that of the Nazis in the political sphere, and this created the opportunity for inter-subjective meaning and successful alliances. Thus, the rural Protestant vote for Hitler was the political equivalent of taking a stand against the growth and institutionalization of a lifeless, rigid, and hierarchical system, in favor of infusing the church and the world with the dynamic, life-affirming, "hot impulses of our time."

The ultimate consequences of voting for Hitler could not have been more ironic. The moral logic which saw the world in terms of heart and system had paltry cultural resources to stand against the Nazis when "purification" ran amok. Most Protestant fellow travelers, to say nothing of the German Christians, were later easily cowed into silence.

REFERENCES

Abel, T. 1986. *Why Hitler Came to Power*. Cambridge: Harvard University Press.

Allen, W. S. 1986. "The Nazi Rise to Power." In *The Rise of the Nazi Regime*. Boulder: Westview.

Barnes, K. 1991. *Nazism, Liberalism, and Christianity*. Lexington: University of Kentucky Press.

Barnett, V. 1992. *For the Soul of the People: Protestant Protest Against Hitler*. New York: Oxford.

Bendix, R. 1952. "Social Stratification and Political Power." *American Political Science Review*. 46(3): 357–375.

Bergen, D. 1991. "One Reich, One People, One Church: the German Christian Movement and the People's Church, 1932–1945." Ph.D. dissertation, Department of History, University of North Carolina, Chapel Hill, NC.

Bethge, E. 1970. *Dietrich Bonhoeffer*. London: Collins.

Bourdieu, P. 1991. "The Genesis and Structure of the Religious Field." *Comparative Social Research*. 13: 1–44.

Bourdieu, P. and L. Wacquant. 1992. *An Invitation to Reflexive Sociology*. Chicago: University of Chicago Press.

Calhoun, C. 1991. "Morality, Identity, and Historical Explanation: Charles Taylor on the Sources of the Self." *Sociological Theory*. 9: 232–263.

Calhoun, C. 1994. "Social Theory and the Politics of Identity" in *Social Theory and the Politics of Identity*. C. Calhoun, ed. Oxford: Blackwell.

Childers, T. 1983. *The Nazi Voter*. Chapel Hill: The University of North Carolina Press.

Dahm, K-W. 1968. "German Protestantism and Politics, 1918–39." *Contemporary History*. 3: 29–50.

Diephouse, D. 1977. "The 'German Catastrophe' Revisited: Civil Religion in the Third Reich." *Fides et Historia*.

Diephouse, D. 1987. *Pastors and Pluralism in Württemberg, 1918–1933*. Princeton: Princeton University Press.

Douglass, P. F. 1935. *God Among the Germans*. Philadelphia: University of Pennsylvania Press.

Falter, J. 1981. "Radicalization of the Middle Classes or Mobilization of the Unpolitical?" *Social Science Information*. 20(2): 389–430.

_____. 1986. "The National Socialist Mobilization of New Voters: 1928–1933" in *The Formation of the Nazi Constituency 1919–1933*. Edited by Thomas Childers. London: Croom Helm.

_____. 1991. *Hitler's Wähler*. München: Beck.

Feige, F. 1990. *The Varieties of Protestantism in Nazi Germany*. Lewiston: Edwin Mellen.

Frey, A. 1938. *Cross and Swastika*. London: Student Christian Movement Press.

Hamilton, R. 1982. *Who Voted for Hitler?* Princeton: Princeton University Press.

Helmreich, E. C. 1979. *The German Churches under Hitler*. Detroit: Wayne State.

Herf, J. 1986. "Comments on Reactionary Modernist Components of Nazi Ideology" in *The Rise of the Nazi Regime*. Charles Maier et al, eds. Boulder: Westview.

Hess, R. 1990. *Selected Speeches*. Translated and published by Karl Hammer.

Hitler, A. 1941. *Mein Kampf*. New York: Reynal & Hitchcock.

Koonz, C. 1986. "Women Between God and Fuhrer" in *The Rise of the Nazi Regime*. Charles Maier et al, eds. Boulder: Westview.

Kornhauser, W. 1959. *The Politics of Mass Society*. New York: The Free Press.

Kuechler, M. 1992. "The NSDAP Vote in the Weimar Republic." *Historical Social Research*. 17: 22–52.

Lease, G. 1995. *"Odd Fellows" in the Politics of Religion*. Berlin: Mouton de Gruyter.

Lipset, S. 1960. *Political Man*. Garden City: Doubleday.

Lohmöller, J-B., and J. Falter. 1986. "Some Further Aspects of Ecological Regression Analysis." *Quality and Quantity*. 20: 109–125.

Loomis, C. and J. A. Beegle. 1946. "The Spread of German Nazism in Rural Areas." *American Sociological Review*. 11(6): 724–734.

Lutzer, E. 1995. *Hitler's Cross*. Chicago: Moody.

Matheson, P. 1981. *The Third Reich and the Christian Churches*. Grand Rapids: Eerdmans.

Merkl, P. 1980. *The Making of a Stormtrooper*. Princeton: Princeton University Press.

Micklem, N. 1939. *National Socialism and Christianity*. New York: Farrar & Rinehart.

Mzimela, S. 1980. *Nazism and Apartheid*. Lewiston: Edwin Mellen.

Noakes, J. 1971. *The Nazi Party in Lower Saxony*. London: Oxford.

Pierard, Ri. 1978. "Why Did Protestants Welcome Hitler?" *Fides et Historia*. 10: 8–29.

Pinson, K. 1934. *Pietism as a Factor in the Rise of German Nationalism*. New York: Columbia.

Pois, R. A. 1986. *National Socialism and the Religion of Nature*. London: Croom Helm.

Prange, G. (ed.). 1944. *Hitler's Words*. Washington, D.C.: American Council on Public Affairs.

Rhodes, J. *The Hitler Movement*. Stanford: Hoover Institution Press.

Reuth, R. G. 1993. *Goebbels*. New York: Harcourt Brace & Company.

Scholder, K. 1987. *The Churches and the Third Reich*. London: SCM Press.

Taylor, C. 1989. *Sources of the Self*. Cambridge: Harvard.

Waite, R. 1977. *The Psychopathic God: Adolf Hitler*. New York: Basic Books.

Warner, S. 1988. *New Wine in Old Wineskins*. Berkeley: University of California Press.

Wright, J. 1974. `Above Parties': The Political Attitudes of the German Protestant Church Leadership 1918–1933*. London: Oxford.

Wright, J. 1977. "The German Protestant Church and the Nazi Party in the Period of the Seizure of Power 1932–3." in Derek Baker (ed.): Renaissance and Renewal in Christian History. Oxford: Bosill Blackwell.

Zabel, J. 1976. *Nazism and the Pastors*. Missoula: Scholars Press.

Ziegler, H. 1989. *Nazi Germany's New Aristocracy*. Princeton: Princeton University Press.

Many Are Called but Few Obey: Ideological Commitment and Activism in Operation Rescue[1]

Rhys H. Williams and Jeffrey Blackburn

The conventional sociological wisdom about abortion as a socio-political issue is that it is an expressive symbol for a wider rift based on cultural worldviews (Luker 1984; Himmelstein 1986; Ginsburg 1989). Analysts see activists on both sides of the issue as less concerned with the practice of abortion as such, than with its meaning in relation to a series of issues that are newly ambiguous in the social, moral, and political landscape of the late twentieth century. Abortion is a symbolic issue condensing a wider debate over morality, gender roles, and the place of women in contemporary society.

For example, Luker (1984) disentangles the socio-logic that the two sets of activists use to justify their actions and reveals the underlying tensions between women's roles in the work world and the family. Ginsburg (1989) understands both pro-life and pro-choice activists as being concerned with what abortion reveals about the proper relationship between men and women. At issue is whether legalized abortion frees women from men's domination or frees men from social responsibility.

This literature is significant for providing important empirical examples of the role and power of symbols in contemporary politics. Symbols are neither totemistic remnants from a pre-modern past nor emblems of a post-modern society lacking substance. Rather, symbols are the currency of politics—ideology, discourse, and political mobilization would be impossible without them.

Nowhere is this more important than in social-movement politics. Social movements are by definition groups of people mobilized to challenge political power from outside the institutionalized corridors of influence. They necessarily rely on symbols to recruit members, neutralize opponents, and influence by-standers and elites.

As a symbol, abortion has become the center of a maelstrom of political and social issues. While movements with the seemingly straightforward titles "pro-life" and "pro-choice" dominate public debate, "the abortion issue" is actually a conglomeration of potentially distinct issues, policies, positions, and players—Condit (1990), for example, documents many possible positions and rationales that could potentially constitute debate on abortion. This chapter demonstrates this complexity through an analysis of interviews with grass-roots activists in one direct-action anti-abortion group. Interviews with activists show that abortion is a "condensed symbol" (Douglas 1973) that often embodies a much wider worldview than even the studies cited above would indicate.

Further, we demonstrate that translating that worldview into formal-movement ideology and practical political strategy can produce wide variation—even within small, tightly-knit, supposedly homogenous social-movement groups. We conclude by discussing the implications for social-movement theory and its recent attention to movement culture and ideology.

OPERATION RESCUE AND ANTI-ABORTION DIRECT ACTION

Recently, Ginsburg (1993) and others (Faludi 1989; Tribe 1990) have written on the religious anti-abortion group Operation Rescue, which exploded on the national scene at the 1988 Democratic convention in Atlanta with its "new" tactic: mass blockades of clinics provoking mass arrests. Subsequent high-profile blockade campaigns—particularly in Wichita, Kansas in 1991—and the diffusion of those tactics, have made Operation Rescue a significant player in the anti-abortion movement. Indeed, Operation Rescue has become so entrenched in abortion politics that a 1995 news report on murders of abortion providers referred to the organization as "an established anti-abortion group" (National Public Radio, "Morning Edition" February 3, 1995). Operation Rescue was a pioneer in developing direct-action tactics.

Ginsburg (1993) analyzes Operation Rescue's ideological reach as going beyond even the expanded borders of the gender and family argument outlined above. Ginsburg claims that the group understands its purpose as "saving America's soul" and restoring the country to a position of righteousness in the eyes of a rigorous and judgmental God (also see Williams 1995). They still understand abortion as more of a means than an end, but the eventual goal is a sweeping indictment of contemporary America. Operation Rescue's high-profile national leader, Randall Terry (quoted in Ginsburg 1993: 558) explicitly professes to be interested in "challenging the entire legitimacy of the secular modern State, withholding allegiance until the nation returns to its religious roots in matters like public prayer and religious education."

Ginsburg's analysis of Terry's writings and media interviews is insightful. Terry proclaims that abortion is but "the tip of the iceberg" (1988: 137), and his 1988 book *Operation Rescue* lays out, not always systematically, a project for thoroughly reforming American culture and a program for accomplishing that end. Operation Rescue's goal is culture reform, and while its immediate tactics involve direct action and clinic blockades, its overall strategy requires more widely-based politico-legal action for change at the societal level.

Thus, at least in Terry's account, abortion is not just a rallying cry for those swept up by rival worldviews, battling over a symbol that has wide expressive connotations, and about which its partisans can only be dimly aware. Rather, abortion is but part of a war of cultural reform, self-consciously tackled with the resources at the group's disposal.

Ginsburg (1993) then generalizes from her analysis of Operation Rescue to the wider anti-abortion movement. She notes that the fight against abortion used to be led by groups such as the National Right to Life Committee, that, while often sponsored by the Catholic Church, were relatively loose coalitions of Catholics and Protestants, many of whom disagreed on other political issues. They pursued a variety of loosely-coordinated activities from letter-writing to picketing, most of them legal and well-recognized methods of promoting political change.

According to Ginsburg, however, the cutting edge of anti-abortion activism has passed to groups willing to use direct action, including extra-legal and illegal means; this includes but is not limited to Operation Rescue. In contrast with the earlier phase, in which loosely-affiliated broadly-based coalitions had a fairly restricted agenda, the new activist organizations are narrow, ideologically conformist movements with broad agendas not limited to abortion.

A clear inference from Ginsburg's work and similar studies (e.g. Blanchard 1994) of groups committed to such a broad agenda and high-risk tactics is that they need a high level of attitudinal consensus in order to function. Such commitment is one of their primary organizational resources. Without large numbers, and often acting outside the bounds of civil political action, the groups must use the high energy and intense commitment of their members for influence.

But is that really the case? Ginsburg's analysis, while clearly superior to journalistic accounts such as Faux's (1990) or Ralston's (1992), similarly relies almost exclusively on the public pronouncements of movement leaders, Randall Terry in particular. Terry's copious writings and willingness to play to the media make this an inviting strategy, but analysts have almost wholly overlooked the views of rank-and-file members (for an exception see Maxwell and Jelen, 1994). Ideological conformity to a broad agenda is simply inferred from Terry's expansive vision and the group's highly-visible and self-stigmatizing tactics.

In contrast, we argue that interviews with rank-and-file activists reveal a more complex ideological picture, as well as distinctions in levels of social-movement commitment. This complexity becomes more evident if one makes distinctions among different types of symbolic resources that social movements use.

SYMBOLIC RESOURCES AND MOVEMENT IDEOLOGY

Our concern here is with what we term the "ideological commitment" among rank-and-file activists identified with Operation Rescue. However, taking our cue from recent work in the sociology of social movements, we recognize the differences between passively held attitudes and ideas powerful enough to motivate activism. Further, the extent to which different members use the same interpretations of movement ideas is an empirical question to be investigated, not assumed.

We make several distinctions among different ideational features associated with social movements and their cultures. A *worldview* is the set of encompassing understandings of life and the world that operate at the level of assumptions. Worldviews provide a sense of "facticity" about humankind and the nature of the good society.[2] To some extent, this includes what Klandermans (1988) calls "consensus formation." This is the "unplanned convergence of meaning in social networks and subcultures" (1988: 175) that in part mark social boundaries. Thus worldviews are both resources from which social movements draw their ideas and the receptivity pool—or cultural field, depending upon your preference in metaphors—into which movements launch their appeals.

A *formal ideology* is the rhetoric of movement leadership that translates elements of the worldview into organizational and activism terms, including the definition of appropriate goals for the movement and the best strategy for achieving those goals. To some extent, we use "formal ideology" in much the same manner as David Snow and his colleagues (et al. 1986; and Benford 1988) use the term "framing." It is a group's diagnosis of problem, prescriptions for change, and motivations for action, as set out by movement elites. In Klandermans' terms, formal ideologies are part of the process of "consensus mobilization (1984; 1988), wherein movements attempt to channel consensus toward participation in the movement's activities.

Operative ideology, on the other hand, is the actual practical understandings activists use to explain their involvement, to themselves and to others. It is akin to what Giddens terms "practical consciousness" (1984: xxiii, 41–45, 290–291); that is, there is a coherence to what people do. They understand their own action, but often not in ways exactly parallel to either the formal ideology of movement leaders or the analyses of scholars. Note that we have adapted Perrow's (1986) distinction between an organization's "formal" goals and its "operative" goals. The former are the goals articulated by organizational leadership and embodied in formal charters and public statements. The latter are the goals that actually operate to orient action within the organization. Activists may or may not explicitly recognize operative goals, and those operative goals may or may not subvert formal goals.

Finally, *symbols* are powerful signs and indicators that can bridge the differences between worldviews, and formal, and operative ideologies by relying more on emotive responses rather than cognitive attitudes or beliefs. Symbols have the ability to produce "solidarity without consensus" (Kertzer 1988: 69), an important tool for motivating movement challenges. Importantly, a movement's symbols need not rely completely on cognitive agreement. In this sense Klandermans' emphasis on "consensus" can be misleading. Consensus does not always precede action (see Ferree 1992) and in many cases remains partial at the level of cognitive attitudes. A crucial process in movement mobilization is the organization of symbolic resources that can both bridge and encompass the worldview and the ideologies.

We turn now to an examination of the movement culture of Operation Rescue. We analyze the formal and operative ideologies of the group, the extent to which they are grounded in a common worldview, and the divergence around questions of translating worldview consensus into political action.

METHODS AND DATA

Our data are drawn from interviews with thirty subjects from southern Illinois and eastern Missouri, chosen for their fervent pro-life views. Twenty-four were Protestants, four were Catholics. While almost all of the interviewees have had at least some involvement with Operation Rescue, the degree of involvement varies. Several interviewees are organizational coordinators; others are moderately or sporadically active in the group; and some are ex-activists who have dropped out of organizational actions for a variety of reasons. Two interviewees, while pro-life in their attitudes, have never been involved with an Operation Rescue activity.

The interviews explored two areas. First, they examined the extent to which interviewees had knowledge of, and felt themselves in accord with, Randall Terry's views on issues ranging from abortion, per se, to broader cultural and political reform. Second, they explored the interviewees' involvement with Operation Rescue as a group, their participation in its activities, and their understanding of the rationale for those actions.

We distilled Terry's views from his book *Operation Rescue* (1988) and from available media interviews. Because Operation Rescue is so thoroughly identified with Terry's direct leadership, we use his writings as representative of the group's formal ideology. They contain all the major elements of a social-movement ideology: an analysis of current social problems in need of action; a prescriptive view of what should be done to alleviate the problems, including appropriate strategies for action; and the requisite motivations for mobilizing action (see Snow and Benford 1988 on social-movement framing). Terry's writings also contain elements of what we describe as the "worldview," the foundation for the organizational ideology.

The interviews with rank-and-file pro-life activists followed an interview schedule structured to elicit responses to all these elements in Terry's writings. Respondents had a fair amount of latitude to take the interview in whatever direction they considered important, but we continued to use prompting questions designed to elicit comments on the formal ideology. Thus we are able to disentangle participants' understanding of what they were doing from Terry's official positions. We call the degree of this congruence "ideological-commitment." We present the formal and operative ideologies in turn.

WORLDVIEW AND FORMAL IDEOLOGY

Randall Terry's *Operation Rescue* contains themes that reflect both worldview and formal organizational ideology. Terry, of course, does not make this distinction, and the text itself mixes concrete organizational goals, strategies, and tactics, with worldview assumptions that undergird and transcend the specifics. Near the front of the book (1988: 15) is a short list of modest goals that center on issues surrounding abortion:

> First, to do everything possible to rescue babies and their mothers from the nightmare of abortion on the very doorstep of local abortion clinics. Second, to show the love of Christ to women in crisis pregnancies by providing whatever help they need to carry their child to term. Third, to re-educate the public and the church to the value of human life from a Bible-based, Christian perspective and to expose the horrors of abortion.

Clearly, Terry recognizes that blockading clinics is but a short-term tactic for the group. Along with physically stopping abortions, Terry calls for attention to women with crisis pregnancies. While the organization is not known for the type of pregnancy care that marks such groups as the pro-life organization, Birthright, the second goal recognizes that abortion is not the sole issue facing women. The third goal offers hints of a broader agenda, calling for a change-oriented campaign aimed at both the church and the broader public. The call, however, is to "re-educate," eschewing any talk of political or legal action.

As a program, these three goals are at the level of formal ideology, describing a problem and what must be done to correct it. But while these are listed systematically, in many other places Terry offers a more expansive and politicized view of Operation Rescue's mission. For example, he calls explicitly for the overturning of *Roe* vs. *Wade*, followed by passage of a Human Life Amendment (1988: 197). Thus there is a strategic agenda stretching from education to direct action, to political and legal change.

As Ginsburg notes, Terry also moves from abortion to a more encompassing vision of cultural reform. He has asserted that "ultimately my goal is to reform this culture...to return to...a Judeo-Christian base" (quoted in Faludi 1989: 26). In another example, Terry (1988: 178) suggests a litany of evils that Operation Rescue will address over time: "We will defeat the abortion holocaust, restore religious and civil liberties to individuals, bring justice to our judicial system, see common decency return, and the godless, hedonistic, sexually perverted mind-set of today will be pushed back into the closet." In another place, Terry (1988: 58) offers a slightly different list of "evils" needing attention: "abortion, infanticide, euthanasia, pornography, and the elimination of Christian witness in the public schools."

Thus cultural-reform goals of Operation Rescue find clear expression in Terry's writings. Also in those writings are themes that help form the Operation Rescue worldview by justifying the focus on abortion as an issue, analyzing the current situation of cultural and moral crisis, and delineating the direct-action tactics Operation Rescue uses in pursuing its aims.

The first theme is clearly a product of Terry's religious beliefs, an assumption that is a basis for much of his other writings. Terry's thought is based on a belief in the inherent depravity of human nature. To be born human is to be born into a condition of original sin, from which God's redemption is the only exit. Flowing from this is the assumption that humans cannot be relied upon to control their own behavior with only their own personalities; self-interest is ever-present and represents a constant temptation to ignore God's will. Fidelity to God requires the harnessing of human nature and control over "humanist" impulses. Terry writes (1988: 159):

> The reason the church has not stood against abortion is because Christians have bowed the knee to America's god—the god of self. Humanism is the worship of man, or self-worship. It makes life man-centered instead of God-centered.

To the extent that people have difficulty controlling their impulses, moral codes must be embodied in social and legal codes—to offer the threat of punishment as well as inducements to moral behavior. Individualist impulses are a profoundly anti-social threat. Therefore, external restraints are necessary for humans to be able to live in an orderly society. This constraint should be moral, of course, and should stem from a particular interpretation of God's word: "The Judeo-Christian ethic is the foundation for our politics, our judicial system, and our public morality…a country whose unmoving bedrock is Higher Laws" (1988: 178).

The second theme moves this same logic to a more abstract level as Terry argues that America as a society has "fallen" into a state of immorality. Reliance on human-centered values has usurped the legitimate authority of God over the nation. America has "becom[e] a guilt-free society" (1988: 135) that seeks "convenience, pleasure and gratification" (1988: 159). This state of gracelessness will surely engender the wrath of God's judgment (1988: 26): "Will America be spared the full fury of God's wrath over this bloodshed? Will we be chastened and restored? Or will we be destroyed?" Restoring the nation to a state of grace will obviously require the imposition of socio-moral constraints on personal behavior (Terry 1988: 188): "As long as God's people are determined to follow man's law above the commands of God, and as long as Christians honor government above God, we cannot win—for this is idolatry."

This leads to a third theme concerning the individual's relationship to society. The accumulation of individual sins, many of them rooted in human nature, has caused the nation to "sin," the clearest sign of which is legalized abortion. These sins result from the unwrapping of traditional moral restraints, evident in the separation of church and State, laws that undermine the family, and lack of faith in God's church. Thus, in order to restore the nation's moral health, a "Judeo-Christian" ethic will have to be reimposed, and be applicable to Christians and non-Christians alike (1988: 53): "we err if we think God does not demand even heathen nations to obey Him."

Terry recognizes that this requires legal action. To be effective, the moral fabric of the country requires legal sanction—although not only legal sanction—to support it. If, however, achieving the end of establishing a legal code consonant with God's will requires short-term tactics of civil disobedience, it is certainly justified. If Christians believe that abortion is murder, they must act as if they do. That may bring them in conflict with the extant legal order, but existing laws are both product and cause of our fallen state. Terry writes (1988: 82, 209, respectively):

> Some of our friends think it is wrong to break the law under any circumstances. But the God of Israel has commanded men and women…to rescue those who are about to die from the hands of the killers. Even if that means violating man-made laws.

> God has called us to take a public stand…as witnesses before the hosts of hell that God still has a people who uphold His law and stand against wickedness.

Finally, Operation Rescue members must maintain a personal relationship with God and draw strength and guidance through prayer—that is, after all, the basis on which they justify all their subsequent beliefs and actions. Terry repeatedly stresses the necessity for daily prayer, Bible study, purity of motive, and faithfulness of personal character. In this regard, it is only Christians who can responsibly lead this wave of social and cultural change. Only those personally close to God and His will can truly guide the nation to do what is right for its moral health. Righteous social change can only come from righteous people.

Much of this moral logic will not sound new to anyone familiar with the history of American religious and political movements. The creation of the "shining city on a hill," to quote Ronald Reagan paraphrasing John Winthrop, is a corporate endeavor, one in which the unsaved may have to be coerced for the nation's, and their own, good. There is also a version of the "necessity" defense to justify civil disobedience, familiar to students of Ghandi and M.L. King—although Operation Rescue's application has been different (see Apel 1991). Finally, hitching the crusade against abortion to a longer litany of evils, beginning with sexuality and gender roles but culminating in the moral transformation of the entire culture, is consistent with many analyses of American history.

Thus the relatively modest formal goals set out in the beginning of Randall Terry's manifesto are eclipsed by a more expansive vision and ambitious scheme for collective action. These are the statements that have inspired so much of the commentary and controversy surrounding Operation Rescue, by activists and scholars alike. They lend themselves easily to an interpretation of Operation Rescue as an ideologically homogenous group with an expansive plan of socio-cultural change. Assessing the degree of ideological commitment among rank-and-file members is our next step.

RANK-AND-FILE MEMBERS AND OPERATIVE IDEOLOGY

We found both consensus and divergence in the ideological commitment of our interviewees. Certainly there is widespread agreement over the "evil" of abortion and the necessity for stopping it. There is also substantial agreement with Terry that abortion is but one practice among a litany of social and moral problems in contemporary America, many caused by a loosening of moral restraints. A list of social conditions offered by one respondent is typical:

> The promiscuity of the youth, the breakdown in morals in the family, the divorce
> rate, the AIDS plague…materialism…education, and the TV. (interview #2)

But the further one moves from those core elements, the more ideological commitment vis-a-vis Terry's vision breaks down. Significantly, some of the most interesting variation is in exactly those areas in which other commentators on Operation Rescue have assumed homogeneity. What follows examines our findings on these issues, moving from those about which there is the most consensus to those where there is the least.

There is least variation on the more "religious" dimensions of Terry's ideology and worldview. None of our respondents denied that they had a personal relationship with God, or that regular prayer was the key to both strength or guidance. Their personal identities as fundamentalist and evangelical Christians were central in that regard. Further, there was consensus on the necessity of an external, and absolute, system of morality in order for society to maintain order. For example, interviewees argued:

> If you don't have a foundation that's based on God or someone bigger than man
> you're going to have Joe Blow and Suzie Q's morality, and their moralities may
> conflict so much that they can't get along…. I don't know how you can function
> successfully. (interview #6)

That's the basic differences in the two sides if you really want to get down to it. I believe man is evil, he is fallen. But you talk to somebody who is pro-abortion and humanistic and everything, and they say man is good.... There has to be restraints, there has to be order. (interview #17)

Without legal constraints, look at what happened to Los Angeles [after the first Rodney King verdicts].... A person would be a fool to be such a libertarian to say let everybody do their own thing. (interview #27)

[The Bible is] God's law and if we don't follow some moral code we will follow anything.... Anything less than [the Bible as the source of truth], when everybody does their own thing, it becomes anarchy. (interview #26)

Additionally, there was widespread agreement about the dimensions of immorality in America's current situation. This immoral condition threatens the nation with God's wrath:

I think [God's wrath] is falling on us now. I think our standard of living is going to go down, we're losing our blessing, we are about to the point that if He doesn't do something to us, He'll have to apologize to Sodom and Gomorrah. (interview #17)[3]

From the evidence, [God's wrath is already] happening. I personally feel that AIDS is a plague that has been placed on us as a result of the open acceptance of homosexual behavior, open drug use, and promiscuous behavior. And I will add to that on the economic front, that if we continue on our course of fiscal irresponsibility, which I feel is a form of immorality, that we are headed to an economic crash. (interview #21)

These responses clearly resonate with Terry's approach. They view the United States as existing in a "covenanted" relationship with God, blessed by Him, but simultaneously charged with keeping His laws. Stepping beyond God's law, or substituting humanly-created—and therefore "humanist"—law, is a transgression that weighs heavily upon the nation as a whole.

So "corporatist" is this vision, that many of our interviewees saw little dilemma in the creation of legal codes that institutionalize their conceptions of morality. Their position was predicated on the assumption that an absolute truth existed beyond subjective human interpretation—as beyond subjective interpretation as the laws of the physical universe:

[God's laws are] like when you go in the house and turn on the light switch; you can either believe in the electricity or not believe in electricity, but it's still there nevertheless. Even though you can't see it, we still have electricity. (interview #4)

One set of interview questions probed whether respondents believed that Christian moral authority should be established as society's legal code, even though many members of society did not practice that faith. Our framing of the issue intended to make this a question about the legal order. A common response, however, was one framed in historical terms, regarding the nation's heritage as a Christian culture:

> I think non-Christians are subjected [to Christian moral authority] whether they want to be or not. For example, in America you can't shoot somebody, well that originally came from the Bible so non-Christians are already subjected.... Our laws were founded on morals in the Bible and Ten Commandments, I mean that's a fact so I think it has to be that way. A good example is Somalia now; we see no government, no law, and we see people just running wild. For those who would like to see these moral laws thrown out, that's a good example of where they'd be headed. (interview #30)

> I think it is necessary for society, because Christian absolutes are really societal absolutes. (interview #15)

> Even those who do not believe in Christianity are the beneficiaries of our forefathers establishing this country on the principles and the guidelines of Scripture in a Christian framework. (interview #11)

However, other respondents answered not in politico-legal terms, but in more "ontological" terms. That is, they treated the question not as a normative inquiry about the organization of society, but as a statement about the facticity and absolute quality of God's law and moral authority:

> Everybody will be subjected to the authority of the Word of God. The Bible says that every knee shall bow, if not in this life, in the hereafter. It is preferable that they do it in this life, because we live in a democratic society that was formed to give light. (interview #27)

> A government based on God's laws is fair for everybody.... You don't have to believe.... But there is no morality outside God's laws. A godly morality brings about social order, social order makes society fair for all. (interview #20)

> The Ten Commandments, it's not just Christian, it is broader than that. (interview #29)

> Actually, it is the natural order of things, the God who created nature is; when we break those laws we are going against nature, we go against ourselves. (interview #28)

> [Non-believers] don't understand how [God's laws] are good for [them] because [they] are short-sighted. The reality is [God's laws] are good for everyone in all situations. (interview #17)

So the problem of pluralism is not a problem of accommodating diverse but equally valid viewpoints within the same society—which implies a relativism viewed as disastrous for social order and the nation's moral health. It is, rather, primarily the problem of non-believers coming to a correct understanding of the content and beneficial consequences of a "biblically-based, Judeo-Christian morality."

However, once the discussion moves beyond these widely-shared aspects of the worldview into aspects of the formal ideology, variations in ideological commitment become more pronounced. Indeed, there may be more variation than either Operation Rescue's leadership—or its critics—would care to admit. We focus on this variation in three specific areas: first, a consideration of the "separation of church and State" in American society and its implication for instituting a Christian moral code; second, whether Operation Rescue's primary strategy should focus on political change or changing hearts and minds; and third, the legitimating rationales for Operation Rescue's tactics of lawbreaking and civil disobedience.

SEPARATION OF CHURCH AND STATE
Randall Terry credits the separation of church and State as a major reason for America's fall from moral grace. It leads Terry to the conclusion that political-legal change is a necessary step in the redemption of the nation. Several respondents agree with that assessment:

> The argument for the separation of church and State is made by people who don't agree with the Scripture, to try to eliminate morality and replace it with their own beliefs. (interview #20)

> I think every country needs a government that articulates God's laws; I think theocracy would be the best of all possible worlds. (interview #11)

However, other respondents continue to accept the separation of church and State as an important principle to uphold, a principle not violated by their activism:

> The church [and] the State should be separated, but I think it was basically so that some church couldn't be forced on you. (interview #23)

> You can't blame all [of America's immorality] on separation of church and State…. I have free speech…they cannot stifle our speech. (interview #2)

> There is something to be said for the separation of the church and the State, in the sense that you should not impose specific doctrines, a state church; there are lines to be drawn. (interview #27)

Notice that when the discussion of the moral bases of law is framed as an issue in church-State relations, an interesting set of ideas emerge. Rank-and-file support for the separation of church and State is at odds with Terry's explicit condemnation of it, but the separation is interpreted rather narrowly. Respondents take separation to mean freedom from the imposition of theological doctrine and specific denominational or church membership.[4] They do not push that separation to the place where it would mean freedom from the moral worldviews and behavioral codes that accompany their form of Christianity.

Thus, on one hand, the connection between religion and proper moral authority is seen as absolute and logically necessary—morality is grounded in Scripture, which is the revealed Word of God, applicable to all people, regardless of subjective belief. Yet, on the other hand, the legal tradition of separation is understood as defending the liberty of conscience regarding doctrine, but not the liberty of action regarding morality. Hence, these respondents are implicitly separating the spheres of theology and morality.

It may well be that this implicit separation is a necessary condition for political mobilization. Conservative Protestants have historically had a difficult time participating in conventional political action because of their reluctance to join in fellowship with those who do not share their theology. Separating theology, in which differences are often many, from morality, where issues such as abortion and homosexuality can produce consensus, allows the coalition-building necessary for social-movement action. While this observation has appeared in other writing on "Christian right" politics (e.g. Liebman and Wuthnow 1983), it casts more doubt on the vision of Operation Rescue as ideologically homogeneous.

This set of interpretations has been termed the "selective" response to the dilemma of reconciling support of church-State separation with a sense of religious duty to reform politics (Williams and Demerath 1991). Selective definitions of what counts as "religion"—in this case meaning doctrine—allows Operation Rescue activists to maintain both the importance of volunteerism, and the necessity of morally-specific legal restraint on individual conduct.

POLITICAL VERSUS EVANGELICAL STRATEGY

While Terry is explicit on the need for action directed at the political system in order to institute legal change, many interviewees were less certain about both the appropriateness and the efficacy of that strategic approach:

> Change will not come about by the law or the Congress, the law or the Supreme Court. It will be by God working through the church to bring change. We have actually made an idol of the ideas of changing Roe vs. Wade and made an idol of political activists. (interview #17)

> Our main goal is to show a sincere love and compassion.... I believe until people change their hearts, you can change all the laws you want and people are still going to seek out abortions. (interview #6)

> You cannot legislate behavior; nor can your legislate pro-life. You cannot legislate good behavior. (interview #5)

> When it comes to some of the things Randall Terry does...in national Operation Rescue, they seem to be more political motives, as far as changing the law. But

I think the Holy Spirit has to move a lot of people, like Joseph Foreman and others, towards teaching the changing of hearts.... That remains the question ultimately. (interview #30)

I think the rescue movement is moving in a new direction as far as just focusing in on the cross and not paying so much attention to what the laws do. After all, Operation Rescue has always preached that we should obey God's laws not man's; why rely on man's laws in the first place? (interview #11)

These concerns demonstrate in another vocabulary the tension between what is considered appropriate "religious" behavior and what is seen as merely political—and thus open to corruption and expediency. While the importance of changing laws is recognized, respondents were reluctant to believe that political-legal change was the answer:

I think having laws is helpful; I don't think that's the entire answer. I think the born-again experience and Christian growth and submitting to the Lord and being involved in a Christian fellowship...is the main issue there.... We believe that we can be an influence, but I'm so disillusioned that we...can force people to become what we think they ought to be.... I would just hope that people individually would see the truth of Scripture and the claims of the Bible. (interview #9)

This issue, of course, is familiar to students of American religion's political history. Protestant churches have often had split responses to their mission of societal reform. Some have emphasized direct social action aimed at societal institutions, while others have focused on evangelism and conversion, counting on changed persons redeeming society. For much of the twentieth century, fundamentalist and evangelical Protestantism has been predominately committed to the later "hearts and minds" approach (see Marty's, 1970 "public" versus "private" distinction).

The surge of conservative Christian activism that became labelled the "New Christian Right" was significant, partly because it countered this pattern. Fundamentalist and evangelical Protestants adopted conventional political action with great enthusiasm and no little expertise in an attempt to shape the public sphere through control of society's mainstream institutions. But, clearly, the transformation has not been complete, and even among committed activists there remains significant traces of this fundamental strategic question.

CIVIL-DISOBEDIENT TACTICS

Randall Terry legitimates Operation Rescue's tactics with a combination of a "Higher Laws" argument and the "necessity" defense. The former is the familiar argument that there exists a transcendent Higher Law that supersedes human laws; when government laws violate Higher Law, they must be held accountable, and civil disobedience is justified (Terry 1988: 54, 178, 283). The necessity defense holds that, on occasion, minor laws must be broken in order to prevent a greater evil from occurring (Apel 1991).

As articulated by Terry and other fundamentalist and evangelical Protestants, there is an important constraint on this rationale. That is, Christians may be justified in breaking unjust human laws, but may do so only if motivated by faith, Christian love, and compassion. Thus, an activist's personal relationship with God is essential—only a righteous individual, pure in motive, can accomplish righteous social change. Civil disobedience may be justified, but this in no way represents a claim that "the ends justify the means" or a license for disrespect for authority.

And yet, this is the area reflecting the greatest discrepancy between Terry's views and those of rank-and-file activists. Issues of tactics, and what they might reveal about motives, were the most conspicuous source of disquiet among our interviewees. Many activists shared Terry's view of the constraints on civil disobedience; and precisely because they did so, they experienced uncomfortable contradictions in some of their actual rescue experiences:

> I've seen the importance of prayer and daily communion with God, because we can do [these rescues] with a wrong motive. We can go out there with a selfish motive, but daily communion with God helps us stay where His heart is. (interview #2)

> [The rescue] didn't seem to me like it was exactly the sort of event that Terry describes.... The people involved in the rescue were definitely human and made some mistakes.... There was some more physical contact than probably there should have been, and also some things the people said. (interview #13)

> There's definitely different leadership styles as far as the national Operation Rescue.... I agree with the tactics of rescuing...with trying to find where the abortionist lives and canvassing their community.... But I think sometimes harassment goes too far; but it depends on how far you go and your motives for doing it. (interview #30)

This concern was not only directed at others. Some responses indicated that Operation Rescue's cultivation of confrontation elicited emotions within themselves that were unsettling:

> I believe [rescuing] needs to be done peacefully and passively; it needs to be done in love and with lots of prayer. It needs to be done with an attitude of love towards the women, and towards the clinic escorts. But that's very difficult to do, it's easier to say that, than to do it. I struggle with that part personally. I don't yell at them, but I have a real hard time with that. (interview #11)

> I was afraid of the way I might react to them because I was pretty mad at the way they were treating some of the rescuers.... I had reached a frustration level that bothered me, so I backed away [and became less active]. (interview #6)

A particular issue with the activists we interviewed was the charge that Operation Rescue members "shout" at women entering clinics and were thus not demonstrating a truly Christian attitude of compassion. Several interviewees were emphatic that shouting did not occur:

> From the standpoint of getting their attention, [we might say] "please don't go in there, please save your baby." I never heard anyone shout any obscenities; they wouldn't be in tune with Operation Rescue. (interview #5)

> If they shout it's not shouting "you're a murderer" or anything, it's shouting because the police have them so far back that they have to shout "we can help you, we've got people to adopt your baby, we've got counselors here...." I've been on some intense rescues, and as far as I can remember, I've never heard anything that I thought was out of line. (interview #30)

Others responded by recasting the terms with which the behavior was discussed, claiming that it was not "shouting" as such, but rather "pleading" or "loud speech." The important distinction seemed to rest on the motivation of the Operation Rescue member engaging in the activity, rather than the interpretation by those who might hear it. A properly-motivated rescuer would not shout, but might indeed have to raise her or his voice:

> Well, I would call it pleading, but sometimes its sounds like shouting. (interview #26)

> To qualify the shouting—it's projecting your voice to be heard against the distance that has been imposed.... It's not shouting in your face.... I prefer "raising one's voice;" shouting has the wrong kind of connotation. (interview #16)

> Sometimes you have to ask yourself if the yelling at the escorts or the women is just loud speech, and what's the attitude behind it. Is it condemnation? Or is it "there's a God who loves you and there are other options?" (interview #11)

Other respondents indicated that the issue of shouting is a matter of internal controversy within Operation Rescue:

> There's not any shouting unless there's some confrontation, the leaders then tell us to pull off.... We're told to not talk at all. (interview #2)

> [Some members were shouting] at the rescue I was at, at the same time they were shouting, there were other members telling them not to shout; so it was interesting. I think it's hard not to shout. (interview #13)

> I agree with [Operation Rescue's] principles; now people unfortunately can't always control other people and not all the people adhere to their objectives. (interview #7)

> Most of the yelling and shouting does come from the group that has been in rescues the longest.... Operation Rescue officials will try to stop the yelling and put a hand on their shoulder and try to talk to them, not because they think it's wrong, but the media always picks on that person and that's what they'll show on the news. (interview #17)

And there are doubts that shouting is effective:

> I don't think [shouting] stops them.... I think it probably more scares the women and maybe even makes them antagonistic towards the rescuers. (interview #13)

> That part is really tough for me because many of the things they are saying is true, but the yelling, I have real doubts that the yelling does any good. (interview #11)

> I think there's more effective things than shouting and our next plan is to use tapes of children singing.... The child singing, that is really effective. (interview #17)

One interview combined all these concerns—tactical effectiveness, intra-movement disagreements, and concern for the women seeking abortions as evidence of a compassionate Christian motivation—in one response:

> I don't [personally approve of shouting] because I believe that it's one thing the media really is attracted to. They want a confrontation.... They want to get something on camera...and that kind of shows the public that we're not as Christ-like as maybe we should be—you know, shouting and saying things that might hurt the women going in. (interview #12)

Finally, the whole issue of civil disobedience is controversial enough to dissuade some pro-life people from actually participating in rescues. A few of our respondents, generally the least active in rescue activities, articulated that experience:

> I haven't resolved if civil disobedience is a Christian's duty.... With a thing such as abortion...I find what I've seen on television on Operation Rescue very violent and very upsetting. I don't like the hype that goes into it, to get the people to the place where they will go to jail for the cause.... That's very manipulative (interview #1)

> I think that Operation Rescue does some damage when they go and picket. I think it is degrading to the people who try to get in.... There's a lot of yelling and screaming rather than a very peaceful demonstration. It becomes a rather vengeful kind of thing.... I am just not sure if disobeying the law is the right means to achieve those goals. (interview #15)

I disagree with their emphasis in that they downgrade the mother, and put her down, and are so hard upon the mothers in trying to get them not to abort.... [I disagree with them] yelling at the women who are going into the clinic, rolling plastic fetuses at them, trying to block the entrances. I don't feel that's the best way.... Just by their actions, just like their attitude changes, it's coming more from a hateful attitude than one of love and support. (interview #22)

There is an irony here: the activists' agreement with Terry on the necessity of pure hearts and motives leads many to have questions about Operation Rescue's very strategy and tactics.

Randall Terry clearly taps into a deep pool of consensus at the level of the worldview—the importance of a personal relationship with God—and substantial agreement on formal ideology—that abortion is a severe enough evil to justify civil disobedience. But this fails to accord completely with the operative ideology developed among many members. That operative ideology holds rescuers to high standards of decorum, and mandates a firm vision of rescues as *religious* actions, not merely political ones. Thus even Operation Rescue itself is sometimes suspected of succumbing to the political expediency for which secular humanist society is criticized.

This is an empirical example of what might be termed a "translation" problem that is a generic concern for collective action and social movement organizations.[5] To build effective movement cultures and persuasive collective-action frames, movement leaders must tap into pre-existing areas of consensus at the worldview level. This then must be tied to a formal ideology, and translated by rank-and-file activists into an operative ideology. This is not an automatic process, however, and even small, tightly-knit movement groups, drawing their cultural resources from a definable subculture—in this case primarily fundamentalist and evangelical Protestantism—can have difficulty accomplishing it completely.

Operation Rescue, at the local level, remains in some important ways a coalition of persons centered around a single issue, abortion. This issue is a symbol for wider concerns, although exactly what those wider concerns entail remains only partially shared. The movement's high-profile leadership is clearly cultural reformist in its agenda, but that has not necessarily produced identical visions among the membership. This suggests once again how important continuing "ideological work" is for movements committed to confrontational or controversial action. Holding a movement together, even among people as generally homogeneous as white, born-again, conservative Protestants is a difficult business. Any consensus mobilization is a fragile and partial accomplishment, needing consistent renewal.

Of course, this renewal can come through actions that result in confrontation or arrest. We heard many stories of activists galvanized by their participation. They take heart from the show of solidarity with fellow activists, and the confrontations and arrests supply a persecution complex that is an effective tool in reinforcing the common notion that they are besieged by a secular society. But these very actions also loosen some of the connections between the underlying worldview and the operative ideology, making ideological commitment something that needs considerable, ongoing construction and maintenance.

CONCLUSIONS

Our findings imply that the study of social movements is more, rather than less, complicated than commonly thought, and that making generalizations about movement membership and commitment are more, rather than less, problematic. But understanding the variation in human action—and the ways movement dynamics can often channel that variation into remarkably homogeneous behavior—is too important a topic to over-simplify.

Clearly, symbols play a key role in both reducing and enhancing the complexities of worldviews and movement ideologies. They simplify by reducing the large numbers of potential problems to be acted upon and targets to be persuaded to a manageable—and highly emotive—core. But they simultaneously make movement culture more complex, by embodying a "multi-vocality" (Kertzer 1988) that allows only partially shared meanings to be translated into communal action.

In particular, the study of social-movement cultures needs to explore further the development of participants' operative ideologies—as distinct from their formal ideologies. Processes of interaction and socialization produce a mutual learning of what it means to be a member. Movements thus develop operative ideologies that "show people how to interpret the world. Collective actors are formed by the process of negotiated meanings" (Tarrow 1989: 14). Operative ideology comprises much of the movement culture. It is not something brought to the movement as individual attributes of the recruits, nor is it only a product of the official ideologies used by movement elites in their attempts to explain the movement to publics—although it includes both those things. Rather, an operative ideology is part of the "collective identity" that makes participants into movement "members" and demarcates them from others.

Studying operative ideology is facilitated by choosing a small social-movement group that draws members from similar social statuses and backgrounds. The amount of variation in operative ideology we have discovered among Operation Rescue participants, and the crucial impact that variation has on its ability to sustain coherent collective action, demonstrates the importance for social movements of the task of constructing and maintaining shared operative ideology.

REFERENCES

Apel, S. 1991. "Operation Rescue and the Necessity Defense: Beginning a Feminist Deconstruction." *Washington and Lee Law Review.* 48: 41–75.

Blanchard, D. 1994. *The Anti-Abortion Movement and the Rise of the Religious Right.* New York: Twayne Publishers.

Condit, C. M. 1990. *Decoding Abortion Rhetoric.* Urbana: University of Illinois Press.

Douglas, M. 1973. *Natural Symbols.* Second Edition. London: Barrie and Jenkins.

Faux, M. 1990. *Crusaders: Voices from the Abortion Front.* New York: Birch Lane Press.

Ferree, M. M. 1992. "The Political Context of Rationality: Rational Choice Theory and Resource Mobilization" in *Frontiers in Social Movement Theory.* A. Morris and C.M. Mueller, eds.: 29–52. New Haven, CT: Yale University Press.

MANY ARE CALLED BUT FEW OBEY **185**

Geertz, C. 1973. *The Interpretation of Cultures*. New York: Basic Books.

Giddens, A. 1984. *The Constitution of Society*. Berkeley: University of California Press.

Ginsburg, F. 1989. *Contested Lives: The Abortion Debate in an American Community*. Berkeley: University of California Press.

_____. 1993. "Saving America's Souls: Operation Rescue's Crusade Against Abortion" in *Fundamentalisms and the State*: 557–588. M. Marty and S. Appleby, eds. Chicago: University of Chicago Press.

Himmelstein, J. 1986. "The Social Basis of Antifeminism: Religious Networks and Culture." *Journal for the Scientific Study of Religion*. 25: 1–16.

Kertzer, D. 1988. *Ritual, Politics, and Power*. New Haven: Yale University Press.

Klandermans, B. 1984. "Mobilization and Participation: Social-Psychological Expansions of Resource Mobilization Theory." *American Sociological Review*. 49: 583–600.

_____. 1988. "The Formation and Mobilization of Consensus." *International Social Movement Research*. 1: 173–196.

Liebman, R. and R. Wuthnow, eds. 1983. *The New Christian Right: Mobilization and Legitimation*. New York: Aldine Publishing.

Luker, K. 1984. *Abortion and the Politics of Motherhood*. Berkeley: University of California Press.

Maxwell, C. and T. Jelen. 1994. "Commandos for Christ: Narratives of Male Pro-Life Activists." Paper presented to the Association for the Sociology of Religion, Los Angeles, August.

Marty, M. 1970 *Righteous Empire*. New York: Dial Press.

Perrow, C. 1986. *Complex Organizations: A Critical Essay*. Third Edition. New York: Random House.

Ralston, J. 1992. "An Inside Look at Operation Rescue." *Ms.* (November/December): 90–91.

Snow, D. and R. Benford. 1988. "Ideology, Frame Resonance, and Participant Mobilization." *International Social Movement Research*. 1: 197–218.

Snow, D., E. B. Rochford, S. Worden, and R. Benford. 1986. "Frame Alignment Processes, Micromobilization, and Movement Participation." *American Sociological Review*. 51: 464–481.

Tarrow, S. 1989. *Struggle, Politics, and Reform: Collective Action, Social Movements, and Cycles of Protest*. Western Societies Program, Occasional Paper #21. Ithaca, NY: Cornell University Center for International Studies.

_____. 1992. "Mentalities, Political Cultures, and Collective Action Frames: Constructing Meanings Through Action." in *Frontiers in Social Movement Theory*. 174–202. eds. A. Morris and C. Mueller. New Haven: Yale University Press.

Terry, R. 1988. *Operation Rescue*. Springdale, PA: Whitaker House.

Williams, R. 1995. "Constructing the Public Good: Social Movements and Cultural Resources." *Social Problems*. 42: 124–144.

Williams, R. and N.J. Demerath III. 1991. "Religion and Political Process in an American City." *American Sociological Review*. 56: 417–431.

PART FIVE

RELIGIOUS IDEOLOGY AND
DISRUPTIVE TACTICS

Popular Christianity and Political Extremism in the United States

James Aho

December 8, 1984. In a shootout on Puget Sound, Washington, involving several hundred federal and local law enforcement officials, the leader of a terrorist group comprised of self-proclaimed Christian soldiers is killed, ending a crime spree involving multi-state robberies, armored car heists, arson attacks, three murders, and a teenage suicide (Flynn and Gerhardt 1989).

Christmas Eve, 1985. A "Christian patriot soldier" in Seattle trying to save America by eliminating the Jewish-Communist leader of the so-called one-world conspiracy, murders an innocent family of four, including two pre-teen children (Aho 1994: 35–49).

August 1992. In northern Idaho, three persons are killed and two others critically injured in the course of a stand-off between federal marshals, ATF officers, the FBI, and a white separatist Christian family seeking refuge from the "Time of Tribulations" prophesied in the Book of Revelations (Aho 1994: 50–65).

Three isolated incidents, twelve dead bodies, scores of young men imprisoned, shattered families, millions of dollars in litigation fees and investigation expenses. Why? What can sociology tell us about the causes of these events that they might be averted in the future? In particular, insofar as Christianity figures so prominently in these stories, what role has this religion played in them? Has Christianity been a cause of right-wing extremism in the United States? Or has it been an excuse for extremism occasioned by other factors? Or is the association between right-wing extremism and Christianity merely anecdotal and incidental? Our object is to address these questions.

EXTREMISM DEFINED

The word "extremism" is used rhetorically in everyday political discourse to disparage and undermine one's opponents. In this sense, it refers essentially to anyone who disagrees with me politically. In this chapter, however, "extremism" will refer exclusively to particular kinds of behaviors, namely, to non-democratic actions, regardless of their ideology—that is, regardless of whether we agree with the ideas behind them or not (Lipset and Raab 1970: 4-17). Thus, extremism includes: (1) efforts to deny civil rights to certain people, including their right to express unpopular views, their right to due process at law, to own property, etc.; (2) thwarting attempts by others to organize in opposition to us, to run for office, or vote; (3) not playing according to legal constitutional rules of political fairness: using personal smears like "Communist Jew-fag" and "nigger lover" in place of rational discussion; and above all, settling differences by vandalizing or destroying the property or life of one's opponents. The test is not the end as such, but the means employed to achieve it.

CYCLES OF AMERICAN RIGHT-WING EXTREMISM

In this chapter we are concerned with the most rabid right-wing extremists, those who have threatened or succeeded in injuring and killing their opponents. We are interested, furthermore, only in such activities as are connected at least indirectly to Christianity. By no means is this limitation of focus intended to suggest that American Christians are characteristically more violent than their non-Christian neighbors. Nor are we arguing that American Christians engage only in right-wing activities. We are focusing on Christianity and on rightist extremism because in America today this connection has become newsworthy and because it is sociologically problematic.

American political history has long been acquainted with Christian-oriented rightist extremism. As early as the 1790s, for example, Federalist Party activists, inspired partly by Presbyterian and Congregationalist preachers, took-up arms against a mythical anti-Christian cabal known as the Illuminati—Illuminati = bringers of light = Lucifer, the devil.

The most notable result of anti-Illuminatism was what became popularly known as the "Reign of Terror": passage of the Alien and Sedition acts (1798). These required federal registration of recent immigrants to America from Ireland and France, reputed to be the homes of Illuminatism, lengthened the time of naturalization to become a citizen from five to fourteen years, restricted "subversive" speech and newspapers—that is, outlets advocating liberal Jeffersonian or what were known then as "republican" sentiments—and permitted the deportation of "alien enemies" without trial.

The alleged designs of the Illuminati were detailed in a three hundred-page book entitled *Proofs of A Conspiracy Against All the Religions and Governments of Europe Carried on in the Secret Meetings of...Illuminati* (Robison 1967 [1798]). Over two hundred years later *Proofs of A Conspiracy* continues to serve as a sourcebook for right-wing extremist commentary on American social issues.[1] Its basic themes are: (1) *manichaenism*: that the world is divided into the warring principles of absolute good and evil; (2) *populism*: that the citizenry naturally would be inclined to ally with the powers of good, but have become indolent, immoral, and uninformed of the present danger to themselves; (3) *conspiracy*: that this is because the forces of evil have enacted a scheme using educators, newspapers, music, and intoxicants to weaken the people's will and intelligence; (4) *anti-modernism*: that the results of the conspiracy are the very laws and institutions celebrated by the unthinking masses as "progressive":

representative government, the separation of church and State, the extension of suf-
frage to the propertyless, free public education, public-health measures, etc.; and (5)
apocalypticism: that the results of what liberals call social progress are increased crime
rates, insubordination to "natural" authorities (such as royal families and property-
owning Anglo-Saxon males), loss of faith, and the decline of common decency—in
short, the end of the world.

Approximately every thirty years America has experienced decade-long popular res-
urrections of these five themes. While the titles of the alleged evil-doers in each era have
been adjusted to meet changing circumstances, their program is said to have remained
the same. They constitute a diabolic *Plot Against Christianity* (Dilling 1952). In the
1830s, the cabal was said to be comprised of the leaders of Masonic lodges: in the
1890s, they were accused of being Papists and Jesuits; in the 1920s, they were the
Hidden Hand; in the 1950s, the Insiders or Force X; and today they are known as
Rockefellerian "one-world" Trilateralists or Bilderbergers.

Several parallels are observable in these periods of American right-wing resurgence.
First, while occasionally they have evolved into democratically-organized political parties holding conventions that nominate slates of candidates to run for office—the
American Party, the Anti-Masonic Party, the People's Party, the Prohibition Party—
more often, they have become secret societies in their own right, with arcane passwords,
handshakes, and vestments, plotting campaigns of counter-resistance behind closed
doors. That is, they come to mirror the fantasies against which they have taken up
arms. Indeed, it is this ironic fact that typically occasions the public ridicule and undo-
ing of these groups. The most notable examples are the Know Nothings, so-called
because under interrogation they were directed to deny knowledge of the organization;
the Ku Klux Klan, which during the 1920s had several million members; the Order of
the Star Spangled Banner, which flourished during the 1890s; the Black Legion of
Michigan, circa 1930; the Minutemen of the late 1960s; and, most recently, the *Bruders
Schweigen*, Secret Brotherhood, or as it is more widely known, The Order.

Secondly, the thirty-year cycle noted above evidently has no connection with economic booms and busts. While the hysteria of the 1890s took place during a nation-
wide depression, McCarthyism exploded on the scene during the most prosperous era in
American history. On close view, American right-wing extremism is more often associated with economic good times than with bad, the 1920s, the 1830s, and the 1980s
being prime examples. On the contrary, the cycle seems to have more to do with the
length of a modern generation than with any other factor.[2]

Third, and most important for our purposes, Christian preachers have played pivotal roles in all American right-wing hysterias. The presence of Dan Gayman, James
Ellison, and Bertrand Comparet spear-heading movements to preserve America from
decline today continues a tradition going back to Jedidiah Morse nearly two centuries
ago, continuing through Samuel D. Burchard, Billy Sunday, G.L.K. Smith, and Fred
Schwarz's Christian Anti-Communist Crusade.

In the nineteenth century, the honorary title "Christian patriot" was restricted to
white males with Protestant credentials. By the 1930s, however, Catholic ideologues,
like the anti-Semitic radio priest Father Coughlin, had come to assume leadership positions in the movement. Today, somewhat uneasily, Mormons are included in the fold.

The Ku Klux Klan, once rabidly anti-Catholic and misogynist, now encourages Catholic recruits and even allows females into its regular organization, instead of requiring them to form auxiliary groups.

CHRISTIANITY: A CAUSE OF POLITICAL EXTREMISM?

The upper Rocky Mountain region is the heartland of American right-wing extremism in our time. Montana, Idaho, Oregon, and Washington have the highest per capita rates of extremist groups of any area in the entire country (Aho 1994: 152–53). Research on the members of these groups shows that they are virtually identical to the surrounding population in all respects but one (Aho 1991: 135–63)—they are not less formally educated than the surrounding population. Furthermore, as indicated by their rates of geographic mobility, marital stability, occupational choice, and conventional political participation, they are no more estranged from their local communities than those with whom they live. And finally, their social status seems no more threatened than that of their more moderate neighbors. Indeed, there exists anecdotal evidence that American right-wing extremists today are drawn from the more favored, upwardly-mobile sectors of society. They are college-educated, professional suburbanites residing in the rapidly-growing, prosperous Western states (Simpson 1983).

In other words, the standard sociological theories of right-wing extremism—theories holding, respectively, that extremists are typically under-educated, if not stupid, transient and alienated from ordinary channels of belonging, and suffer inordinately from status insecurity—find little empirical support.[3] Additionally, the popular psychological notion that right-wing extremists are more neurotic than the general population, perhaps paranoid to the point of psychosis, can not be confirmed. None of the right-wing political murderers whose psychiatric records this author has accessed have been medically certified as insane (Aho 1991: 68–82; Aho 1994: 46–49). If this is true for right-wing murderers, it probably also holds for extremists who have not taken the lives of others.

The single way in which right-wing extremists *do* differ from their immediate neighbors is seen in their religious biographies. Those with Christian backgrounds generally, and Presbyterians, Baptists and members of independent fundamentalist Protestant groups specifically, all are over-represented among intermountain radical patriots (Aho 1991: 164–82).[4] Although it concerns a somewhat different population, this finding is consistent with surveys of the religious affiliations of Americans with conservative voting and attitudinal patterns (Lipset and Raab 1970: 229–232, 359–361, 387–392, 433–437, 448–452; Shupe and Stacey 1983; Wilcox 1992).

Correlations do not prove causality. Merely because American extremists are members of certain denominations and sects does not permit the conclusion that these religious groups compel their members to extremism. In the first place, the vast majority of independent fundamentalists, Baptists, and Presbyterians are not political extremists, even if they are inclined generally to support conservative causes. Secondly, it is conceivable that violently-predisposed individuals are attracted to particular religions because of what they hear from the pulpit; and what they hear channels their *already* violent inclinations in political directions.

Today, a man named Gary Yarbrough, gaunt-faced and red-bearded, languishes in federal prison because of his participation in the *Bruders Schweigen*. Although he was recruited into terrorism from the Church of Jesus Christian—Aryan Nations—it was not the church itself that made him violent, at least not in a simplistic way. On the contrary, Yarbrough was the offspring of a notorious Pima, Arizona family that one reporter (Ring 1985) describes as "very volatile—very anti-police, anti-social, anti-everybody." Charges against its various members have ranged from burglary and robbery to witness-intimidation.

Lloyd, Steve, and Gary Yarbrough are sons of a family of drifters. Red, the father, works as an itinerant builder and miner. Rusty, his wife, tends bar and waitresses. Child rearing, such as it was, is said to have been "severely heavy handed." Nor was much love lost between the parents. Fist fights were common and once Rusty stabbed Red so badly he was hospitalized. Not surprisingly, "the boys did not get very good schooling." Still, mother vehemently defends her boys. One night, she jumped over a bar to attack an overly inquisitive detective concerning their whereabouts.

After a spree of drugs, vandalism, and thievery, Gary, like his brothers, eventually found himself behind bars at the Arizona State Prison. It was there that he was contacted, first by letter and later personally, by the Aryan Nations prison ministry in Idaho. He was the kind of man the church was searching for: malleable, fearless, sentimental, tough. Immediately upon release, Yarbrough moved with his wife and daughter to Idaho to be close to church headquarters. He had finally found his calling: working with like-minded souls in the name of Christ to protect God's chosen people, the white race, from mongrelization.

Yarbrough purchased the requisite dark blue twill trousers, postman's shirt, Nazi pins, Sam Browne holster-belt, and 9 mm. semi-automatic pistol. The pastor of the church assigned him to head the security detail. At annual church conventions, he helped conduct rifle training. But Yarbrough was a man of action; he soon became bored with the routine of guarding the compound against aliens who never arrived. He met others in the congregation who shared his impatience. Together in a farm building, deep in the woods, over the napping figure of one of the member's infant children, they founded the *Bruders Schweigen*, swearing together an oath to war against what they called ZOG—Zionist Occupation Government (Flynn and Gerhardt 1989).

The point is not that every extremist is a violent personality searching to legitimize criminality with religion. Instead, the example illustrates the subtle ways in which religious belief, practice, and organization all play upon individual psychology to produce persons prepared to violate others in the name of principle. Let us look at each of these factors separately, understanding that in reality they intermesh in complicated, sometimes contradictory ways that can only be touched upon here.

BELIEF

American right-wing politics has appropriated from popular Christianity several tenets: the concept of unredeemable human depravity, the idea of America as a specially chosen people, covenant theology and the right to revolt, the belief in a national mission, millennialism, and anti-Semitism. Each of these in its own way has inspired rightist extremism.

THE NEW ISRAEL

The notion of America as the new Israel, for example, is the primary axiom of a fast growing religiously-based form of radical politics known as Identity Christianity. Idaho's Aryan Nations Church is simply the most well-known Identity congregation. The adjective "identity" refers to its insistence that Anglo-Saxons are in truth the Israelites. They are "Isaac's-sons"—the Saxons—and hence the Bible is *their* historical record, not that of the Jews (Barkun 1994). The idea is that after its exile to what today is northern Iran around seven hundred B.C., the Israelites migrated over the Caucasus mountains—hence their racial type, "caucasian"—and settled in various European countries. Several of these allegedly still contain mementos of their origins: the nation of Denmark is said to be comprised of descendants from the tribe of Dan; the German-speaking Jutland, from the tribe of Judah; Catalonia, Scotland, from the tribe of Gad.

COVENANT THEOLOGY

Identity Christianity is not orthodox Christianity. Nevertheless, the notion of America as an especially favored people, or as Ronald Reagan once said, quoting Puritan founders, a "city on a hill," the New Jerusalem, is widely shared by Americans. Reagan and most conservatives, of course, consider the linkage between America and Israel largely symbolic. Many right-wing extremists, however, view the relationship literally as an historical fact and for them, just as the ancient Israelites entered into a covenant with the Lord, America has done the same. According to radical patriots America's covenant is what they call the "organic Constitution." This refers to the original articles of the Constitution plus the first ten amendments, the Bill of Rights. Other amendments, especially the 16th establishing a federal income tax, are considered to have questionable legal status because allegedly they were not passed according to constitutional strictures.

The most extreme patriots deny the constitutionality of the 13th, 14th, and 15th amendments—those outlawing slavery and guaranteeing free men civil and political rights as full American citizens. Their argument is that the organic Constitution was written by white men exclusively for themselves and their blood descendants (Preamble 1986). Non-caucasians residing in America are considered "guest peoples" with no constitutional rights. Their continued residency in this country is entirely contingent upon the pleasure of their hosts, the Anglo-Saxon citizenry. According to some, it is now time for the property of these guests to be confiscated and they themselves exiled to their places of origin (Pace 1985).

All right-wing extremists insist that if America adheres to the edicts of the organic Constitution, She, like Israel before her, shall be favored among the world's nations. Her harvests shall be bountiful, her communities secure, her children obedient to the voices of their parents, and her armies undefeated. But if she falters in her faith, behaving in ways that contravene the sacred compact, then calamities, both natural and human-made, shall follow. This is the explanation for the widespread conviction among extremists today for America's decline in the world. In short, the federal government has established agencies and laws contrary to America's divine compact: these include the Internal Revenue Service; the Federal Reserve System; the Bureau of Alcohol, Tobacco and Firearms; the Forest Service; the Bureau of Land Management; Social

Security; Medicare and Medicaid; the Environmental Protection Agency; Housing and Urban Development; and the official apparatus enforcing civil rights for "so-called" minorities.

Essentially, American right-wing extremists view the entire executive branch of the United States government as little more than "jack-booted Nazi thugs," to borrow a phrase from a National Rifle Association fund-raising letter: a threat to freedom of religion, the right to carry weapons, freedom of speech, and the right to have one's property secure from illegal search and seizure.

Clumsy federal-agency assaults, first on the Weaver family in northern Idaho in 1992, then on the Branch Davidian sect in Waco, Texas in 1993, followed by passage of the assault weapons ban in 1994, are viewed as indicators that the organic Constitution presently is imperiled. This has been the immediate impetus for the appearance throughout rural and Western America of armed militias since the Summer of 1994.[5] The terrorists who bombed a federal building in Oklahoma City in the Spring of 1995, killing one hundred sixty-eight, were associated with militias headquartered in Michigan and Arizona. One month after the bombing, the national director of the United States Militia Association warned that after the current government falls, homosexuals, abortionists, rapists, "unfaithful politicians," and any criminal not rehabilitated in seven years will be executed. Tax evaders will no longer be treated as felons; instead they will lose their library privileges (Sherwood 1995).

MILLENNIALISM

Leading to both the Waco and Weaver incidents was a belief on the victims' parts that world apocalypse is imminent. The Branch Davidians split from the Seventh-Day Adventists in 1935 but share with the mother church its own millenarian convictions. The Weaver's received their apocalypticism from *The Late Great Planet Earth* by fundamentalist lay preacher Hal Lindsey (1970), a book that has enjoyed a wide reading on the Christian right.[6]

Both the Davidians and the Weavers were imbued with the idea that the thousand-year-reign of Christ would be preceded by a final battle between the forces of light and darkness. To this end both had deployed elaborate arsenals to protect themselves from the anticipated invasion of "Babylonish troops." These, they feared, would be comprised of agents from the various federal bureaucracies mentioned above, together with UN troops stationed on America's borders awaiting orders from Trilateralists. Ever alert to "signs" of the impending invasion, both fired at federal officers who had come upon their property; and both ended up precipitating their own martyrdom. Far from quelling millenarian fervor, however, the two tragedies were immediately seized upon by extremists as further evidence of the approaching End Times.

Millenarianism is not unique to Christianity, nor to Western religions; furthermore, millenarianism culminating in violence is not new—in part because one psychological effect of end-time prophesying is a devaluation of worldly things, including property, honors, and human life. At the end of the first Christian millennium (A.D. 1000) as itinerant prophets were announcing the Second Coming, their followers were taking-up arms to prepare the way, and uncounted numbers died (Cohn 1967). It should not surprise observers if, as the second millennium draws to a close and promises of Christ's imminent return increase in frequency, more and more armed cults flee to the mountains, there to prepare for the final conflagration.

ANTI-SEMITISM

Many post-Holocaust Christian and Jewish scholars alike recognize that a pervasive anti-Judaism can be read from the pages of the New Testament, especially in focusing on the role attributed to Jews in Jesus' crucifixion. Rosemary Ruether, for example, argues that anti-Judaism constitutes the "left-hand of Christianity," its archetypal negation (Ruether 1979). Although pre-Christian Greece and Rome were also critical of Jews for alleged disloyalty, anti-Semitism reached unparalleled heights in Christian theology, sometimes relegating Jews to the status of Satan's spawn, the human embodiments of Evil itself.

During the Roman Catholic era, this association became embellished with frightening myths and images. Jews—pictured as feces-eating swine and rats—were accused of murdering Christian children on high feast days, using their blood to make unleavened bread, and poisoning wells. Added to these legends were charges during the capitalist era that Jews control international banking and by means of usury have brought simple, kind-hearted Christians into financial ruin (Hay 1981 [1950]). All of this was incorporated into popular Protestant culture through, among other vehicles, Martin Luther's diatribe, *On the Jews and Their Lies*, a pamphlet that still experiences brisk sales from patriot bookstores.[7] This is one possible reason for a survey finding by Charles Glock and Rodney Stark that created a minor scandal in the late 1960s. Rigidly orthodox American Christians, they found, displayed far higher levels of Jew-hatred than other Christians, regardless of their education, occupation, race, or income (Glock and Stark 1966).

In the last thirty years there has been "a sharp decline" in anti-Semitic prejudice in America, according to Glock (1993: 68). Mainline churches have played some role in this decline by facilitating Christian-Jewish dialogue, de-emphasizing offensive scriptural passages, and ending missions directed at Jews. Nevertheless, ancient anti-Jewish calumnies continue to be raised by leaders of the groups that are the focus of interest in this chapter. Far from being a product of neurotic syndromes like the so-called Authoritarian (or fascist) Personality, the Jew-hatred of many right-wing extremists today is directly traceable to what they have absorbed from these preachments, sometimes as children.

HUMAN DEPRAVITY

There is none righteous, no not one;...there is none that doeth the good, no, no one. Their throat is an open sepulchre. With their tongues they have used deceit; the poison of asps in under their lips. In these words of the apostle Paul, John Calvin says God inveighs not against particular individuals, but against all mankind. "Let it be admitted, then, that men...are...corrupt...by a depravity of nature" (Calvin 1966: 34–35; see Romans 3:11–24).

One of the fundamentals of Calvinist theology, appropriated into popular American Christianity, is this: a transcendent and sovereign God resides in the heavens, relative to whom the earth and its human inhabitants are utterly, hopelessly fallen. True, Calvin only developed a line of thought already anticipated in Genesis and amplified repeatedly over the centuries. However, with a lawyer's penetrating logic, Calvin brought this tradition to its most stark, pessimistic articulation. It is this belief that accompanied the Pilgrims in their venture across the Atlantic, eventually rooting itself in the American psyche.

From its beginnings, a particular version of the doctrine of human depravity has figured prominently in American right-wing extremist discourse. It has served as the basis of its perennial misogyny, shared by both men and women. The female, being supposedly less rational and more passive, is said to be closer to earth's evil. Too, the theology of world devaluation is the likely inspiration for the right-wing's gossipy preoccupation with the body's appetites and the "perilous eroticism of emotion," for its prudish fulminations against music, dance, drink, and dress, and for its homophobia. Here, too, is found legitimation for the right-wing's vitriol against Satanist ouigi boards, "Dungeons and Dragons," and New Age witchcrafters with their horoscopes and aroma-therapies, and most recently, against "pagan-earth-worshippers" and "tree hugging idolaters" (environmentalists). In standing tall to "Satan's Kids" and their cravenness, certain neo-Calvinists in Baptist, Presbyterian, and fundamentalist clothing accomplish their own purity and sanctification.

CONSPIRATORIALISM

According to Calvin, earthquakes, pestilence, famine, and plague should pose no challenge to faith in God. We petty, self-absorbed creatures have no right to question sovereign reason. But even in Calvin's time, and more frequently later, many Christians have persisted in asking: if God is truly all-powerful, all-knowing, and all-good, then how is evil possible? Why do innocents suffer? One perennial, quasi-theological response is conspiratorialism. In short, there are AIDS epidemics, murderous holocausts, rampant poverty, and floods because counter-poised to God there exists a second hidden force of nearly equal power and omniscience: the Devil and His human consorters—Jews, Jesuits, Hidden Hands, Insiders, Masons, and Bilderbergers.

By conspiratorialism, we are not referring to documented cases of people secretly scheming to destroy co-workers, steal elections, or run competitors out of business. Conspiracies are a common feature of group life. Instead, we mean the attempt to explain the entirety of human history by means of a cosmic Conspiracy, such as that promulgated in the infamous *Protocols of the Learned Elders of Zion*. This purports to account for all modern institutions by attributing them to the designs of twelve or thirteen—one representing each of the tribes of Israel—Jewish elders (Aho 1994, 68–82). *The Protocols* enjoys immense and endless popularity on the right; and has generated numerous spin-offs: *The International Jew*, *None Dare Call It Conspiracy*, and the *Mystery of [Jewish] Iniquity*, to name three.

To posit the existence of an evil divinity is heresy in orthodox Christianity. But, theological objections aside, it is difficult indeed for some believers to resist the temptation of intellectual certitude conspiratorialism affords. This certainty derives from the fact that conspiratorialism in the cosmic sense can not be falsified. Every historical event can, and often is, taken as further verification of conspiracies. If newspapers report a case of government corruption, this is evidence of government conspiracy; if they do not, this is evidence of news media complicity in the conspiracy. If the media deny involvement in a cover-up, this is still further proof of their guilt; if they admit to having sat on the story, this is surely an admission of what is already known.[8]

PRACTICE

Christianity means more than adhering to a particular doctrine. To be Christian is to live righteously. God-fearing righteousness may either be understood as a *sign* of one's salvation, as in orthodox Christianity or, as in Mormonism, a way to *earn* eternal life in the celestial heavens.

Nor is it sufficient for the faithful merely to display righteousness in their personal lives and businesses, by being honest, hard-working, and reliable. Many Christians also are obligated to witness to, or labor toward, salvation in the political arena; to work with others to remake this charnel-house world after the will of God; to help establish God's kingdom on earth. Occasionally this means becoming involved in liberal causes— abolitionism, civil rights, the peace and ecological movements; often it has entailed supporting causes on the right. In either case it may require that one publicly stand up to evil. For, as Saint Paul said, to love God is to hate what is contrary to God.

Such a mentality may lead to "holy war," the organized effort to eliminate human fetishes of evil (Aho 1994: 23–34). For some, in cleansing the world of putrefaction their identity as Christian is recognized, it is re-known. This is not to argue that holy war is unique to Christianity, or that all Christians participate in holy wars. Most Christians are satisfied to renew their faith through the rites of Christmas, Easter, baptism, marriage, or mass. Furthermore, those who *do* speak of holy war often use it metaphorically to describe a private spiritual battle against temptation, as in "I am a soldier of Christ, therefore I am not permitted to fight" (Sandford 1966). Lastly, even holy war in the political sense does not necessarily imply the use of violence. Although they sometimes have danced tantalizingly close to extremism (in the sense defined earlier—neither Pat Robertson nor Jerry Falwell, for example, have advocated non-democratic means in their "wars" to avert America's decline.

Let us examine the notion of Christian holy war more closely. The sixteenth-century father of Protestant reform, Martin Luther, repudiated the concept of holy war, arguing that there exist two realms: holiness, which is the responsibility of the Church, and warfare, which falls under the State's authority (Luther 1974). Mixing these realms, he says, perverts the former while unnecessarily hamstringing the latter. This does not mean that Christians may forswear warfare, according to Luther. In his infinite wisdom, God has ordained princes to quell civil unrest and protect nations from invasion. Luther's exhortations to German officials that they spare no means in putting down peasant revolts are well known. Indeed, few theologians have "so highly praised the virtues of the State as Luther," says Ernst Troeltsch. Nevertheless, State violence is at best "sinful power to punish sin" for Luther. It is not a sacred instrument (Troeltsch 1960: 539–44, 656–77). To this day, Lutherans generally are less responsive to calls for holy wars than many other Christians.

John Calvin, on the other hand, rejected Luther's proposal to separate church from State. Instead, his goal was to establish a Christocracy in Geneva along Roman Catholic lines, and to attain this goal through force, if need be, as Catholicism had done. Calvin says that not only is violence to establish God's rule on earth permitted, it is command-ed. "Good brother, we must bend unto all means that give furtherance to the holy cause" (Walzer 1965: 17, 38, 68–87, 90–91, 100–109; see Troeltsch 1960: 599–601, 651–652, 921–922 n. 399). This notion profoundly influenced Oliver Cromwell and his English revolutionary army known as the Ironsides, so named because of its righteously cold bru-tality (Solt 1971). And it was the Calvinist ethic, not that of Luther, that was imported to America by the Puritans, informing the politics of Presbyterians and Congregational-ists—the immediate heirs of Calvinism—as well as some Methodists and many Baptists.[9] Hence, it is not surprising that those raised in these denominations are often over-repre-sented in samples of "saints" on armed crusades to save the world for Christ.

Seminal to the so-called pedagogic or educational function of holy war are two requirements. First, the enemy against whom the saint fights must be portrayed in terms appropriate to his status as a fetish of evil. Second, the campaign against him must be equal to his diabolism. It must be terrifying, bloodthirsty, uncompromising.

"Prepare War!" was issued by the now defunct Covenant, Sword and the Arm of the Lord, a fundamentalist Christian paramilitary commune headquartered in Missouri. A raid on the compound in the late 1980s uncovered one of the largest private arms caches ever in American history. Evidently, this arsenal was to be used to combat what the pamphlet calls "Negro-beasts of the field...who eat the flesh of men.... This canni-balistic fervor shall cause them to eat the dead *and* the living during" the time of Tribulations, prophesied in The Book of Revelations (CSA n.d.: 19]).[10] The weapons were also to be directed against "Sodomite homosexuals waiting in their lusts to rape," "Seed-of-Satan Jews, who are today sacrificing people in darkness," and "do-gooders who've fought for the 'rights' of these groups" (CSA n.d.: 19). When the Lord God has delivered these enemies into our hands, warns the pamphlet quoting the Old Testament, "thou shalt save alive nothing that breatheth: but thou shalt utterly destroy them" (CSA n.d.: 20; see Deuteronomy 20: 10–18).

The 1990s saw a series of State-level initiatives seeking to deny homosexuals civil rights. Although most of these failed by narrow margins, one in Colorado was passed (later to be adjudged unconstitutional), due largely to the efforts of a consortium of fundamentalist Christian churches. One of the most influential of these was the Laporte, Colorado Church of Christ, America's largest Identity congregation (more on Identity Christianity below). Acknowledging that the title of their pamphlet "Death Penalty for Homosexuals" would bring upon them the wrath of liberals, its authors insist that "such slanderous tactics" will not deter the anti-homosexual campaign. "For truth will ultimately prevail, no matter how many truth-bearers are stoned." And what precisely is this truth? It is that the Lord Himself has declared that "if a man also lie with mankind, as he lieth with a woman, both of them have committed an abomina-tion: they shall surely be put to death; their blood shall be upon them"(Peters 1992: i; see Leviticus 20:13).

Like "Prepare War!," "Death Penalty for Homosexuals" is not satisfied merely to cite biblical references. To justify the extremity of its attack, it must paint the homo-sexual in luridly terrifying colors. Finding and citing a quote from the most extreme of radical gay activists, their pamphlet warns (CSA n.d.: 19):

[They] shall sodomize [our] sons.... [They] shall seduce them in [our] schools,...in [our] locker rooms,...in [our] army bunkhouses...wherever men are with men together. [Our] sons shall become [their] minions and do [their] bidding.... All laws banning homosexual activity will be revoked. Instead, legislation shall be passed which engenders love between men.... [They] shall stage plays in which man openly caresses man.... The museums of the world will be filled only with paintings of...naked lads.... Love between men [will become] fashionable and de rigueur. [They] will eliminate heterosexual liaisons.... There will be no compromises.... Those who oppose [them] will be exiled. [They] shall raise vast private armies...to defeat [us].... The family unit...will be abolished.... All churches who condemn [them] will be closed.... The society to emerge will be governed by...gay poets.... Any heterosexual man will be barred from...influence. All males who insist on remaining...heterosexual will be tried in homosexual courts of justice."[11]

What should Christians do in the face of this looming specter, asks the pamphlet? "We, today, can and should have God's Law concerning Homosexuality and its judgment of the death penalty." For "they which commit such things," says the apostle Paul, "are worthy of death" (CSA n.d.: 15; see Romans 1:27–32). Extremism fans the flames of extremism.

ORGANIZATION

Contrary to popular thinking, people rarely join right-wing groups because they have a prior belief in doctrines such as those enumerated above. Rather, they come to believe because they have first joined. That is, people first affiliate with right-wing activists and only then begin altering their intellectual outlooks to sustain and strengthen these ties. The original ties may develop from their jobs, among neighbors, among prison acquaintances, or through romantic relationships.

Take the case of Cindy Cutler, who was last seen teaching music at the Aryan Nations Church academy (Mauer, 1980). Reflecting on the previous decade she could well wonder at how far she had come in such a short time.

Cindy had been raised Baptist. "I was with the Jesus Christ thing, that Jesus was my savior and God was love. We'd go to the beach up to a perfect stranger and say, 'Are you saved?'" Such was the serene existence of an uncommonly pretty thrice born-again teenager then residing in San Diego—until she met Gary Cutler, a Navy man stationed nearby. Gary was fourteen years Cindy's senior and seemed the "good Christian man" she had been looking for when they met one Sunday at Baptist services.

Gary and Cindy were already dating when he discovered Identity Christianity. Brought up as a Mormon, he had left the church when it began granting priesthood powers to Black members during the 1970s. After several years searching for a new religious home, Gary claims to have first heard the Identity message one evening while randomly spinning the radio dial. An Identity preacher was extolling the white race as God's chosen people. Gary says the sermon gave him "new found pride."

In the meantime, Cindy's fondness for Gary was growing. The only problem was his espousal of Identity beliefs. As part of her faith, Cindy had learned that Jews, not Anglo-Saxons, were from Israel, and that Jesus was Jewish. Both of these notions were in conflict with what Gary was now saying. Perhaps, Cindy feared, she and Gary were incompatible after all. How could she ever find intellectual consensus with her fiance?

Gary and Cindy routinely spent time together in Bible study. One evening Cindy saw the light. She had already learned from church that Jews were supposedly "Christ killers." It was this information that enabled her to overcome what she calls her prideful resistance to Identity. The occasion of her conversion was this passage: "My sheep know me and hear my voice, and follow me" (John 10: 27). "That's how I got into Identity," she later said. "I questioned how they [the Jews] could be God's chosen people if they hate my Christ." Having discovered a shared theological ground upon which to stand, Gary and Cindy could now marry.

The point of this story is the sociological truth that the way in which some people become right-wing extremists is indistinguishable from the way others become vegetarians, peace activists, or members of mainline churches (Lofland and Stark 1965; Aho 1991: 185–211). *Their affiliations are mediated by significant others already in the movement.* It is from these others that they first learn of the cause; sometimes it is through the loaning of a pamphlet or videotape; occasionally it takes the form of an invitation to a meeting or workshop. As the relationship with the other tightens, the recruit's viewpoint begins to change. At this stage old friends, family members, and cohorts, observing the recruit spending inordinate time with "those new people," begin their interrogations: "What's up with you, man?" In answer, the new recruit typically voices shocking things: bizarre theologies, conspiracy theories, manichaeistic worldviews. Either because of conscious "disowning" or unconscious avoidance, the recruit finds the old ties loosening, and as they unbind, the "stupidity" and "backwardness" of prior acquaintances becomes increasingly evident.

Pushed away from old relationships and simultaneously pulled into the waiting arms of new friends, lovers, and comrades, the recruit is absorbed into the movement. Announcements of full conversion to extremism follow. To display commitment to the cause, further steps may be deemed necessary: pulling one's children out of public schools where "secular humanism" is taught; working for radical political candidates to stop America's "moral decline;" refusing to support ZOG with taxes; renouncing one's citizenship and throwing away social security card and drivers license; moving to a rugged wilderness to await the End Times. Occasionally it means donning camouflage, taking-up high-powered weaponry, and confronting the "forces of satan" themselves.

There are two implications to this sociology of recruitment. First and most obviously, involvement in social networks is crucial to being mobilized into right-wing activism. Hence, contrary to the claims of the estrangement theory of extremism mentioned above, those who are truly isolated from their local communities are the last and least likely to become extremists themselves. My research (Aho 1991, 1994) suggests that among the most important of these community ties is membership in independent fundamentalist, Baptist, or Presbyterian congregations.

Secondly, being situated in particular networks is largely a matter of chance. None of us choose our parents. Few choose their co-workers, fellow congregants, or neighbors,

202 DISRUPTIVE RELIGION: THE FORCE OF FAITH IN SOCIAL-MOVEMENT ACTIVISM

and even friendships and marriages are restricted to those available to us by the happenstance of our geography and times. What this means is that almost any person could find themselves in a Christian patriot communications-network that would position them for recruitment into right-wing extremism.

As we have already pointed out, American right-wing extremists are neither educationally nor psychologically different from the general population. Nor are they any more status insecure than other Americans. What makes them different is how they are socially positioned. This positioning includes their religious affiliation. Some people find themselves in churches that expose them to the right-wing world. This increases the likelihood of their becoming right-wingers.

CONCLUSION

Throughout American history, a particular style of Christianity has nurtured right-wing extremism. Espousing doctrines like human depravity, white America as God's elect people, conspiratorialism, Jews as Christ killers, covenant theology and the right to revolt, and millennialism, this brand of Christianity is partly rooted in orthodox Calvinism and in the theologically questionable fantasies of popular imagination. Whatever its source, repeatedly during the last two centuries, its doctrines have served to prepare believers cognitively to assume hostile attitudes toward "un-Christian"—hence un-American—individuals, groups, and institutional practices.

This style of Christianity has also given impetus to hatred and violence through its advocacy of armed crusades against evil. Most of all, however, the cults, sects, and denominations wherein this style flourishes have served as mobilization centers for recruitment into right-wing causes. From the time of America's inception, right-wing political leaders in search of supporters have successfully enlisted clergymen who preach these principles to bring their congregations into the fold in "wars" to save America for Christ.

It is a mistake to think that modern Americans are more bigoted and racist than their ancestors were. Every American generation has experienced right-wing extremism, even that occasionally erupting into vigilante violence of the sort witnessed daily on the news today. What is different in our time is the sophistication and availability of communications and weapons technology. Today, mobilization to right-wing causes has been infinitely enhanced by the availability of personal computer systems capable of storing and retrieving information on millions of potential recruits. Mobilization has also been facilitated by cheap short-wave radio and cable-television access, the telephone tree, desk-top publishing, and readily available studio-quality recorders. Small coteries of extremists can now activate supporters across immense distances at the touch of a button. Add to this the modern instrumentality for maiming and killing available to the average American citizen: military-style assault weaponry easily convertible into fully automatic machine guns, powerful explosives manufacturable from substances like diesel oil and fertilizer, harmless in themselves, hence purchasable over-the-counter. Anti-tank and aircraft weapons, together with assault vehicles, have also been uncovered recently in private-arms caches in the Western states.

Because of these technological changes, religious and political leaders today have a greater responsibility to speak and write with care regarding those with whom they disagree. Specifically, they must control the temptation to demonize their opponents, lest, in their declarations of war they bring unforeseen destruction not only on their enemies, but on themselves.

REFERENCES

Aho, J. 1991. *The Politics of Righteousness: Idaho Christian Patriotism.* Seattle: University of Washington Press.

_____. 1994. *This Thing of Darkness: A Sociology of the Enemy.* Seattle: University of Washington Press.

Barkun, M. 1994. *Religion and the Racist Right: The Origins of the Christian Identity Movement.* Chapel Hill: North Carolina University Press.

Calvin, J. 1966. *On God and Man.* F.W. Strothmann (ed.). New York: Ungar.

Cohn, N. 1967. *The Pursuit of the Millennium.* New York: Oxford University Press.

CSA. n.d. "Prepare War!" Pontiac, Missouri: CSA Bookstore.

Dilling, E. 1952. *The Plot Against Christianity.* n.p.

Flynn, K. and G. Gerhardt. 1989. *The Silent Brotherhood: Inside America's Racist Underground.* New York: Free Press.

Glock, C. 1993. "The Churches and Social Change in Twentieth-Century America." *Annals of the American Academy of Political and Social Science,* 527: 67–83.

Glock, C. and R. Stark. 1966. *Christian Beliefs and Anti-Semitism.* New York: Harper and Row.

Hay, M. 1981 (1950). *The Roots of Christian Anti-Semitism.* New York: Anti-Defamation League of B'nai B'rith.

Lindsey, H. 1970. *The Late Great Planet Earth.* Grand Rapids: Zondervan.

Lipset, S.M. and E. Raab. 1970. *The Politics of Unreason: Right-Wing Extremism in America, 1790–1970.* New York: Harper and Row.

Lofland, J. and R. Stark. 1965. "Becoming A World-Saver: A Theory of Conversion to A Deviant Perspective." *American Sociological Review* 30: 862–875.

Luther, M. 1974. *Luther: Selected Political Writings,* J.M. Porter, ed. Philadelphia: Fortress Press.

Mannheim, K. 1952. "The Problem of Generations" in *Essays in the Sociology of Knowledge.* London: Routledge and Kegan Paul.

Mauer, D. 1980. "Couple Finds Answers in Butler's Teachings." *Idaho Statesman.* Sept. 14.

Nisbet, R. 1953. *The Quest for Community.* New York: Harper and Brothers.

Pace, J.O. 1985. *Amendment to the Constitution.* Los Angeles: Johnson, Pace, Simmons and Fennel.

Peters, P. 1992. *Death Penalty for Homosexuals.* LaPorte, Colorado: Scriptures for America. Preamble. 1986. "Preamble to the United States Constitution: Who Are the Posterity?" Oregon City, Oregon: Republic vs. Democracy Redress.

Ring, R.H. 1985. "The Yarbrough's." *The Denver Post.* Jan. 6.

Robison, J. 1967 (1798). *Proofs of A Conspiracy....* Los Angeles: Western Islands.

Ruether, R. 1979. *Faith and Fratricide: The Theological Roots of Anti-Semitism.* New York: Seabury.

Sandford, F.W. 1966. *The Art of War for the Christian Soldier.* Amherst, New Hampshire: Kingdom Press.

Schlesinger, A. 1986. *The Cycles of American History.* Boston: Houghton Mifflin.

Sherwood, "Commander" S. 1995. quoted in *Idaho State Journal.* May 21.

Shupe, A. and W. Stacey. 1983. "The Moral Majority Constituency" in *The New Christian Right,* R. Liebman and R. Wuthnow. eds. New York: Aldine.

Simpson, J. 1983. "Moral Issues and Status Politics" in *The New Christian Right,* R. Liebman and R. Wuthnow, eds. New York: Aldine.

Solt, L. 1971. *Saints in Arms: Puritanism and Democracy in Cromwell's Army.* New York: AMS Press.

Stark, R. and William Bainbridge. 1985. *The Future of Religion: Secularization, Revival and Cult Formation.* Berkeley: University of California Press.

Stouffer, S.A. 1966. *Communism, Conformity and Civil Liberties.* New York: John Wiley.

Troeltsch, E. 1960. *Social Teachings of the Christian Churches.* Trans. by O. Wyon. New York: Harper and Row.

Walzer, M. 1965. *The Revolution of the Saints.* Cambridge, Massachusetts: Harvard University Press.

Wilcox, C. 1992. *God's Warriors: The Christian Right in Twentieth Century America.* Baltimore, Maryland: Johns Hopkins University Press.

A Comparison of the Political Behavior of Faith-Based and Secular Peace Groups

Ron Pagnucco

Throughout United States history, religious groups have engaged in political activities.[1] However, while there have been some very informative case studies of the activities of particular faith-based groups (see, for example, Morris 1984; Gusfield 1986; Rader 1986; Hertzke 1988; Holsworth 1989; Epstein 1990; Yarnold, ed. 1991; McNeal 1992), there have been few systematic, quantitative studies of the political behavior of faith-based social-movement organizations (see Donnelly 1987; McAdam, McCarthy and Zald 1988). This chapter will examine the political behavior—with special focus on tactics—of a national sample of faith-based and secular social movement organizations working for peace in the late 1980s in the United States. They were all part of what is called "the peace movement," and so will be called "peace movement organizations" (PMOs).[2]

The American peace movement has always included a strong core of religious activists and groups. Throughout American history, the historic peace churches, primarily the Quakers, have played key roles in the emergence of anti-war activism during wartime and have been carriers of the movement in less active times (see DeBenedetti 1980; DeBenedetti and Chatfield 1991; Pagnucco 1992; Chatfield 1992). There have also been other groups working for peace, such as the Fellowship of Reconciliation (FOR) and Clergy and Laity Concerned (CALC), which are not formally a part of a church structure, but work with religiously motivated constituencies, largely from mainstream American religious denominations.

Faith-based PMOs have unique characteristics which have contributed to their prominent role in one of the United States' oldest social movements. As movement "halfway houses" (Morris 1984), many faith-based organizations provided a consistent supply of resources for activism through their connections with formal religious organizations. Meeting spaces, access to interpersonal networks, and financial resources are among the key assets provided by formal religious structures (see DeBenedetti 1980; Chatfield 1992; Epstein 1990; Zald and McCarthy 1987). Perhaps more importantly, however, these institutions—both traditional churches as well as alternative, ecumenical religious groups—also helped to build and sustain a sense of motivation or inspiration for activism among their members (Morris 1984; Epstein 1990, 1991). Key values and beliefs, such as social justice and nonviolence, cultivated through formal religious structures and rituals were the very ones that faith-based peace activists sought to foster in the world.

Do these kinds of factors make faith-based peace activism different from that of secular PMOs? Are the foundations of religiously motivated peace activism likely to lead faith-based PMOs to use tactics that significantly differ from those used by secular interest groups, political lobbyists, and secular PMOs? The case studies of Epstein (1990) and Rader (1986), which focused on several United States faith-based peace groups in the 1980s, suggest that the moral and religious orientation and identity of these groups inclined them to be skeptical of the standard political process and the conventional methods of political pressure—i.e., voter mobilization, lobbying letters, and visits to members of Congress—and to use instead the "unruly" tactics of nonviolent direct action (see Pagnucco 1992). According to these studies, these groups are more likely to engage in what has been called a "politics of moral witness" (Epstein 1990) and the "parabolic deed" (Yoder 1992: 58). In these cases, "political...action is the expression of an individual's responsibility to his or her own conscience" (Epstein 1991: 196), and "one rejects what the moral law rejects, without calculating one's chances of getting away with it or of achieving a change in public policy" (Yoder 1992:57). In such a politics, the "rejection of the present evil is valid for its [own] sake, and this must be said by word and deed" (Yoder 1992: 59). One must reject and visibly oppose immoral policies now and not wait for the government to change them through a legislative process often dominated by powerful interests that support them. Parabolic deeds include "unruly" or "unconventional" direct-action tactics such as war-tax resistance and civil disobedience, that constitute moral acts of noncooperation with evil and forms of public witness that challenge the consciences of the American people. For those engaging in the politics of moral witness, parabolic deeds, and not the conventional tactics of political bargaining, will help to bring about personal and social transformation. One must say in word and deed a pure and uncompromising "no" to immoral government policies.

Other studies, however, have shown that some faith-based peace groups are not averse to political compromise and the use of conventional political tactics, such as lobbying Congress and the Executive branch. The study by Hertzke (1988) of religious lobbies in Washington, D.C. during the 1980s indicates that certainly not all faith-based groups working for peace are reluctant to use conventional political tactics. However, Hertzke notes the tension within many of these groups between "winning and witnessing" (1988: 75). Similarly, in his study of grass-roots faith-based groups, Holsworth (1989) noted that although the activists were somewhat skeptical of the political system, they nevertheless used conventional, as well as unruly, tactics. Clearly, then, there are faith-based groups skeptical of the political bargaining process that engage in the politics of moral witness and parabolic deeds, and those that are less skeptical, that use conventional political-pressure tactics. But which type of faith-based group is more typical? What is the general pattern of political behavior of faith-based peace groups, as compared to secular groups? Is religious orientation strongly correlated with the use of certain tactics? These are the questions I address here by analyzing comparative data from a national sample of faith-based and secular peace-movement organizations.

DATA AND METHOD

The data I use to explore these questions come from a 1988 survey of 483 PMOs with annual budgets over $30,000. Questionnaires were mailed to the entire population of these groups listed in the Topsfield Foundation's *Grassroots Peace Directory* (1987) and returned at a 56 percent response rate (n=273) (see Smith 1994). The survey was directed by Dr. Mary Anna Colwell, and is hereafter referred to as the 1988 Colwell Survey. While these data are limited in that they present only a small subset of the population of PMOs, the relatively large budgets of these groups make them the groups that are most widely known as well as most likely to endure.[3]

The survey asked "Are your members primarily part of a specific category of people (e.g. women, religious denomination, occupational or regional group)?" Responses which indicated a specific denomination, church, or religious group as well as religious orders were included in the faith-based category (n=55). All other groups (n=218) were included in the "secular" comparison group.

The 1988 PMO survey consisted of some 225 questions on tactics, organizational characteristics, and goals and values. Drawing from peace group organizing manuals, studies of social movements, and Schlozman and Tierney's (1986) comprehensive study of interest groups, a list of 38 tactics was included in the questionnaire and respondents were asked to indicate whether or not their group used the tactic. The 38 tactics were divided into two categories: 28 tactics were listed under "political and educational activities," which included such activities as visiting a member of congress or engaging in civil disobedience. Respondents were asked to indicate whether or not their organization used the tactic in the previous year. Ten tactics were listed under "electoral activities," which included voter registration and taking voters to the polls on election day. In order to include electoral cycles, respondents were asked to indicate whether or not they used the tactic in the 1986–1987 time period.

Activist groups generally utilize a limited number of different tactics from a tactical "repertoire" that exists in a country in a particular historical period (Tilly 1979; Marullo 1990); and tend to employ a particular combination of related tactics (Gais and Walker 1991; Pagnucco 1992). In order to determine whether PMOs that used certain tactics were also likely to use related tactics, a factor analysis was performed on responses to the 38 questions on tactics.[4] This analysis resulted in five tactics "clusters," which I labeled "local legislative," "citizen action," "electoral," "national legislative," and "unruly" (see Table 1). The first four clusters involve conventional tactics of political bargaining. The fifth cluster, involving such tactics as civil disobedience and boycotts, is unconventional; they comprise the tactical repertoire of moral witness. If the "moral witness" hypothesis about the relationship between religious identity and political tactics is correct, we should find a high percentage of faith-based groups scoring high on the unruly tactics scale, and scoring significantly higher than the secular groups on the scale. We should also find faith-based groups scoring low on the four conventional—"citizen action," "national legislative," "local legislative," and "electoral"—tactics scales, and scoring significantly lower than the secular PMOs on these scales.

The multi-item factors presented in Table 1 were scaled for this analysis. The more tactics in the cluster that were employed by a PMO, the higher its score on the scale.

TABLE 1: *Rotated Varimax Factor Analysis: PMO Tactics*

TACTIC	FACTOR LOADING
State/Local Legislative	
Testified at state/local government hearing	.78
Consulted with state/local official to plan legislative strategy	.75
Helped draft state/local legislation	.69
Visited state/local officials	.69
Had influential constituent contact state/local official	.66
Alpha=.839	
Citizen Action	
Monitored foreign policy legislation	.72
Monitored the voting records of members of Congress	.70
Had influential constituent contact Congressperson's office	.60
Monitored arms control legislation	.55
Visited members of Congress	.55
Encouraged members to write letters to a local newspaper	.54
Participated in letter-writing campaign	.51
Alpha=.812	
Electoral	
Encouraged members to join local political party	.75
Encouraged members to participate in party primaries/caucuses	.73
Encouraged members to work and/or contribute money to electoral campaign of peace-minded candidates	.71
Helped get voters to the polls on election day	.65
Encouraged members to give money to a political party	.61
Made public endorsements of a candidate for office	.60
Conducted a voter registration campaign	.56
Participated in initiative or referendum	.51
Held a public meeting for political candidates	.51
Alpha=.837	
National Legislative	
Helped draft national legislation	.73
Testified at Congressional hearing	.67
Filed suit or otherwise engaged in litigation	.66
Consulted with national official to plan legislative strategy	.50
Alpha=.749	
Unruly Tactics	
Provided war-tax resistance information	.72
Participated in boycott	.68
Participated in vigil or prayer service	.68
Provided nonviolence training	.66
Engaged in civil disobedience	.62
Participated in rally or demonstration	.55
Provided draft counseling	.50
Alpha=.754	

Source: 1988 Colwell Survey

TABLE 2: *Comparison of PMO Mean Scores for Repertoires*

	FAITH-BASED	SECULAR	T VALUE
Unruly	.596	.332	-6.03**
Citizen Action	.768	.657	-2.32*
National Legislative	.217	.251	.70
Local Legislative	.335	.409	1.23
Electoral	.168	.208	1.00

*** $p<.01$ * $p<.05$; Source: 1988 Colwell Survey.*

TABLE 3: *Comparative Use of Alternative Tactical Repertoires* (percents)

USE OF TACTICAL REPERTOIRES	FAITH-BASED PMOS	SECULAR PMOS
UNRULY		
None	2	22
Some	34	52
Extensive	64	26

p-value < .01, Chi Square 31.51 (d.f.2)

CITIZEN ACTION		
None	2	7
Some	11	22
Extensive	87	70

p < .05, Chi square 6.35 (d.f.2)

NATIONAL LEGISLATIVE		
None	53	50
Some	34	32
Extensive	13	18

n.s., Chi square .632 (d.f.2)

Local Legislative		
None	39	31
Some	29	32
Extensive	33	37

n.s., Chi square .936 (d.f. 2)

Electoral		
None	40	48
Some	53	32
Extensive	8	20

p< .05, Chi square 9.50 (d.f. 2); Source: 1988 Colwell Survey

The scores of the faith-based PMOs and the secular PMOs on each scale were then subjected to a comparison of mean scores (Table 2). The scores for the faith-based and secular PMOs were then divided into a three-level category of repertoire usage—none, some, and extensive—and compared using a Chi-Square statistical test of significance (Table 3).[5]

FINDINGS

The data presented in Tables 2 and 3 allow us to test the hypothesis that faith-based peace movement organizations, because of their religious identities and moral claims, are more likely than secular PMOs not to use conventional tactics of political bargaining, but to use more unconventional, unruly tactics of "moral witness." In Table 2 we see the comparison of mean scores for repertoire usage. As hypothesized, faith-based PMOs were significantly more likely than secular PMOs to use unruly tactics. This finding supports the argument that faith-based groups have a preference for the tactics of "moral witness." However, the findings for the other tactical repertoires do not support the hypothesis that faith-based PMOs are disinclined to use conventional tactics of political bargaining. As we can see from the mean scores, faith-based PMOs were as likely as secular groups to use national legislative, local legislative, and electoral tactics, and were significantly more likely than secular groups to use citizen-action tactics.

In Table 3 we see the percentage of faith-based and secular PMOs that make no use, some use, and extensive use of each of the tactical repertoires. We see that the majority of faith-based PMOs made extensive use of unruly tactics. In contrast, only one fourth (26 percent) of the secular groups made extensive use of such tactics, and over one-fifth (22 percent) made no use at all of unruly tactics. This robust finding strongly supports the argument that faith-based PMOs have a strong preference for unruly tactics. However, the remaining data falsify the hypothesis that faith-based PMOs are disinclined to use conventional tactics. We see that the overwhelming majority of faith-based PMOs made extensive use of citizen action tactics, and were significantly more likely than secular PMOs to utilize this repertoire. We also see that faith-based PMOs were as likely as secular PMOs to use national legislative and local legislative tactics. These findings are consistent with the results of the comparison of mean scores (Table 2).[6]

In order to understand better the statistical findings noted above and the process of tactical choice within faith-based PMOs, I turn now to examine briefly the case of one of the respondents in the 1988 Colwell survey: Pax Christi USA, the largest Roman Catholic peace movement organization in the United States. This faith-based PMO was one of the 64 percent that made extensive use of the unruly tactical repertoire listed in Table 1, and one of the 87 percent that made extensive use of the citizen action tactical repertoire. These make it a particularly revealing case to study.

A CASE STUDY: PAX CHRISTI USA

Pax Christi USA (PCUSA) was founded in 1972 as the United States branch of Pax Christi International, itself founded in 1948. An increasingly visible advocate for peace and justice in the Roman Catholic Church and the broader society, PCUSA, the largest Catholic peace group in the United States, has grown steadily since its founding. By 1976, it had 365 members, including fifteen Roman Catholic bishops; by 1982, it had grown to 5,500 members, with forty-six bishops (see McNeal 1992: 236). By 1988, the time of the Colwell survey, PCUSA had approximately 7,500 members, 134 of whom were Roman Catholic bishops (Clark 1995).[7] Through this case study, we will try to gain an understanding of why faith-based groups in general were significantly more likely than secular ones to use nonviolent, unruly tactics and citizen action tactics.

WHY PCUSA WAS FOUNDED

Pax Christi USA was founded to transform the U.S. Catholic Church into an advocate for peace, nonviolence, and social justice, and to mobilize Catholics to work for peace and justice in the broader society. From its beginning PCUSA was concerned with disarmament and arms control; militarism; the promotion of nonviolence; building support for and strengthening the role of the United Nations in the world; upholding the right of conscientious objection, including selective conscientious objection,[8] to war; and promoting a spirituality and theology of peace among its members and the Roman Catholic Church. It has always had ties with the institutional church, witnessed by the fact that two bishops were among its earliest members.

PCUSA's work within the church has been somewhat successful: it has recruited a number of bishops and lay people alike, and played a major role in the conception and development of the bishops' pastoral, *The Challenge of Peace: God's Promise and Our Response*, which was issued in 1983. Its theological and educational materials have been read by tens of thousands of people, and it has mobilized a number of Catholics, clergy and lay, to oppose the United States government's policies on such issues as nuclear arms, the military draft, Central America, and Haiti.

Although, as we shall see, PCUSA was founded with a mission to promote nonviolence and support nonviolent direct action, PCUSA has also advocated the use of conventional political tactics to change United States policies. It has also worked with the United Nations, providing the personnel and their financial support for Pax Christi International's work with the United Nations in New York. PCUSA is not averse to conventional political tactics and institutions; indeed, as we saw above, it made extensive use of the Citizen Action tactical repertoire. However, as we also saw, PCUSA made extensive use of the unruly tactical repertoire.

WHY NONVIOLENT ACTION?

Like the majority of faith-based PMOs, PCUSA has used more unruly nonviolent tactics than nearly 75 percent of the secular PMOs. Why? Both faith-based and secular PMOs operate in the same sociocultural and political environment and often pursue some of the same goals—e.g., anti-intervention in Central America and nuclear disarmament. The United States foreign policymaking process is just as closed and unresponsive to faith-based groups as it is to secular groups (see Pagnucco and Smith 1992). So, presumably, both sets of groups would have the same degree of incentive to use unruly nonviolent tactics. It would thus appear that variation in the use of unruly nonviolent tactics is not explained by differences in the political opportunity structure alone, or solely by the organizational structures of the two sets of groups (Pagnucco 1992).[9] Rather, the variation in tactical choice would appear to be due to a complex interaction between the political opportunity structure and organizational cultures and values, which are related to the particular histories and memberships of the organizations.[10]

An historical analysis of the faith-based peace movement reveals that extensive use of nonviolent action by faith-based groups is a somewhat recent phenomenon. Indeed, most of the faith-based peace groups in the 1950s, for example, made little—if any— use of nonviolent direct action (Fahey 1995). Thus, it would be ahistorical to claim that a faith-orientation alone is responsible for the use of such tactics. A more dynamic process must be responsible for our findings. It is likely that historical experiences, unresponsiveness of the political system, theological developments, and the network of people from which a group draws its members all contribute to changes in organizational values and culture and the organization's choice of tactics.

This process is evident, for example, in the adoption of nonviolent tactics by the American civil rights movement. Leaders such as Martin Luther King, Jr. drew from a particular sub-tradition in African-American Christianity to fashion a religious orientation that incorporated the philosophy and practice of nonviolence. Such an explicitly Christian nonviolent orientation was not prevalent in the African-American opposition to racial inequality before the mid-1950s (see Meier and Rudwick 1989). A particular configuration of historical, social, political and theological factors contributed to the development of Christian nonviolence as the prevalent orientation in the movement from the mid-1950s to the mid-1960s (see Morris 1984; McAdam 1982). Faith-based groups experienced a similar evolution in their employment of unruly nonviolent tactics during the anti-Vietnam War movement, a process in which the experiences and religious discourse of the civil rights movement played an important role (see McNeal 1992; Hall 1990; Meconis 1979).

The experiences of the African-American civil rights and the anti-Vietnam War movements played a role in the PCUSA's adopting a nonviolent orientation, which was founded as both of those movements were winding down in 1972. Many of those who founded PCUSA had been actively involved in both of those movements. They were also either involved in or strongly influenced by the Catholic Worker, the Catholic Peace Fellowship, and the Community for Creative Nonviolence—three small groups of Roman Catholic pacifists that represent the minority pacifist tradition in the Roman Catholic Church (see McNeal 1992; Vanderhaar 1995). While many if not all of the founders of PCUSA were pacifists (Fahey 1995), the organization reflected the larger international organization, Pax Christi International, of which it was a branch, and recruited both pacifists *and* advocates of the just war tradition, by far the most established tradition in the Church. PCUSA, unlike its three predecessors mentioned above, was not founded as a pacifist organization. Nevertheless, from its founding through the early 1990s, there has always been an influential contingent of pacifists in the organization, many of whom have held leadership positions.

The original members of PCUSA were part of the Catholic peace and justice network that flourished in the 1960s that was comprised of a small number of Catholic clergy and lay people. Situated in the context of the civil rights and anti-Vietnam War movements, and following the opening in the Roman Catholic Church that took place in Vatican Council II (1963–1965), many members of this vibrant network discussed in essays, meetings, and retreats, the ethics of violence, the history of Christian pacifism and nonviolence, and the role of nonviolent direct action in bringing about peace and justice. Many began using nonviolent direct action to oppose racism and war. This was a period of renaissance in Catholic thought and action on war and peace. In 1968, Catholic activist and academic Jim Douglas published a book that would become a mainstay of PCUSA philosophy, *The Non-Violent Cross* (Macmillan), which was one of the first extended treatments of Christian nonviolence by an American Catholic (McNeal 1992). Also, in 1968, following a new draft law established in 1967 and the escalation of the Vietnam War, some Catholic activists, frustrated with the government's unresponsiveness to those opposed to the war, pushed nonviolent direct action another step as they destroyed draft registration records at several draft boards (McNeal 1992). This small but growing network of radical Catholics, known as the "Catholic Resistance," brought a new urgency to Catholic activists' discussions of the philosophy and practice of nonviolence. PCUSA was a child of this renaissance and carried its spirit into the 1970s, 80s, and 90s.

Many PCUSA leaders were committed to promoting nonviolence from the organization's start, though PCUSA itself did not formally advocate or organize nonviolent direct action. The theme of the founding assembly of PCUSA in October 1973 was "Gospel Nonviolence: A Catholic Imperative;" the organization's introductory brochure (quoted in McNeal 1992: 234) described PCUSA as "an association of Catholics and others committed to the exploration of Gospel Nonviolence for our time. We seek to permeate the Catholic consciousness and the Catholic structure with this rich tradition and witness." One of PCUSA's major goals was "to move into the mainstream of Catholic life with a realistic approach to nonviolence" (quoted in McNeal 1992: 234). Besides being active on the broader political scene, PCUSA intended to reach out to bishops and people in the pews alike, and to move the Roman Catholic Church to a commitment to nonviolence and peacemaking. According to one of its founders, Eileen Egan, PCUSA would "lay stress on peace education.... The activism of demonstrations would be the work of other peace organizations" (quoted in McNeal 1992: 230). However, from its beginning, PCUSA supported absolute and selective conscientious objection and individual objectors, as well as the refusal to pay war taxes, though it did not officially advocate these acts (Vanderhaar 1995). PCUSA's hesitancy to advocate these and other forms of nonviolent direct action was based largely on the concern that doing so would make it difficult to recruit bishops and ordinary parishioners into the organization (Fahey 1995). The continuous growth of PCUSA throughout the 1970s may have been related to this strategy of moderation.

In spite of this concern about nonviolent direct action, the theme of the second annual national assembly, held in 1975, was again on nonviolence: "Christian Nonviolence: Challenge to American Life." The keynote speaker was Detroit's Auxiliary Bishop Thomas Gumbleton, who was the President of the organization. Significantly, the third and fourth annual national assemblies featured as keynote speakers two veterans of the civil rights movement: Julius Lester and James Lawson, the later a former associate of Martin Luther King, Jr. The fourth annual national assembly was held in Memphis,

Tennessee with Lawson giving a keynote address on "Nonviolence in a Violent World." The assembly featured a special commemoration of Martin Luther King, Jr. The nonviolent orientation of PCUSA was becoming institutionalized.

Although the national organization did not formally advocate and organize nonviolent direct action, after the election of Ronald Reagan and the re-escalation of the Cold War in the early 1980s, an increasing number of individual members and local chapters began doing so. And the national organization did not stop them. This increase in nonviolent activism is reflected in the organization's magazine, which increasingly provided a forum for members who advocated nonviolent direct action to express their views in its pages. For example, in January of 1982, Raymond Hunthausen, the Archbishop of Seattle, announced that he would engage in war tax resistance, withholding half of his income tax in protest of United States nuclear policy. Hunthausen's statement was printed in the Pax Christi newsletter. While not endorsing war tax resistance as a corporate body, PCUSA was clearly publicizing it as an option. Workshops on a variety of nonviolence topics, such as war-tax resistance, were held in the annual national assemblies. The March 1983 issue of PCUSA's magazine published a sample letter to the Internal Revenue Service to be included with 1982 income tax returns that explained why the writer was withholding part of their income tax in protest. PCUSA also encouraged members to support the World Peace Tax Fund bill under consideration in Congress. The legislation would have legally permitted those opposed to their tax money being used by the military to direct their taxes for peaceful purposes.

In 1979, the United States military draft was reinstituted. In 1980, the Center for Law and Pacifism was established by Gordon Zahn under the auspices of PCUSA to provide literature and counseling for Catholic objectors. In 1982, responding to the fact that some Catholic young men were not registering, the National Council of PCUSA passed a resolution (quoted in McNeal 1992: 238) that read:

> Although we neither advise nor encourage such action, Pax Christi USA recognizes non-registration for the draft based on conscientious objection to conscription and opposition to growing militarization of this nation as a valid Christian witness deserving the respect and support of the entire Christian community.

In the March 1983 issue of their magazine, PCUSA expressed support of those Catholic young men who registered as conscientious objectors, and those who refused to register at all. They advised all those who considered themselves to be COs, whether they registered or not, to make use of PCUSA draft counselors, and to create a file documenting their CO sentiments and give it to a religious organization, including PCUSA. PCUSA also launched a letter-writing campaign to members of Congress in support of legislation to end draft registration.

In the early 1980s, PCUSA as an organization was careful not formally to endorse or call for nonviolent action. But it did continue to propagate Christian nonviolence. It produced publications and study guides and held retreats and workshops on nonviolence. PCUSA helped to organize the Nuclear Weapons Freeze Campaign, opposed the Reagan administration's policies in Central America, and lobbied the United States Catholic bishops to write a strongly anti-nuclear, pro-nonviolence pastoral letter. Partly because of its bishop members and the efforts of PCUSA leaders, Bishop Gumbleton was one of the five members assigned to the drafting committee for the pastoral letter.

PCUSA continued to promote nonviolence in the mid-1980s. The March 1985 issue of their magazine announced in its pages "Pax Christi Action: Disarm the Heart/Disarm the Nations," a program of actions to commemorate the 40th anniversary of the atomic bombings of Hiroshima and Nagasaki. In this issue of the magazine, PCUSA further deepened and institutionalized its nonviolent orientation inviting members publicly to take a vow of peace, which committed them to a lifestyle of Christian nonviolence. This project makes clear that, for PCUSA, nonviolence was not only a political tactic but a personal act of faith "with a powerful potential to birth a peace church" (Kownacki 1985: 5). The opening line of the vow is a statement of individual repentance: "Recognizing the violence in my own heart, yet trusting in the goodness and mercy of God, I vow for one year to practice the nonviolence of Jesus" (PCUSA 1985a: 5). Individuals and groups vowed to follow the nonviolent Jesus (PCUSA 1985a: 5):

> By striving for peace within myself and seeking to be a peacemaker in my daily life; by accepting suffering rather than inflicting it; by refusing to retaliate in the face of provocation and violence; by persevering in nonviolence of tongue and heart; by living conscientiously and simply so that I do not deprive others of the means to live; by actively resisting evil and working nonviolently to abolish war from my own heart and from the face of the earth.

With this vow PCUSA was hoping to foster and give expression to a commitment to Christian nonviolence among its members.

But the organization did not merely advocate a vow, as significant as the repercussions of such a vow ardently followed could be. In the March 1985 issue of its magazine, PCUSA published a call for civil disobedience at the nuclear weapons test site in Nevada, though it stopped short of officially advocating this action. PCUSA was also, by this time, participating in the Pledge of Resistance network, which consisted of individuals and groups pledging "to engage in acts of nonviolent resistance if the United States invades, bombs, sends combat troops, or otherwise significantly escalates its intervention in Nicaragua or El Salvador" (PCUSA 1985b: 5). PCUSA also issued a statement of support for the Sanctuary movement, praising those religious groups and individuals that took in illegal refugees from the United States-backed wars in Central America (see Smith 1996). But nonviolent action was not the only tactic that PCUSA mentioned for each of these issues. It also encouraged its members to contact the White House and Congress and to organize letter-writing campaigns on these issues as well.

Although individual members and local chapters of PCUSA were increasingly employing nonviolent, unruly tactics throughout the 1980s, it was not until May, 1987, on the fourth anniversary of the bishops' peace pastoral, that the national PCUSA organization formally sponsored and organized civil disobedience. In preparation for the event, the National Council approved a statement on Civil Disobedience at its March meeting, which was printed in the Winter issue of Pax Christi magazine. The statement explicitly endorsed civil disobedience and claimed that it had played a central role in the church's history. PCUSA lamented the "significant levels of lawlessness within our government's present policies" (PCUSA 1987a: 7). According to the statement, the Reagan administration had taken the United States in an immoral, illegal, and dangerous direction. Under such circumstances, civil disobedience was warranted (PCUSA 1987a: 7):

> [W]e look about and see forms of weaponry and weapon-making which embody imminent danger of indiscriminate destruction. We see acts of warmaking which, we believe, violate international law regarding civilian immunity....All of these policies carry in their wake laws and practices which seem to us to deserve the name 'unjust.' Pax Christi USA protests such policies not only for the sake of the integrity of individual conscience, but also as responsible civic action compatible with our country's best traditions in its nurturing of the common good. Thus our nonviolent civil disobedience not only seeks to preserve a personal faith integrity, but also aims to correct unjust policies and to cultivate the gift of a humane democratic society.

The National Council also acknowledged that nonviolent actions by individuals and local groups in PCUSA had positively affected them.[11] It was with this mindset that PCUSA organized the event in which two Roman Catholic bishops and ninety-six other participants illegally entered the nuclear weapons test in Nevada and were arrested.[12] One of the organizers of and participants in the action, Bishop Thomas Gumbleton, invited PCUSA members to participate, saying, "It is time to resist our participation in government policies that conflict with the gospel. We must change public policy in accord with the clear teaching of the peace pastoral" (PCUSA 1987b: 1). Bishop Charles Buswell echoed these sentiments. He had hoped to see a change in United States foreign policy after the peace pastoral was issued in 1983. However, he (quoted in Leddy 1987: 4) said that his hope,

> has not been realized.... On the contrary, so far as our country's administration is concerned, the Challenge of Peace is no challenge. Its moral demands have been ignored. The Nevada test site and its activity are proof of this fact.

A grass-roots activist in PCUSA, Sr. Connie Ostrander, explained why she participated: "I did not come planning to commit civil disobedience but did so because nuclear warfare is so clearly against the scriptural mandate to choose life" (quoted in Leddy 1987: 7).

The nonviolent direct action drew widespread support among PCUSA members and friends. Over two hundred people came to participate in the celebration of the Mass and the other activities that surrounded the action. Thirteen other bishops endorsed the action, and two hundred PCUSA local chapters organized supportive actions throughout the country. PCUSA also organized a complementary legislative campaign, asking members to contact their Senators and Congresspersons and urge them to support legislation under consideration in Congress that would have banned nuclear testing.

The act of trespassing at the Nevada test site was intended to be a "parabolic deed," a symbolic "No!" to United States policy. The rich liturgical practice of the Roman

Catholic church lends itself readily to the enactment of the parabolic deed. Leddy (1987:6) described the event in Nevada:

> The civil disobedience action took place after a time for personal meditation and a Eucharistic liturgy in the desert. During the sign of peace, at the end of the [Mass], participants formed into their...groups and then lined themselves up along the side of the road leading to the test site. Then, one by one, the groups walked down the road leading to where the local sheriff and his assistants were waiting. Some groups sang, other groups prayed, as they walked.

In reading this description, it is difficult to determine when the liturgy actually ended and the protest began—a typical intermingling of sacred and political in PCUSA groups using nonviolent action.

The influence of the liturgical tradition on PCUSA's thinking on nonviolent action was discussed in a booklet written by PCUSA national staff member Tom Cordaro (1990: 12):

> For Catholics and other Christians who have a sacramental and liturgical tradition, word, symbol and action have a special meaning. In our sacramental life we understand that word, symbol and action have the power to transform.... It is word and water which is poured that makes baptism sacramental. Nonviolent direct actions that have the power to transform are those that choose word, symbol and action carefully. In this sense, nonviolent direct action becomes a form of liturgy where people are called together to share a word and to participate in a symbolic action which points to a truth greater than the act itself.

Cordaro continued (1990: 12): "A well planned nonviolent direct action is like a well planned liturgy. It creates a space for conversion to take place."

In the Catholic tradition, rich in public ritual and symbolism, it is a small step for some to apply the logic of liturgy to the parabolic deed and the drama of protest. Thus, embedded in a particular Catholic tradition sustained by an active community, and challenged by what were to its members the increasingly problematic social and political issues of the day, PCUSA eventually put its nonviolent values into action.

WHY CITIZEN ACTION TACTICS?

Unlike nonviolent direct action, citizen-action tactics were officially advocated and organized by PCUSA from its very beginning. Thus we have less to describe and explain. These tactics are the basic, familiar tactics of citizenship in the United States, so it is not surprising that many individuals and groups use them. However, the question we are faced with is: why were faith-based groups significantly more likely than secular groups to use these tactics?

Contradicting what is expected by the politics-of-moral-witness theory noted earlier, faith-based PMOs in the Colwell survey used both conventional and nonviolent unruly tactics, combining the use of parabolic deeds with the use of conventional tactics of political bargaining. This was certainly true in the case of PCUSA.

We saw no differences between secular and faith-based PMOs in their use of the conventional-electoral, national-legislative, and local-legislative tactical repertoires. Not many PMOs used these repertoires, for reasons mostly related more to organizational capacity and political opportunity structure (see Pagnucco 1992). However, faith-based PMOs were significantly more likely to use citizen-action tactics, such as monitoring foreign policy legislation, visiting members of Congress, and participating in letter-writing campaigns.

The case of PCUSA suggests possible explanations as to why, statistically, faith-based PMOs were significantly more likely to use citizen-action tactics. In PCUSA, a Christian moral commitment and a sense of crisis underlay the use of nonviolent, unruly tactics—seen, for example, in the civil disobedience at the Nevada test site. However, the same commitment and sense of crisis underlay PCUSA's use of citizen action tactics, also seen in the Nevada action. Both tactical repertoires stem from the same source—an understanding of responsible Christian citizenship. This understanding, explicitly cultivated by PCUSA, sees the individual as having a personal involvement in, and responsibility for, what happens in the world.[13] According to this view, unwittingly or not, we often cooperate with immoral policies and structures, but have a responsibility to cease cooperating with them, to oppose them, and try to change them by peaceful means. Such means may include nonviolent unruly tactics and conventional tactics. Whatever means are choosen, Christians must engage the world and try to change it. This is the imperative of responsible Christian citizenship. Inaction and indifference in this perspective are unacceptable.

Faith commitment and an understanding of responsible Christian citizenship not only provide strong motivation for taking some form of action however. They also encourage to see "political issues" primarily in moral terms. Many members confront the daunting political problems of the day with a sustaining, faith-based spirit of hope and a biblical vision of the just and peaceful society (Robinson 1995b). This sustaining hope and vision helps to explain why PCUSA has retained eighty percent of its members throughout the 1980s (Robinson 1995a). This hope and vision lay behind a popular saying in PCUSA: "We are called to be faithful, not effective." For many PCUSA members, this saying does not mean that they should not use tactics that might change government policies. Rather, it means that they must work for peace and justice even if they are not at the moment "winning."

But if a belief in responsible Christian citizenship requires action, which actions will be taken? Here a structural analysis will help provide an explanation. Both the unruly and citizen action tactical repertoires reflect an important factor in common: they are readily accessible to local groups of committed activists—compared to the national and state legislative, and to some degree electoral, tactical repertoires, which require a higher level of resources, knowledge, and skills. PCUSA is composed of many local groups. We know from research on social movements that individuals integrated into groups are more likely to be mobilized for collective action than are unintegrated individuals, especially for nonviolent direct action. The use of unruly nonviolent tactics is facilitated by membership in a group: the presence of supportive others makes risk-taking easier and helps the individual take care of personal and family matters after they are arrested (Laffin 1995; McAdam 1988).[14] Groups also provide an important base for the use of citizen action tactics. For example, in 1986 PCUSA worked with twelve dioceses to mobilize a comprehensive nuclear test ban petition drive. The relative simplicity and low cost of these tactics make them ideal for widespread use and helps to account for the survey finding that twenty-three percent more faith-based PMOs made extensive use of citizen action tactics than unruly tactics (see Table 3).

CONCLUSION

Though faith-based PMOs have a moral understanding of political issues and do engage in the politics of moral witness and parabolic deeds, they are not averse to using the conventional tactics of political bargaining. Indeed, faith-based PMOs were significantly more likely than secular PMOs to use nonviolent unruly tactics and conventional citizen action tactics. Since both sets of PMOs operate in the same relatively unresponsive political system, and the differences in tactical choice cannot be explained by a range of organizational characteristics, it appears that a religious orientation explains much of the differences. The case of PCUSA showed how the time period and the experiences and beliefs of its founders gave the organization an orientation to nonviolence, while advocating the use of conventional political tactics. It always supported its members who employed nonviolent tactics—though initially the national PCUSA did not officially advocate them, fearing that such official advocacy would make the recruitment of bishops and lay Catholics more difficult. The Reagan administration's policies in the 1980s, which PCUSA considered immoral, lawless, and dangerous, and the increasing use of unruly tactics by some grass-roots members, however, eventually led the national organization to officially organize its first act of civil disobedience in 1987. This case study, then, shows that PCUSA made extensive use of both citizen action and unruly tactics because of its understanding of responsible Christian citizenship, its perception of moral and political crisis, its structure of local groups, its ties with the local church, and because of the accessibility of these tactics to its members. These findings should help us to understand better the political behavior of the other faith-based PMOs in the Colwell Survey and beyond, and why their behavior differed from that of secular PMOs.

REFERENCES

Colwell, M. A. 1990. "Defining Social Movements: Questions and Problems Arising From a 1988 Survey of Groups and Organizations Working for Peace." Paper presented at the American Sociological Association Annual Meetings, Washington, D.C.

_____. 1989. *Organizational and Management Characteristics of Peace Groups*. San Francisco, CA: Institute for Nonprofit Organization Management, University of San Francisco. Working Paper No. 8.

Chatfield, C. 1992. *The American Peace Movement: Ideals and Activism*. New York: Twayne.

_____. ed. 1975. *The Americanization of Gandhi*. New York: Garland.

Clark, J. 1995. Interview with author, PCUSA national office, Erie, PA, January 5.

Cordaro, T. 1990. *To Wake the Nation: Nonviolent Direct Action for Personal & Social Transformation*. Erie, PA: Pax Christi USA.

DeBenedetti, C. 1980. *The Peace Reform in American History*. Bloomington, IN: Indiana University Press.

DeBenedetti, C. and C. Chatfield. 1990. *An American Ordeal: The Antiwar Movement of the Vietnam Era*. Syracuse, NY: Syracuse University Press.

Donnelly, B. 1987. "The Social Protest of Christian and Nonreligious Groups: The Importance of Goal Choice." *Journal for the Scientific Study of Religion*. 26 (3): 309–326.

Edwards, B., and S. Marullo. 1995. "Organizational Mortality in a declining Movement: The Demise of Peace Movement Organizations in the End of the Cold War." Manuscript.

Epstein, B. 1990. "The Politics of Moral Witness: Religion and Nonviolent Direct Action," in *Peace Action in the Eighties: Social Science Perspectives*. J. Lofland and S. Marullo, eds. New Brunswick, NJ: Rutgers University Press: 106–124.

Fahey, J. 1995. Letter to the author, dated March 21, Bronx, New York.

Freeman, J. 1979. "Resource Mobilization Strategy: A Model for Analyzing Social Movement Organization Actions," in *The Dynamics of Social Movements: Resource Mobilization, Social Control and Tactics*. Mayer Zald and J. D. McCarthy, eds. Cambridge, MA: Winthrop Publishers: 167–189.

Gais, T., and J. Walker, Jr. 1991. "Pathways to Influence in American Politics," in *Mobilizing Interest Groups in America: Patrons, Professions, and Social Movements*. Ann Arbor, MI: University of Michigan Press: 103–121.

Gusfield, J. R. 1986. *Symbolic Crusade: Status Politics and the American Temperance Movement*. 2nd edition. Chicago: University of Illinois Press.

Hall, M. K. 1990. *Because of Their Faith: CALCAV and Religious Opposition to the Vietnam War*. New York: Columbia University Press.

Hertzke, A. 1988. *Representing God in Washington: The Role of Religious Lobbies in the American Polity*. Knoxville: The University of Tennessee Press.

Holsworth, R. 1989. *Let Your Life Speak: A Study of Politics, Religion, and Antinuclear Weapons Activism*. Madison, WI: University of Wisconsin Press.

Kownacki, M. L. 1985. "Vow of Nonviolence: Potential to Birth a Peace Church." *Pax Christi* magazine (September): 4–5.

Laffin, A. 1995. Untitled presentation. Workshop on the Role of Religious Groups. International Assembly to Stop the Spread of Weapons, April 21, New York, New York.

Leddy, M. J. "The Church is Crossing the Line." *Pax Christi* magazine (Summer): 4–7.

Marty, W. R. 1991. "The Role of Religious Organizations in the Peace Movement Between the Wars," in Yarnold, Barbara, ed. *The Role of Religious Organizations in Social Movements*. Westport, CT: Praeger: 47–70.

Marullo, S. 1990. "Patterns of Peacemaking in the Local Freeze Campaign," in *Peace Action in the Eighties: Social Science Perspectives*. J. Lofland and S. Marullo, eds. 1991. New Brunswick, NJ: Rutgers University Press: 246–263.

McAdam, D., J. McCarthy, and M. Zald. 1988. "Social Movements," in *Handbook of Sociology*. Niel J. Smelser, ed. Beverly Hills: Sage.

McAdam, D. 1988. *Freedom Summer*. New York: Free Press.

McNeal, P. 1995. Interview with author, Notre Dame, IN, January 16.

———. 1992. *Harder Than War: Catholic Peacemaking in Twentieth-Century America*. New Brunswick, NJ: Rutgers University Press.

Meconis, C. A. 1979. *With Clumsy Grace: The American Catholic Left 1961–1975*. New York: The Seabury Press.

Meier, A., and E. Rudwick. 1989. "The Origins of Nonviolent Direct Action in Afro-American Protest: A Note on Historical Discontinuities," in *We Shall Overcome: The Civil Rights Movement in the United States in the 1950's and 1960's*. Vol. 3. David Garrow, ed. New York: Carlson: 833–915.

Morris, A. 1984. *The Origins of the Civil Rights Movement*. New York: The Free Press.

Pagnucco, R. 1992. *Tactical Choice Among Groups Working for Peace in the Contemporary U.S.: The Ruly/Unruly Divide*. Ph.D. Dissertation, Department of Sociology, The Catholic University of America, Washington, D.C.

———. 1987b. "Challenge for Peace: Ban Nuclear Testing." Pax Christi Collection, Box 8, Folder "National Assembly (Chicago) 1987, University of Notre Dame Archives, Notre Dame, IN.

———. 1986. "Recommendations from General Assembly." Box 8, Folder 61, "Organizational Details," Pax Christi Collection,University of Notre Dame Archives, Notre Dame, IN.

———. 1985a. "Vow of Nonviolence." *Pax Christi* (September): 5.

———. 1985b. "Pledge of Resistance." *Pax Christi* (March): 5.

———. 1982. "Pax Christi Survey Results." Box 8, File "National Council 1982," Pax Christi Collection, University of Notre Dame Archives, Notre Dame, IN.

Pagnucco, R. and J. Smith. 1993. "The Peace Movement and the Formulation of U.S. Foreign Policy." *Peace and Change: A Journal of Peace Research*. 18:2: (April): 157–181. [Pax Christi USA. 1987. "On the Meaning of Civil Disobedience." *Pax Christi* magazine (Winter): 7.]

Rader, V. 1986. *Signal Through the Flames: CCNV, Mitch Snyder and America's Homeless*. Kansas City, MO: Sheed and Ward.

Robinson, D. 1995a. Untitled presentation. Workshop on the Role of Religious Groups. International Assembly to Stop the Spread of Weapons, April 21, New York, New York.

———. 1995b. Interview with the author, PCUSA national office, Erie, PA, January 5.

Schlozman, K. L., and J. T. Tierney. 1986. *Organized Interests and American Democracy*. New York: Harper and Row.

Smith, C. 1996. *Resisting Reagan: The U.S. Central America Peace Movement.* Chicago: University of Chicago Press.

Smith, J. 1994. "An Analysis of Response Bias in the 1988 Survey of Organizations Working for Peace." Unpublished manuscript. Kroc Institute for International Peace Studies, University of Notre Dame, Notre Dame, IN.

Tilly, C. 1979. "Repertoires of Contention in America and Britain, 1750–1830," in *The Dynamics of Social Movements: Resource Mobilization, Social Control, and Tactics.* M. Zald and J. D. McCarthy, eds. Cambridge, MA: Winthrop Publishers: 126–155.

Topsfield Foundation. 1987. *Grassroots Peace Directory.* Topsfield Foundation: Pomfert, CT.

Vanderhaar, G. A. 1995. Letter to the author, dated April 15, Memphis, TN.

Yarnold, B. M., ed. 1991. *The Role of Religious Organizations in Social Movements.* Westport, CT: Praeger.

Yoder, J. H. 1992. *Nevertheless: Varieties of Religious Pacifism.* Scottsdale, PA: Herald Press.

Zald, M., and J. D. McCarthy. 1987. *Social Movements in an Organizational Society.* New Brunswick, NJ: Transaction Books.

NOTES

INTRODUCTION

1. Inattention to religion's role in disruptive politics in the academic literature on social movements is not due to lack of notice or suggestion by some visible scholars. Mayer Zald and John McCarthy, for example, invited research into disruptive religion with their 1982 *Review of Religious Research* article, "Theological Crucibles: Social Movements in and of Religion." Yet few scholars seem to have accepted these invitations or followed their leads; nor is the inattention in the social-movement literature due to a scarcity of works on religion, politics, protest, and revolution. This chapter's bibliography alone suggests the many relevant works available. Yet, social-movement scholars appear to have made little effort to locate and utilize these works.

2. And, what was viewed as structural-functionalism's main antidote, dialectical materialism, also devalued the social importance of religion.

3. These are the Society for the Scientific Study of Religion, which publishes the *Journal for the Scientific Study of Religion*; the Association for the Sociology of Religion, which publishes *Sociology of Religion* (formerly *Sociological Analysis*); and the Religious Research Association, which publishes *Review of Religious Research*.

4. My reliance on Berger (1967) and Geertz (1973) in the following section is clear.

5. One solution to this dilemma is to conflate the absolute into the relative, by declaring—as did some Roman emperors—that Caesar himself is god.

6. More precisely, this occurs in situations of opening political opportunity structures for, increasing organizational strength of, and developing insurgent consciousness among social-movement protagonists (McAdam 1982; Smith 1991).

7. Morris (1984) calls these organizations "movement halfway houses."

8. It should also be recognized, however, that, for other reasons, in other cases, urbanization and geographical concentration are prerequisites for the emergence of social movements (see, e.g., McAdam 1982; Smith 1991; McAdam, McCarthy and Zald 1988: 703).

CHAPTER 3

1. My thanks to Lis Clemens, Jan Kubik, Antoni Sulek, and Sidney Tarrow for their insightful questions and comments. This research was supported, in part, by a grant from IREX.

2. Archiwum Archidiecezjalne w Gdańsku (Archdiocesan Archives in Gdańsk) [hereafter: AAG], syg. III KB/III 69, Dekanat Gdańsk I, Wrzeszez, par. sw. Krzyza, Nawiedzenie 11–12.X.1960. All translations from Polish language texts are those of the author.

3. In particular, the Second Republic (1918–1939) was vilified as a bourgeois state

and the Polish Peoples' Republic acclaimed as "the victory of the Polish working class in solidarity with the working peoples of the Soviet Union"—and, of course, their representative the CPSU. At that time, the story of the "miracle at the Vistula" gained great popularity among Poles. According to the legend, Pilsudski's victory over the Russians at the shores of the Vistula River in 1920—on the feast of Our Lady of Czestochowa, the Black Madonna—was further proof of miraculous intercession by the Virgin.

4.   The success of the Novena's initial phase and the demand from other dioceses for visitation by the Black Madonna encouraged the episcopate to extend the Novena until 1980.

5.   This refers to the consolidation of Polish lands into a kingdom by King Mieszko I, Poland's first Christian ruler in 966.

6.   AAG, 29–30 September, 1960, syg. III KB/III 69, Dekanat Gdańsk I, Gdańsk par. Niepokolane Poczęcie N.M.P. 29–30 IX.

7.   The results of pastoral mobilization were impressive. In the six deaneries of the Gdańsk archdiocese, the painting of the Black Madonna visited fifty-eight parishes and nine rectoral churches. During the visitation of the Painting, 154,185 people received the sacrament of confession (74% of those obligated); 268,788 went to communion; 22% of communicants were people coming to participate in the ceremonies from outside the parish. AAG, 1960, syg. III/KB, III 69. "Diecezja Gdańska–Zestawienie danych z nawiedzenia M.B."

8.   "Przebieg Uroczystosci—Wspomnienia Uczestnika: Zatrzymanie Obrazu Nawiedzenia—20 VI 1966," Warszawa (23–24 VI 1966) (Great Novena archival documents published in Raina 1991: 252).

9.   "Przebieg Uroczystosci—Wspomnienia Uczestnika: Centralne Nabozenstwo Milenijne w Archikatedrze (24 VI 1966)," Warszawa (23–24 VI 1966) (Great Novena archival documents published in Raina 1991: 265).

CHAPTER 8

1.   This is a much revised version of a paper presented at the 1993 annual meeting of the Midwest Sociological Society, Chicago. The authors also thank the members of Yale University's Interdisciplinary Seminar in Law and Deviance for their discussion and suggestions.

2.   Note that while we borrow the term "worldview" from Geertz, we merge his definitions of "ethos" and "world view" (Geertz 1973: 89-90, 127–128).

3.   Interestingly, three separate respondents in three separate interviews used the line about "apologizing to Sodom and Gomorrah." We are unsure as to its origins.

4.   Only four of the interviewees in our sample were Catholic. Three of those four offered an interpretation of church-state relations that emphasized that doctrine or church membership cannot be forced on the individual. In conjunction with other comments about Protestant-Catholic tensions among O-R participants, one can believe that Catholics have a sense of minority status and find the protection from theological or doctrinal coercion attractive.

5. Tarrow (1992) outlines theoretically a similar scheme for understanding the levels of culture of relevance to social movements; he calls them "mentalities," "political culture," and "collective action frames."

CHAPTER 9

1. Thus, in Ralph Epperson's traveling workshop, "The Unseen Hand—An Introduction to the Conspiratorial View of History," *Proofs of A Conspiracy* is invoked to show that the French Revolution, Communism, the Civil War, the Federal Reserve Act, the Bolshevik Revolution, both World Wars, the United Nations, and the Civil Rights movement, ultimately are traceable to the machinations of the Illuminati. Epperson's lectures are sponsored by the John Birch Society.

2. Sociologically, "generation" refers to a type of collective identity. Specifically, it is a shared belief on the part of an aggregate that its political character is due to its temporal location in society. To be a member of a social class, it is not enough to have a particular income. Likewise, to be a member of a generation, it is not sufficient merely to be a particular age (Mannheim 1952). For the application of this notion to American political history see Schlesinger (1986).

3. The classic statements of the educational, alienation, and status insecurity theories are found, respectively, in Stouffer (1966), Nisbet (1953), and Lipset and Raab (1970).

4. Utah aside, the upper Rocky Mountain and West Coast states constitute the American "unchurched belt." Per capita conventional church membership here is the lowest in the country. Indications are that it is also the center of American cultism and a major locale of sectarianism. Many right-wing extremist groups have both a cultic and a sectarian flavor, including most of those mentioned by name in this chapter. See Stark and Bainbridge (1985).

5. For excellent journalistic coverage of the militia movement, see *Christian Science Monitor*, April 20 and 26, 1995; *USA Today*, April 24, 1995; and *The Seattle Post-Intelligencer*, April 28, 1995.

6. The cover claims: "No. 1 non-fiction bestseller of the decade.... Over 10,000,000 copies in print!"

7. For example, reprints of Luther's pamphlet are available from the Church of Israel Missionary and Literature Room for $2.00. Also for sale are *Anne Frank's Diary, A Hoax; The International Jew; Satan's Kids (The Jews); The Talmud Unmasked; The Zionist Connection*, and *The Protocols*. The Aryan Nations Church and the Laporte Church of Christ carry analogous lists.

8. For an article "proving" that the Oklahoma City federal building bombing in April 1995 was part of a Clinton-Reno conspiracy, see *Scriptures for America*, volume 11, 1995.

9. A theological tradition in America at least as dominant as Calvinism has been Arminianism, after Jacob Arminius. Arminianism democratized the predestinarian exclusivity of Calvinism by making salvation available in principle to all persons, contingent upon their free acceptance of grace. By taking involvement in political campaigns against private and public corruption as a sign of righteousness,

Methodist forms of Arminianism have historically been congenial to the idea of moralistic crusading. This has found expression in both liberal reformism and in right-wing politics.

10. No such prophecy actually appears in Revelations.

11. The pronouns in this quote have been changed to give a clearer sense of the homosexual threat.

CHAPTER 10

1. I would like to thank Joe Fahey, Gerry Vanderhaar, Christian Smith, and Jackie Smith for their helpful comments on this essay. I also want to thank Joe Fahey, Dave Robinson, Gerry Vanderhaar, Jo Clark, Fr. Richard McSorley and Nancy Small of Pax Christi USA, and Ben Schennink of Pax Christi Netherlands, for their helpful comments and materials on Pax Christi and some of the issues discussed in this essay. Thanks, too, to Sharon Sumpter, Archives Associate at the Notre Dame Archives. This essay was written while I was a Visiting Faculty Fellow at the Kroc Institute for International Peace Studies, University of Notre Dame.

2. For a discussion of the composition of the "peace movement" and the nature of "peace movement organizations," see Colwell (1990) and Pagnucco (1992).

3. For further information on the 1988 PMO survey, see Colwell (1989, 1990). Further research is needed to clarify the relationship of budget size to tactical choice. In his study using data from the Colwell 1988 PMO survey, Pagnucco (1992) concluded that the variation in the use of unruly tactics found among PMOs with annual budgets of $30,000 and above was not due to budget size; budget size was not a good predictor of their use. For a study of the mortality rates of PMOs, see Edwards and Marullo (1995).

4. Scales are standardized and range from 0 to 1.

5. Repertoire usage scores were coded as follows: usage scores of 0 were coded as "none"; usage scores of above 0 to .49—usage of 1 to under 50% of the tactics in the scale—were coded as "some"; and usage scores of .50 and more—indicating usage of over 50% of the tactics in the repertoire—were coded as "extensive."

6. However, the Table 3 data on Electoral Tactics appear to diverge from these results. This discrepancy can be explained upon closer inspection. The electoral-tactics scale has the largest number of tactics (9); groups falling into the extensive-usage category used five or more of those tactics. Twice as many secular PMOs as faith-based groups made extensive use of the repertoire. However, more than half (53%) of the faith-based PMOs and only 32% of the secular PMOs made some use of the repertoire, a difference of 21%. Similarly, a larger percentage of secular PMOs than faith-based groups made no use of the repertoire at all. This ovearll pattern does not support the hypothesis that faith-based PMOs are disinclined to use the conventional repertoire of electoral tactics.

7. The 1982 and 1988 membership figures are under-reported because these figures represent both individual and "corporate" members, which include religious orders and intentional communities of several or more people. The 1988 figure also includes Catholic parishes. The growth in membership has continued through the

early 1990s (Clark 1995), which contradicts the general trend of decline in PMO membership reported by Edwards and Marullo (1995).

8. Selective conscientious objection refers to the opposition to a specific war because the individual finds it morally objectional. The individual need not be morally opposed to all wars and violence to be a selective objector. In 1968, the Roman Catholic bishops in the United States recognized the right of Catholics to be selective conscientious objectors, though the United States government still does recognize this right.

9. Tests for variation between the two subsets on key organizational characteristics such as tax status, staff size, organizational type and membership participation in organizational decisions show no significant variations that would influence our results.

10. Other national branches of Pax Christi do not use nonviolent action nearly as much as PCUSA. For example, the author's discussions with Dutch and American members of Pax Christi strongly indicates that the content of religious identity and tactical choice is related to the structure of political opportunities. PCUSA's interest in a "spirituality of resistance" was difficult for some Dutch members to understand because they felt they had relatively open access to, and some influence on, government officials who make foreign policy. As one Dutch member queried, "resistance to what?" For a discussion of the relatively inaccessible process of foreign policymaking in the United States, see Smith and Pagnucco (1993).

11. There is evidence that many grass-roots members wanted the national organization to organize nonviolent direct action. For example, of one hundred ninety-eight recommendations from the membership at the 1986 national assembly, 20% wanted an act of "public witness" included as part of the annual national assemblies (PCUSA 1986: 3). Patricia McNeal, an historian of PCUSA, believes that the support for and use of nonviolent direct action at the local level contributed to the decision of the National Council to organize civil disobedience in 1987. Another factor contributing to this decision was that some local activists who had been arrested for civil disobedience had been elected to the National Council.

12. This was only the second time that a U.S. Catholic Bishop was arrested for civil disobedience. In 1986, another Bishop was arrested for protesting apartheid (see Leddy 1987).

13. Holsworth (1989) described a similar orientation, which he called "personalism," among the faith-based PMOs he studied in Richmond, Virginia. Not coincidentally, among the groups he studied was a local Pax Christi chapter.

14. Results from the 1982 membership survey indicate the extent to which members are integrated into their local parish communities and the institutional church: 93% of those surveyed claimed to participate regularly in a parish, and approximately 30% were employed by the church (PCUSA 1982:1,3).

INDEX

Printed in Great Britain
by Amazon

36730295R00139